BEST PRACTICE IN
MOTIVATION AND MANAGEMENT
IN THE CLASSROOM

ABOUT THE AUTHORS

Dennis Gene Wiseman holds the Ph.D. and M.A. degrees from the University of Illinois at Urbana-Champaign (1974, 1970) and the B.A. degree from the University of Indianapolis (1969). He is a Distinguished Professor Emeritus at Coastal Carolina University, Conway, South Carolina, where formerly he held the positions of Dean of the Spadoni College of Education and Associate Provost for Academic Affairs. He has taught with the Champaign, Illinois, and Indianapolis, Indiana, public schools systems. He is coauthor of *Effective Teaching: Preparation and Implementation* (4th edition), *Best Practice in Motivation and Management in the Classroom* (2nd edition); *The Middle Level Teacher's Handbook: Becoming a Reflective Practitioner, The Modern Middle School: Addressing Standards and Student Needs*; editor of *The American Family: Understanding its Changing Dynamics and Place in Society*; and coeditor of *Teaching at the University Level: Cross-Cultural Perspectives from the United States and Russia; Family and Childrearing: Russia and the USA, A Cross-Cultural Analysis*; and *Youth and the Socio-Cultural Environment: Russia and the USA*. Dr. Wiseman has also authored numerous articles in professional journals. His fields of specialization are curriculum and instruction, social studies education, and educational psychology.

Gilbert Harrison Hunt holds the Ph.D. and M.Ed. degrees from the University of North Carolina at Chapel Hill (1975, 1971) and the B.S. degree from Campbell University (1969). He is a Distinguished Professor Emeritus at Coastal Carolina University, Conway, South Carolina, where formerly he held the positions of Dean of the Spadoni College of Education and Singleton Chaired Professor and Research Scholar. Dr. Hunt taught at the middle school level with the Harnett County, North Carolina, public school system prior to beginning his career at Coastal Carolina University. He is coauthor of *Effective Teaching: Preparation and Implementation* (4th edition); *Best Practice in Motivation and Management in the Classroom* (2nd edition); *The Middle Level Teachers' Handbook: Becoming a Reflective Practitioner, The Modern Middle School: Addressing Standards and Student Needs*; and coeditor of *Teaching at the University Level: Cross-Cultural Perspectives from the United States and Russia*. Dr. Hunt also has authored numerous articles in professional journals and delivered numerous presentations at professional conferences.

Third Edition

BEST PRACTICE IN MOTIVATION AND MANAGEMENT IN THE CLASSROOM

By

DENNIS G. WISEMAN, Ph.D.

Distinguished Professor Emeritus
Coastal Carolina University

and

GILBERT H. HUNT, Ph.D.

Distinguished Professor Emeritus
Coastal Carolina University

CHARLES C THOMAS • PUBLISHER, LTD.
Springfield • Illinois • U.S.A.

Published and Distributed Throughout the World by

CHARLES C THOMAS • PUBLISHER, LTD.
2600 South First Street
Springfield, Illinois 62704

© 2014 by CHARLES C THOMAS • PUBLISHER, LTD.

ISBN 978-0-398-08770-8 (paper)
ISBN 978-0-398-08771-5 (ebook)

Library of Congress Catalog Card Number: 2013026155

With THOMAS BOOKS *careful attention is given to all details of manufacturing
and design. It is the Publisher's desire to present books that are satisfactory as to their
physical qualities and artistic possibilities and appropriate for their particular use.*
THOMAS BOOKS *will be true to those laws of quality that assure a good name
and good will.*

Printed in the United States of America
SM-R-3

Library of Congress Cataloging-in-Publication Data

Wiseman, Dennis.
  Best practice in motivation and management in the classroom / by Dennis
G. Wiseman and Gilbert H. Hunt. -- Third edition.
    pages cm
  Includes bibliographical references and index.
  ISBN 978-0-398-08770-8 (pbk.) -- ISBN 978-0-398-08771-5 (ebook)
  1. Motivation in education. 2. Classroom management. 3. Effective teaching.
I. Hunt, Gilbert. II. Title.

  LB1065.W57 2014
  370.15'4--dc23

                                                                    2013026155

This text is dedicated to those students who enter schools each day and bring with them, or encounter there, problems and challenges in motivation and behavior management and to the many dedicated educators who continue to seek ways to meet both the personal and learning needs of these students.

PREFACE

There is no question that teachers today must have an in-depth understanding of the subjects that they teach. Students will not achieve at high levels without teachers who are experts themselves in the subject matter that they are charged to teach their students. Teacher knowledge of subject matter alone, however, is not sufficient to ensure that instruction will be effective or that students will be successful in their learning. Teachers interact on a daily basis with students in their classrooms who often see little value in what they are being taught and feel uncomfortable or out-of-place in the school environment that frequently is so very different from that of their homes and communities. Many students have difficulty controlling their own behaviors and focusing on what is expected of them in the classroom. Many bring with them to school a host of issues and concerns about who they are today as well as who they will become in the future.

Today's teachers are expected to provide high quality instruction and services to all of their students, schools, and communities to a degree that would never have been considered even ten years ago. Likewise, teachers are held accountable for their own performance and the performance of their students in ways and through means that also would not have received serious consideration in years past. The demand for additional and higher levels of performance and accountability comes at a time when the challenges that teachers face each day in their schools and classrooms are greater than at any previous time in the history of the teaching profession.

Beyond the need to have an in-depth understanding of their subject matter, teachers must be able to teach this subject matter at a level and in ways that their students find understandable, engaging, challenging, interesting, and relevant. If students do not see what they are learning as being of value, if they do not recognize it as being relevant to their lives now and/or in the future, if they are not meaningfully connected to it, and if they do not understand it to the degree that they can be successful, they will not achieve at their greatest potentials. In today's classrooms and schools, teachers are expected to be effective in getting their students to learn, and students are expected to be successful in demonstrating what they have learned.

Additionally, to be effective and meet the demands of society today, teachers also must understand their students' interests, styles of learning, and backgrounds, both academic and personal. Teachers cannot meet the unique needs of their students if they do not know their unique needs. Having the ability to manage the learning environment, motivate students in the environment, and offer instruction that itself is motivating and which contributes to students learning what they need to learn and acquiring skills they need to acquire characterizes effective teachers. To meet the many and varied expectations held for them, teachers need to have highly developed skills as instructional specialists, motivators, managers, and problem solvers.

This text offers practical information and vicarious practice for beginning as well as veteran teachers to become more knowledgeable, skilled, and effective in their work. Through study, application of what has been studied, and the analysis and evaluation of the end result of this application, teachers who care to improve can improve. And, teachers who are already successful in their teaching can be even more successful. Beyond what they know and are able to do at any particular point in time, to be effective, teachers must continue to be active learners. This text provides a specific context and focus for this active learning in the areas of student motivation, classroom management, and instruction which are considered essential for best practice in classrooms today.

Dennis G. Wiseman
Gilbert H. Hunt

CONTENTS

BEST PRACTICE IN
MOTIVATION AND MANAGEMENT
IN THE CLASSROOM

Chapter 1

MOTIVATION AND MANAGEMENT: TWO SIDES OF THE SAME COIN

When a classroom population ranges from twenty to forty students from disparate backgrounds, peaceable and productive learning environments depend on the management of explicit standards and expectations to which all adhere. Schools need to set up management structures that promote prosocial behaviors and educators must be prepared to teach replacement behaviors that are prosocial. A major flaw in school management has been that of erasing negative behaviors without teaching prosocial replacement behaviors. (Froyen & Iverson, 1999, p. 6)

The knowledge base of motivation is so extensive that the crucial factor is making the best choice for a particular problem. If we have not learned the extensive motivational knowledge base, then our choices are limited. (Alderman, 2008, p. 22)

THE INTERRELATEDNESS OF MOTIVATION AND MANAGEMENT

Annual polls conducted by the Gallup organization in conjunction with Phi Delta Kappa have consistently identified classroom management to be an especially important concern of both veteran and novice teachers alike. Beginning in the late 1960s, *discipline* was identified as one of the most significant problems that teachers face. From 1986 to 1992, *discipline* ranked third only to *drugs* and *inadequate funding* as the most significant problem. In 1994 and 1995, *discipline* was again the number one problem (Elam & Rose, 1995); *discipline* was sec-

3

ond to *drug abuse* in 1996 (Elam, Rose, & Gallup, 1996); tied for first
with *lack of financial funding* in 1997 (Rose, Gallup, & Elam, 1997); second to *fighting, violence,* and *gangs* in 1998 (Rose & Gallup, 1998); first in
1999 (Rose & Gallup, 1999); and second to *lack of financial support* in
2000 (Rose & Gallup, 2000). In more recent years, the most significant
problem identified with America's public schools has been lack of financial support and funding followed by *discipline* or *overcrowded schools*
being second or third in importance. Each poll also identified *fighting,
violence, gangs,* and *use of drugs* as being among the top five concerns that
teachers face (Rose & Gallup, 2003; Rose & Gallup, 2004; Rose &
Gallup, 2005; Rose & Gallup, 2006; Rose & Gallup, 2007). Between
2008 and 2012, the five most significant problems facing America's
public schools have been: (1) lack of financial support, (2) lack of discipline, (3) overcrowding, (4) fighting/gang violence, and (5) drugs
(Bushaw & Lopez, 2012). With the question asked being, *What do you
think are the biggest problems with which the public schools of your community
must deal with?*, and with *discipline, violence, fighting,* and *drugs* being rated on a consistent basis as highly significant problems, educators, those
involved in educator preparation, and even communities at large, must
give greater attention than ever before to addressing what clearly are
important national issues. Table 1.1 identifies the ranking of the major
problems being faced in today's schools over the last five years.

Table 1.1.

**What do you think are the biggest problems that the
public schools of your community must deal with?**

School Problems	2008	2009	2010	2011	2012
Lack of Financial Support	1	1	1	1	1
Lack of Discipline	2	2	2	2	2
Overcrowded Schools	3	3	3	2	3
Fighting/Gang Violence	3	5	–	4	4
Drugs	4	4	–	5	5

Source: From Bushaw, W., & Lopez, S. (2012). The 44th annual Phi Delta Kappa/Gallup Poll of the
public's attitudes toward the public schools. *Phi Delta Kappan, 94*(1), pp. 8–25.

Problems of discipline and management in schools and classrooms
are no longer problems of only public perception. Such issues impact
teacher recruitment and teacher retention as well. It is commonly accepted that, in many instances, the student behavior problems that

teachers face in their schools and classrooms are directly related to the teacher shortage problems also being faced by many states and school districts. These problems in particular have contributed to the reduction in the number of teachers entering the profession. Such problems also are believed by many to be a part of the reason for the shorter length of time that many teachers stay in teaching. It might be asked, *Why would one desire to enter a work environment that on a daily basis reflects stress, frustration, and, in some cases, fear?* While teacher preparation programs are dedicating more time to the study of classroom management and working with challenging students, such programs alone cannot successfully address the myriad issues that teachers face in motivating students and addressing student behavior problems. After they have entered the profession, teachers themselves must remain active learners and continue to develop their skills in working with their students to develop classrooms that are active, positive, safe, and successful learning environments. Whether from a student achievement or school staffing perspective, motivating students and managing student behavior are challenges of critical importance to today's teaching profession. Skills in classroom management are important factors in enhancing student achievement and in schools successfully serving very diverse students (Poplin, Rivera, Durish, Hoff, Kawell, Pawlak, Hinman, Straus, & Veney, 2011; Ratcliff, Jones, Costner, Savage-Davis, Sheehan, & Hunt, 2010).

In addition to its impact on practicing teachers, potentially being confronted with problems of managing student behavior has been identified as one of the most important concerns of pre-service teachers or those preparing to enter the teaching profession. Beginning teachers share many common concerns such as being able to maintain classroom discipline, motivate students, accommodate for differences among students, appropriately evaluate student work, work with parents, and develop positive relationships with other teachers (Conway & Clark, 2003; Melnick & Meister, 2008; Veenman, 1984). Historically, pre-service and beginning teachers have felt least well prepared to deal with issues related to classroom management and discipline (Kher-Durlabhji, Lacina-Gifford, Jackson, Guillory, & Yandell, 1997). This perception is especially important as teachers who are effective managers have been identified as having greater job satisfaction. Teachers who are not successful during their first years of teaching report students who continually misbehave as their primary cause for job-related stress (Feitler & Tokar,

1992). Teachers who report that they would not choose the teaching profession again were much more likely to have experienced discipline problems than teachers who would choose teaching again as a profession given the opportunity to do so (National Institute of Education, 1980).

Over the past few years, managing student behavior has gone from being an issue associated only with involving students in effective instruction to being an issue associated with classroom and school safety. School-based tragedies across the country involving student violence have captured the national attention with outcries for immediate action and demands for safer schools. Beginning teachers today are faced with the daunting challenge of offering instruction of high quality in what are often very unpredictable and, at times, unsafe environments. The following eight problems have been most frequently identified by teachers with classroom discipline and motivating students being first and second on the list (Veenman, 1984).

1. Classroom discipline
2. Motivating students
3. Dealing with individual differences
4. Assessing student work
5. Relationships with parents
6. Organization of class work
7. Insufficient and/or inadequate teaching materials and supplies
8. Dealing with problems of individual students

Clement (1998) reported on ten common problems faced by first-year teachers, noting that student motivation and classroom management and discipline are first and third on the list. It is also observed that problems two, four, six, seven, eight, and nine can all impact problems related to student motivation and classroom management.

1. Student motivation
2. Handling students' social and emotional problems
3. Maintaining classroom management and discipline
4. Overenrolled classrooms
5. Book and supply shortages
6. Uncomfortable classroom environments (size, temperature, cleanliness)
7. Working with special education or inclusion students
8. Grading students' work

9. Communicating with parents
10. School or district administration

Although problems of student behavior in schools are easily and in some ways well documented, the major tenet of this text does not view the management of student behavior as a stand-alone issue. Rather, problems of managing student behavior are looked at more inclusively as these problems relate to both student motivation and effective teaching practice. Because of these special relationships, it is not advisable to separate solving a student behavior management problem from the challenge of motivating students and the importance of delivering effective teaching. Separating managing student behavior, motivating students, and using effective teaching practices only serves to oversimplify and bring about an incomplete understanding of each area as an important concern for teachers in establishing successful learning environments in their classrooms. While it is possible to study student management separately from student motivation and effective teaching, treating the three in isolation from one another misdirects their most meaningful, synergistic understanding. This understanding and the importance of these three constructs in establishing positive school environments go together, and, in fact, rely on one another. The close relationship between classroom management, effective classroom instruction and student achievement is well documented (Jones & Jones, 2013). Teachers must carefully analyze whether the content they are teaching and the teaching methods they are using are actively and meaningfully engaging their students and leading to a genuine increase in student achievement. Lessons that encourage students' active participation and that address their individual interests, needs, and backgrounds are not only more likely to foster academic achievement, they also are more likely to generate the good will, respect, and cooperation needed to establish and maintain a productive learning environment.

Problems that teachers face in managing student behavior often are fundamentally problems of student motivation, or, management and motivation problems occurring simultaneously. This text explores student motivation, classroom management, and effective teaching as they relate to each other, and influence each other, rather than as discretely separate aspects of the teaching and learning process. To help conceptualize this relationship, one might think of the entire teaching and learning enterprise as a three-legged stool with one leg being management, one leg being motivation, and one leg being effective teaching practice.

No teacher should leave school at the end of the day lamenting how difficult it was to manage his or her students without also reflecting on how he or she might become better able to motivate them. Though perhaps not in all, in many cases in classrooms where there are student behavior problems, there also is the absence of needed levels of student motivation. It has been reported that some teachers spend as much as 25% to 80% of their time addressing discipline problems (Levin & Nolan, 2010). This figure serves to reinforce the special relationship that exists between motivation, management, and effective teaching. To be successful, teachers must be able to establish appropriate student behavior in their classrooms to maximize the time that they and their students spend on learning.

ESTABLISHING A COMMON LANGUAGE FOR UNDERSTANDING MOTIVATION AND MANAGEMENT

Because understanding the relationship between student *motivation* and student *management* is critical to establishing successful teaching practices, it is essential that teachers have a clear understanding of the meaning of both concepts as they relate to the work of the teacher in the classroom. Though the terms are used frequently, they often are used in different ways with different meanings. It is also important to address the meaning of the concept *discipline* as the term discipline is often used interchangeably with *management*. This is unfortunate as the two are not the same. As clear communication and understanding are essential to effective teaching practice, they also are essential to the successful understanding and study of this practice.

The following definitions of *motivation* and *management* found in the literature today are presented here for a better understanding and illustration of these two concepts.

Motivation

- processes that can arouse and initiate student behavior, give direction and purpose to behavior, help behavior to persist, and help the student choose a particular behavior (Burden, 2010);

- an energizing or activating of behavior, a directing of behavior, and a regulating persistence of behavior (Alderman, 2008);
- an inner drive that focuses behavior on a particular goal or task and causes the individual to be persistent in trying to achieve the goal or complete the task successfully (Levin & Nolan, 2010);
- an internal state that arouses one to action, pushes one in a particular direction, and keeps one engaged in certain activities (Elliott, Kratochwill, Cook, & Travers, 2000);
- something that energizes, directs, and sustains behavior; it gets students moving, points them in a particular direction, and keeps them going (Ormrod, 2011).

Management

- actions teachers take to create an environment that supports and facilitates both academic and social-emotional learning (Evertson & Weinstein, 2006);
- all things that a teacher does to organize students, space, time, and materials so that instruction in content and student learning can take place (Wong & Wong, 2009);
- teacher actions to create a learning environment that encourage positive social interaction, active engagement in learning, and self-motivation (Burden & Byrd, 2013);
- the use of rules and procedures to maintain order so that learning may result (Elliott et al., 2000);
- teacher actions to create a learning environment that encourages positive social interaction, active engagement in learning, and self-motivation (Burden & Cooper, 2004).

Based on the definitions presented here, *motivation* may be seen as that which the teacher initiates or seeks to bring about so that students become and stay positively and actively engaged in the teacher's learning activities. *Management*, on the other hand, may be looked upon as an action or actions that the teacher takes in relation to the classroom environment to make optimum levels of student achievement possible.

Motivation and management go hand in hand. For the purposes of this text, **motivation** is *an internal state that arouses students to action, directs them to certain behaviors, and assists them in maintaining that arousal and action with regard to behaviors important and appropriate to the learning environment.* **Management** is *a system of organization that addresses all ele-*

ments of the classroom (i.e., students, space, time, materials, and behavioral rules and procedures) that enables the teacher to reach optimum levels of instruction and establish a foundation for student learning. How then does student discipline relate to student motivation and management? The following are common definitions of *discipline.*

Discipline

- teachers' responses to student misbehavior (Eggen & Kauchak, 2013);
- the required action by a teacher or school official toward a student (or group of students) after the student's behavior disrupts the ongoing educational activity or breaks a pre-established rule or law created by the teacher, the school administration, or the general society (Wolfgang, 1999);
- teachers' efforts to maintain classroom decorum and secure students' cooperation in learning and exercising self-control (Charles, 2011);
- the process of enforcing standards and building cooperation so that disruptions are minimized and learning is maximized (Jones, 1987);
- the act of responding to misbehaving students in an effort to restore order (Burden, 2010).

Considering these definitions, *discipline* is what the teacher engages in when efforts to motivate students and manage the classroom have not been successful. For many, with its emphasis on dealing with student misbehavior, attention to discipline has been replaced by a more current and comprehensive body of knowledge that emphasizes increasing student achievement through the creation of classroom environments that meet the student's personal as well as academic needs (Jones & Jones, 2013). While the terms discipline and punishment, like management and discipline, are also sometimes used interchangeably, they likewise are not the same (Coloroso, 1994). Punishment is considered to be adult oriented, imposes power from without, can arouse anger and resentment, and invite conflict. Punishment can wound rather than heal by focusing on blame and pain and demonstrates the teacher's ability to control a student rather than teach a student. The following teacher actions are important to keep in mind any time the use of punishment is being considered (Burden, 2010).

1. Discuss and reward acceptable behaviors.
2. Clearly specify the behaviors that will lead to punishment.
3. Use punishment only when rewards or nonpunitive interventions have not worked, or if the behavior must be decreased quickly because it is dangerous.
4. Administer punishment in a calm, unemotional manner.
5. Deliver a warning before punishment is applied to any behavior.
6. Apply punishment fairly to everyone who exhibits the targeted behaviors.
7. Apply punishment consistently after every occurrence of the targeted misbehavior.
8. Use punishment of sufficient intensity to suppress the unwanted behaviors.
9. Select a punishment that is effective, that is not associated with a positive or rewarding experience, and that fits the situation.
10. Avoid extended periods of punishment.

Important differences exist between discipline and punishment. The process of discipline does four things that the act of punishment does not do (Coloroso, 2000). Discipline:

1. shows students what they should have done,
2. gives students as much ownership of the problem as they are able to handle,
3. gives students options for solving the problem, and
4. leaves students with their dignity in-tact.

For purposes of this discussion, **discipline** is *action taken on the part of the teacher to enforce rules and respond to student misbehavior.* Misbehavior is behavior considered to be inappropriate and unwanted and includes any student action that is perceived by the teacher to compete with or threaten the classroom environment at a particular moment (Burden & Byrd, 2013). A clear understanding for both students and teachers of what behaviors represent discipline problems is essential for effective classroom management to be established (Levin & Nolan, 2010). In the absence of this understanding, it is impossible for the teacher to: (1) design and communicate to students rational and meaningful classroom guidelines, (2) recognize misbehavior when it occurs, and (3) use intervention strategies effectively. Misbehavior creates disruptions in the progress of planned classroom activities. Charles (2011) pointed out that classroom misbehavior occurs intentionally, not inadvertently, and that student misbehavior interferes with teaching or learning, threatens or intimidates others, and oversteps society's standards of moral, ethical, or legal behavior. In exhibiting misbehavior, students do things on purpose that they know they should not do. Thirteen types of student misbehavior, felt to be in an increasing order of seriousness, are identified in Table 1.2.

Table 1.2
Misbehavior Types in an Increasing Level of Seriousness

Misbehavior	Misbehavior Explanation
Inattention	daydreaming, doodling, looking out the window, thinking about things irrelevant to the lesson
Apathy	a disinclination to participate, sulking, not caring, fear of failure, not wanting to try or do well
Needless talk	chatting during instructional time about things unrelated to the lesson
Moving about the room	getting up and moving about without permission, congregating in parts of the room
Annoying others	provoking, teasing, picking on, calling names
Disruption	shouting out during instruction, talking and laughing inappropriately, using vulgar language, causing "accidents"
Lying	falsifying to avoid accepting responsibility or admitting wrongdoing, or to get others in trouble
Stealing	taking things that belong to others
Cheating	making false representations for personal benefit or wrongly taking advantage of others
Sexual harassment	making others uncomfortable through touching, sex-related language, or sexual innuendo
Aggression and fighting	showing hostility toward others, threatening, shoving
Malicious mischief	doing intentional damage to school property or the belongings of others
Defiance of authority	talking back to the teacher, ignoring the teacher, or hostilely refusing to do as requested

Source: From Charles, C.M. (2011). *Building classroom discipline* (10th ed.), Boston: Pearson, pp. 15–16.

While it is important for the teacher to be prepared for discipline problems when they arise, when the teacher uses strategies to discipline students the teacher has entered into more of a reactive than proactive mode of behavior. As with exhibiting good teaching practice, teachers need to be poised, confident, capable, and focused when using discipline strategies in response to student misbehavior. When a teacher uses discipline strategies, it may be concluded that the teacher's approach(es) to student motivation and management were not fully effective.

Management issues or problems are a very real part of schools and classrooms today. In a survey by the American Federation of Teachers (AFT), 17% of the teachers surveyed indicated that they had lost four or more hours of teaching per week due to disruptive students; 19% reported having lost two to three hours; 43% said they had students in their classes with discipline problems (Walker, Ramsey, & Gresham, 2004). Although disruptive students engage in antisocial behavior, such students actually represent a rather small percentage of students in today's schools. Nevertheless, aggressive and disruptive behavior waste teaching time, disrupt the learning of all students, threaten safety, and overwhelm teachers. Although direct early intervention may not be as common as it should be, when used, early intervention can make a significant difference and bring about positive change in student behavior. When dealing with disruptive, antisocial behavior, a combination of the following strategies is recommended to bring about desired behavior change:

1. adopt a consistently enforced schoolwide behavior code,
2. engage in social-skills training,
3. incorporate appropriately-delivered adult praise for positive behavior,
4. provide reinforcement contingencies and response costs, and
5. use time-out.

This proactive approach to dealing with disruptive behavior can make a significant difference and have a successful impact on student actions and the overall classroom environment.

BEST PRACTICE IN MOTIVATION AND MANAGEMENT

Teachers who are able to maximize student learning minimize student misbehavior at the same time. Acknowledging this, the relationship between effective practice in teaching and effective practice in motivation and management cannot be ignored. *Why is it that effective teachers typically have many fewer discipline problems to address when compared to ineffective teachers?* The reason is not particularly complicated and the answer to this question lies in the teacher's: (1) attitude, (2) readiness and preparedness, (3) ability to manage the totality of the learning environment, and (4) offering meaningful and relevant instruction to all students. Teachers who are well prepared for their teaching, motivating, and managing responsibilities have fewer classroom problems than those who are not. It has been observed that half of what a teacher will accomplish in a day is determined before the teacher even leaves home; three-fourths of what will be accomplished is determined before the teacher enters the school door (Wong & Wong, 2005). Being prepared is the key to success for any teacher. Effective teachers are characterized by having their rooms ready, their work ready, and themselves ready.

In a classic study, Kounin (1970) identified that effective teachers are basically no different from ineffective teachers in their ability to respond to and deal with student misbehavior *after the misbehavior has occurred.* Significant differences are apparent, however, in the behaviors of effective and ineffective teachers *before the misbehavior takes place.* Kounin found that it was the ongoing behavior of teachers in carrying out their instruction that determined whether they were effective or ineffective. Kounin's research pointed out that ineffective teachers simply were not fully ready for all that was expected of them or needed to occur in their classrooms. This lack of readiness led to confusion, confusion led to uncertainty, uncertainty led to mixed messages with lack of clarity in communication and understanding of expectations, and all of these, in total, led to student misbehavior. The ineffective teachers, virtually daily, became more and more stressful, disorganized, frustrated, negative, and held others responsible for the problems that they experienced. Kounin concluded that the key to maintaining orderly classrooms lies not in the teacher's ability to handle inappropriate student behavior once it occurs, but in the teacher's ability to prevent behavior problems from occurring in the first place. This observation led to the separation of the concept *classroom management,* which represents the teacher's organized system and strategies used to create and maintain an orderly learning environment, and the concept *discipline,* which represents the teacher's reactions to and ways of dealing with student misbehavior.

Effective teachers are prepared for the many things, some predictable and some unexpected, that come into play in the job of teaching. The effective teacher's classroom is ready, meaningful learning activities are ready, and the students are ready to learn when they enter the classroom. Effective teachers are so well prepared through their prior practices and planning that they are able to prevent most student misbehavior, certainly most serious misbehavior, from ever occurring. It perhaps sounds all too simple. The reason that effective teachers are effective is that they have fewer student behavior problems and, consequently, are better able to get their students to work (be engaged), stay on task, and achieve. In turn, effective teachers incur less stress as a consequence of having to deal with fewer behavior problems. They are able to leave school each day having been more productive and feeling more satisfied with their work than those teachers who are seen as not being effective. Kounin's conclusions have been validated over the years by other educators and researchers (Brophy & Evertson, 1976; Evertson, 1980).

Most textbooks on teaching methodology include a section on the need for the teacher to be prepared and ready when entering the classroom. Being ready for teaching frequently is explored with respect to the teacher being well planned to teach lessons to students. The term *plan* most often is used in the context of the teacher's plan for instruction. It is important, however, to expand this outlook toward planning to include more than just the teacher's instructional plan. In pursuit of the well-managed classroom and motivated students, four types of plans should be considered. These are the teacher's:

1. instructional plan,
2. motivation plan,
3. management plan, and
4. discipline plan.

While it may sound awkward to think of the teacher as a discipliner, it is not at all awkward to think of the teacher as a motivator and a manager. The effective teacher is a motivator with a plan to motivate and a manager with a plan to manage. Effective teachers also are capable of dealing with student misbehavior or discipline problems if they arise. Following this line of thought, effective teachers have plans to discipline. Not only do they have such plans, they know when and how to use them successfully.

THE TEACHER AS A MOTIVATOR

Many different qualities come to mind when thinking of the characteristics of effective teachers. Effective teachers are organized, flexible, have a deep knowledge of the subjects that they teach, are clear in their communications, task-oriented, enthusiastic and energetic, and dynamic in their work. Such teachers have the ability to create positive learning environments where students are actively engaged in their own learning. They enrich their teaching and the learning of their students by establishing positive climates in their classrooms. School climate includes the feelings that students and staff have about the school environment (Peterson & Skiba, 2001). These feelings have to do with how comfortable each individual student feels in the environment and whether each student believes that the environment is supportive of learning, teaching, appropriately organized, and safe. Comfortable and supportive environments help provide a foundation for effective teaching and learning as well as positive student behavior and attitudes. Educational research identifies that effective teachers are able to motivate students and establish positive, motivating learning environments. Above all else, effective teachers are characterized as being motivational in their approaches to teaching. The main constraint in assisting students to achieve is not with respect to some fixed capacity that they bring with them to the classroom or school, but with respect to the degree to which they are purposefully engaged in working on their learning and achievement (Sternberg, 1999; 1985). This also involves the degree to which their teachers are actively engaged in helping them. Working toward achievement involves experiences with effective instructional practices, active participation on the part of the student, role modeling on the part of the teacher, and reward. Sternberg (1999) identified a model for developing expertise and achievement in students with the following key elements: (1) metacognitive skills, (2) learning skills, (3) thinking skills, (4) knowledge, and (5) motivation. All of these elements are dependent on the context for learning that has been established in the classroom. Critical to these elements is motivation. Nothing happens in the absence of motivation. Motivation helps bring about the development of metacognitive skills which then influence the development of learning and thinking skills. Learning and thinking skills provide feedback for the further development of metacognitive skills enabling the student's level of understanding to increase. Motivation is central to this process.

One of the myths associated with motivation is that teachers really do motivate their students (Elliott et al., 2000). Some believe that the best that teachers can do is establish conditions for learning which are as attractive and stimulating as possible and that match learning tasks to student abilities and interests. When these conditions have been established, students will be motivated. It may be the conditions, then, that create the motivation and not the teacher. Regardless of the source of the motivation, whether students are motivated by the conditions present in the classroom environment or by the teacher in the process of teaching and in establishing the conditions, motivation is a critical part of the learning process.

Considering the myriad challenges that teachers face in schools today, the **mastery-focused classroom** that focuses on continuous improvement, understanding and effort represents the kind of environment most suitable for promoting student motivation (Eggen & Kauchak, 2013). This is as opposed to the **performance-focused classroom** that emphasizes high grades, public displays of ability, and performance and achievement compared to others. The important consideration in this analysis is on the relationship between the mastery-focused classroom and student motivation. This relationship is illustrated in Table 1.3 by comparing mastery-focused and performance-focused classrooms on selected criteria.

Student motivation increases when teachers establish classrooms where students are at the center of all learning activities; this typifies the mastery-focused classroom. As identified in the Model for Promoting Student Motivation, the mastery-focused classroom is characterized by three important components: *Teacher, Learning Climate,* and *Instruction.*

Teacher

- **Personal Teaching Efficacy**: the belief that teachers can have an important, positive effect on student learning; the more this is believed, the more it will happen.
- **Modeling and Enthusiasm**: teachers present information enthusiastically resulting in increased student self-efficacy, attributions of effort and ability, self-confidence and achievement, and through their own behaviors display or project positive learning models.

Table 1.3
Mastery-Focused and Performance-Focused Classrooms

Criteria for Comparison	Mastery-Focused Classroom	Performance-Focused Classroom
Definition of Success	Mastery and improvement	High grades and doing better than others
What is Valued	Effort and improvement	High grades and the demonstration of high ability
Reasons for Satisfaction	Meeting challenges and hard work	Doing better than others and success with minimum effort
Teacher Orientation	Student learning	Student performance
View of Errors	A normal part of learning	A basis for concern and anxiety
Reason for Effort	To increase understanding	To receive high grades and demonstrate doing better than others
Student Ability	Incremental and alterable	An entity that is fixed
Reasons for Assessment	To measure progress toward preset criteria and to provide feedback	To determine grades and to compare students to one another

Source: From Eggen, P., & Kauchak, D. (2013). *Educational psychology: Windows on classrooms* (9th ed.). Boston: Pearson, p. 365.

- **Caring**: teachers empathize with and invest in the protection and development of their students.
- **Positive Expectations**: teacher expectations are clearly linked to student achievement and become a part of the self-fulfilling prophecy; teacher expectations influence interactions with students; teachers treat students they believe to be high achievers differently from those they believe to be low achievers.

Learning Climate

- **Order and Safety**: students learn and engage more in the learning activities when they see the environment as physically and psychologically safe; order and safety influence a climate variable that creates a predictable learning environment and promotes feelings of physical and emotional security.
- **Success**: success is one of the most significant factors that contribute to students' believing in themselves. Situations where students are successful contribute to ongoing success.

- **Challenge**: success alone is not sufficient to increase student motivation; students need to experience success on tasks that they perceive as challenging.
- **Task Comprehension**: learning increases when students understand the relevance of the task and see it as worth understanding.

Instruction

- **Introductory Focus**: the teacher's lesson beginning attracts student attention and provides a conceptual framework for the lesson that follows.
- **Personalization**: the teacher's lessons and topics are seen as personally meaningful and intellectually and/or emotionally relevant.
- **Involvement**: the extent to which students are directly participating in an activity; student involvement is related to student achievement.
- **Feedback**: providing information to students helps them understand their own personal progress in learning.

In addition to assessing the classroom environment, Snowman, McCown, and Biehler (2012) offered seven recommendations for teacher behaviors related to motivating students to learn. These recommendations include teacher actions, student perceptions, and environmental concerns. In motivating students to learn, the teacher should:

1. use behavioral techniques to help students exert themselves and work toward remote goals,
2. make sure that students know what they are to do, how to proceed, and how to determine when they have achieved goals,
3. encourage low-achieving students to attribute success to a combination of ability and effort and failure to insufficient effort,
4. encourage students to think of ability as a set of cognitive skills that can be added to and redefined, rather than as a fixed entity that is resistant to change, by praising the processes they use to succeed,
5. encourage students to adopt appropriate learning goals,
6. maximize factors that appeal to both personal and situational interest, and

7. try to make learning interesting by emphasizing activity, investigation, adventure, social interaction, and usefulness.

Teaching strategies and behaviors related to student motivation in learning have also been organized into considerations being given to the following basic classroom conditions (Woolfolk, 2013).

1. The classroom must be relatively organized and free from constant interruptions and disruptions.
2. The teacher must be a patient, supportive person who never embarrasses students because they made mistakes.
3. The student's work must be challenging, but reasonable.
4. The student's learning tasks must be authentic.

These classroom conditions provide a focused way to consider teacher behaviors specifically in the context of the classroom environment and improved student motivation. The desired end result of addressing these conditions and in displaying these recommended teacher behaviors is a classroom where students are motivated to learn. As the teacher is responsible for his or her own teaching behaviors, in fulfilling this responsibility the teacher is able to take responsibility for the development of the motivational richness of the learning environment.

After these conditions are met, the influences on students' motivation to learn in a particular situation can be summarized in exploring the responses to four specific student-posed questions.

I. Can I succeed at this task? – Building Confidence and Positive Expectations

Encouragement cannot substitute for real accomplishment. To ensure genuine progress, teachers need to:

1. begin work at the student' level and move forward in small steps,
2. make sure learning goals are clear, specific, and possible to reach in the near future,
3. stress self-comparison and not comparison with others,
4. communicate to students that academic ability is improvable, and
5. model good problem solving.

II. Do I want to succeed? – Seeing the Value in Learning

Teachers may use both intrinsic and extrinsic motivation strategies to help students see the value of the learning task. Teachers need to link the learning task with the needs and interests of students to establish attainment or intrinsic value. Strategies for doing this include:

1. tie class activities to student interests,
2. arouse curiosity,
3. make the learning task fun and enjoyable, and
4. make use of novelty and familiarity.

When assisting the student to see a task's attainment as possible or when intrinsic value seems especially difficult, teachers may need to rely on the use of the instrumental value of tasks, i.e., showing the need for mastery of the task. For example:

- when connections are not obvious for students to figure out themselves, explain the connections to them,
- in some situations, provide incentives and rewards for learning, and
- use ill-structured problems and authentic tasks such as connecting problems in school to real problems outside of school.

III. What do I need to do to succeed? – Staying Focused on the Task

It is inevitable that students will face difficulties from time to time if they are working on a challenging level. When this occurs, for success to follow it is important that they maintain their focus directly on the learning task. Strategies helpful to assist students in maintaining their attention on the task may include:

1. give students frequent opportunities to respond,
2. when possible, have students create a finished product,
3. avoid heavy emphasis on grades and competition,
4. reduce the task risk without oversimplifying it,
5. model motivation to learn, and
6. teach the particular learning strategies student will need to master the material.

IV. Do I belong? – Feeling Connected to and Safe in the Environment

No individual works at his or her best in an environment characterized by discomfort rather than comfort and that pushes away rather than invites in. This is especially true for students in classrooms. If a student's answer to the question, *Do I belong?* is *No,* the teacher may be faced with a serious problem in motivating that student to succeed at his or her highest level. The quality of the learning community that has been established in the classroom is critical for any student to succeed to his or her fullest potential, and establishing an appropriate learning community is both a challenge and a teacher responsibility. Points to consider in addressing this challenge and meeting this responsibility include:

1. maintain authority without being rigid or harsh,
2. apply rules in a fair and consistent manner,
3. establish an authentic classroom, i.e., a classroom that links the environment to the student's culture,
4. make sure that each student is engaged in something that he or she sees as being of value,
5. ensure that each student has a meaningful way to establish some kind of positive connectedness to the classroom and the activities that take place there, and
6. create an environment where students can make choices and ensure that those choices lead to something seen as positive by the student.

In addition to the analysis of the classroom and the teacher's teaching strategies, the reason for poor student motivation can sometimes be found in problems in the relationship that exists between the teacher and the student (Glasser, 1997). A positive student-to-teacher relationship rests, in part, on the perception held by the student as to whether or not the teacher actually cares for him or her. Students who are destined to fail, and in many cases destined to be unmotivated, often believe that no one (in this case their teachers) cares about them as individuals. This belief is often based on their own analysis of the teacher behaviors that they observe. The classroom environment needs to reflect sensitivity through positive interpersonal relationships. A poll by the Association for Supervision and Curriculum Development (2007) asked the question, *What's the most effective way for schools to be safe and secure?*, with the top three responses being: (1) connect every student with a caring adult, (2) ensure that the school staff emphasizes and models mutual respect, and (3) foster identity/community by listening to kids. Establishing these three qualities in schools will not only help to create safer schools, but it will also help to create a more relaxed learning atmosphere in the classroom where students will experience greater opportunities for success. This will help to instill confidence in students and make them emotionally equipped and ready to be actively involved in the learning process.

A good explanation of the relationship among motivation, management, and student success is that teachers make success definite when they make failure impossible (DiGiulio, 2000). Teachers can help to ensure student success when they know their students' strengths, their weaknesses, what interests and what does not interest them, and when they establish a positive relationship with them. The three axioms that follow are recommended as a guide for ensuring such student success.

1. Students who feel successful are seldom behavior problems.
2. To feel successful, students must actually be successful.
3. To actually be successful, students must first do something of value.

THE TEACHER AS A MANAGER

It would be naïve to suggest that if a teacher has a classroom management plan that this by itself will guarantee there will be no student behavior problems. No such guarantee is possible. Nevertheless, teachers can establish and manage the learning environment in such a way as to greatly diminish the possibility of problems with student misbehavior. To do this, teachers must be able to first develop and then implement well-conceived plans for managing their classrooms. The effectiveness of such plans and their implementation rests to a large extent on the teacher's understanding of the characteristics of positive learning environments and having the necessary skills to create them. The better the understanding of positive learning environments, the better the teachers' skills will be to establish them in their classrooms. Classroom management historically has been seen largely as controlling students and getting them to respond to teacher demands, needs, and goals (McCaslin & Good, 1998). For many teachers, the control of student behavior is still the primary foundation of good classroom management. Though this view may be prevalent in some settings, it is not the proper foundation upon which to build a positive learning environment. Rather than focus on control of the environment and students, teachers should focus on promoting the goal of students developing their own capacity for self-regulation. **Self-regulation** is *the process of using one's own thoughts and actions to reach academic learning goals and to govern one's own behaviors.* Self-regulation includes taking responsibility for one's own learning to identify goals, develop strategies for reaching them, and monitor progress toward their attainment. Self-regulation for most students improves over time, although in the early grades, girls may be better at self-regulation than boys (Matthews, Ponitz, & Morrison, 2009). Self-regulation is supported by the two social processes of co-regulation and shared regulation. Co-regulation is a transitional phase where students gradually develop self-regulated learning and skills through such activities as modeling, direct teaching and coaching from teachers, parents, or peers. Shared regulation takes place when students work together to regulate each other through such activities as giving reminders, prompts, and other guidance (Woolfolk, 2013).

Students should not behave in certain ways or be regulated merely as a response to a control system that the teacher has created. Reinforcing its complexity and multi-faceted nature, classroom management should be seen as a gestalt (ASCD, 2006), dependent on several interdependent components, such as the teacher: (1) developing an engaging curriculum; (2) working with anger, projection, and depression; (3) guiding students to be and treating students as responsible citizens; (4) serving as a self-knowing model; (5) utilizing effective classroom management skills; (6) working with resistance, conflict, and stress; and (7) offering robust instruction on a consistent basis. The quality of teacher-student relationships in the classroom is the key to all other aspects of classroom management (Marzano & Marzano, 2003). Although some may see the foundation of teacher-student relationships as being the student's view of the teacher as a person (e.g., a friend, nice person, sociable), the most effective teacher-student relationships are characterized by specific teacher behaviors such as exhibiting appropriate levels of dominance, showing appropriate levels of cooperation, and being aware of and appropriately working with high-needs students. The most effective classroom managers do not treat all students the same, but treat all students equitably and tend to use different strategies with different types of students. Effective managers use what the situation calls for while considering the student and the student's needs.

Considering the classroom environment with respect to student behavior management, teachers must be proactive in their work and able to clearly define and communicate the expectations that they hold for their students (Gathercoal, 1993). The importance of clarity and consistency in communicating rules and expectations to students cannot be overstated. If students do not know what their teachers expect of them, there is little reason to believe that they will be consistent in exhibiting those behaviors that their teachers desire.

Rules help to clarify the expectations that teachers have for their students and the clear statement of even a few important rules of conduct can contribute to the prevention of many student behavior problems. The following guidelines are included here to aid teachers in identifying and listing their classroom rules (Hensen & Eller, 1999).

1. Establish the list during the first few class meetings.
2. Keep the list short.
3. State each rule simply and in language the student can understand.
4. Include only those rules that are considered necessary and be prepared to explain why each rule is needed.
5. Involve students in setting rules.
6. Focus on student behavior needed to achieve lesson goals.
7. State consequences for breaking rules so that students will know what will happen if rules are broken.
8. State rewards for following rules.

It is commonly accepted that the characteristics of a well-managed classroom need to be understood and/or agreed upon by students as well as teachers and not complicated to understand (Wong & Wong, 2005). Simplicity in the characteristics of the classroom is a positive quality of both the teacher and the environment. Consider the following characteristics of a well-managed classroom:

- students are deeply involved with their work, especially with academic, teacher-led instruction,
- students know what is expected of them and are generally successful,
- there is relatively little wasted time, confusion, or disruption, and
- the climate of the classroom is work-oriented but relaxed and pleasant.

The well-managed classroom is physically arranged to facilitate productive work and has a positive climate. Students are on task, cooperative and respectful of one another. All of these qualities are within the sphere of control of the teacher and should be established early in the school year.

While many different rules are possible, a long list of rules is not recommended and is unnecessary to ensure a well-organized and well-managed classroom. A set of five or six rules normally is sufficient to cover most important areas of classroom behavior (Emmer, Evertson, & Worsham, 2006). The following general rules that encompass many classroom behaviors are typical of well-managed classrooms.

1. Bring all needed materials to class.
2. Be in your seat and ready to work when the bell rings or when the class begins.
3. Respect and be polite to everyone.
4. Listen and stay seated when someone is talking.
5. Respect other people's property.
6. Obey all school rules.

Wong and Wong (2005) suggested that five rules should be considered as a maximum number and that the rules need to be stated in a positive manner when possible. The following are examples of such rules.

1. Follow directions the first time they are given.
2. Raise your hand and wait for permission to speak.
3. Stay in your seat unless you have permission to do otherwise.
4. Keep hands, feet, and objects to yourself.
5. No cursing or teasing.

Common teacher problems in establishing well-managed classrooms are often the result of students suffering from inconsistent teacher messages. Teachers frequently manage for obedience while professing to be teaching for exploration and risk taking. For example:

> Educators have created an oxymoron: a curriculum that urges problem solving and critical thinking and a management system that requires compliance and narrow obedience. The management system at least dilutes, if not obstructs, the potential power of the curriculum for many of our students. Students are asked to think and understand, but in too many classrooms they are asked to think noiselessly, without

peer communication or social exchange. And the problems they are asked to think about must be solved, neatly, within (at most) forty-five minute intervals. In the problem-solving curriculum, in too many cases, the teacher sets the performance goals, identifies relevant resources, establishes criteria for evaluation, and eventually announces winners and losers. Students generally gain recognition and approval by paying close attention to recommended procedures and by taking few academic risks (e.g., reading and extensively footnoting fifteen secondary sources rather than venturing their own informed opinions). (McCaslin & Good, 1998, p. 173)

The conflict that can be seen in this observation between what teachers say and what they do is obvious. If teachers desire that students develop successful work habits and certain behavior characteristics, it is necessary for them to have the opportunity and guidance to meaningfully think about and explore how they learn and to actively participate in their own learning; this includes participating in the development of classroom rules.

While different, it is clear that there is a close relationship between classroom management and discipline. Teachers are reacting to student behavior problems when they engage in the use of discipline strategies and are seeking to prevent them when they develop their systems of management. In the popular *The First Days of School,* Wong and Wong (1991) identified the following eleven Principles of Effective Discipline as a framework for addressing student problems and establishing an environment to prevent them. The principles themselves reinforce the relationship between management and discipline.

1. Treat students with dignity and respect.
2. Effective teaching reduces discipline problems.
3. Students need a limited say in what happens in the classroom.
4. It takes time to develop an effective discipline plan and style.
5. Teachers create most of their discipline problems by how they teach and treat people.
6. Bored students become discipline problems.
7. Lack of self-esteem is the major reason why students act up.
8. No one wants or likes to fail; a student would rather be bad than be stupid.
9. Anything a teacher can do to make students feel good about themselves will help to minimize discipline problems.

10. Students who feel powerless will find ways of expressing their lack of power (e.g., not knowing what has been assigned to them).
11. Teachers deny most the students who need to learn responsibility by denying them the experience to have responsibility (e.g., student council, athletics, music, etc.).

Teacher behavior has been identified as the single most important factor in determining the quality of the learning environment (Levin & Nolan, 2010). Intended or not, the verbal and nonverbal behaviors of teachers influence student behaviors. In accepting the role of instructional leader, teachers need to use techniques and strategies and institute programs that maximize student on-task behavior. Teachers who have classrooms with a high percentage of on-task student behavior: (1) understand the relationship between effective teaching and student discipline, (2) understand the factors that motivate student behavior, (3) understand their own personal expectations for student behavior, and (4) have a systematic plan to manage misbehavior. Student learning and on-task behavior are maximized when teaching strategies are based on what educators know about student development, how people learn, and what constitutes effective teaching.

The potential for disruptive behavior is reduced when the classroom environment is appropriately structured for learning. Students are more likely to follow established classroom guidelines if the teacher models appropriate behavior. This includes explaining the relationship of the guidelines to expectations in the classroom, expecting mutual student-teacher respect, and valuing the protection and safety of property and individuals. Increased student commitment may also be found in such environments. The more that classroom guidelines and rules reflect a connection to the culture of students' homes and communities, the more the chance of improved student behavior increases. This is also the case when the teacher creates group/classroom norms that are supportive of and promote engagement in learning activities.

Important principles of classroom management may be organized by behavior or by problem (Levin & Nolan, 2010). Two important categories of this organization include *Understanding the Nature of the Discipline Problem* and *Understanding Why Children Misbehave*. Each principle in these categories presents a valuable perspective for understanding the role of the teacher as an effective classroom manager.

Understanding the Nature of the Problem

1. A discipline problem exists whenever a behavior interferes with the teaching act, interferes with the rights of others to learn, is psychologically or physically unsafe, or destroys property.
2. For effective teaching to take place, teachers must be competent in influencing appropriate student behavior so as to maximize the time spent on learning. Such teachers enjoy teaching more and have greater confidence in their ability to affect student achievement.

Understanding Why Children Misbehave

1. An awareness of the influences of misbehavior, which are often beyond the schools' control, enables teachers to use positive intervention techniques rather than negative techniques, which stem from erroneously viewing misbehavior as a personal affront.
2. Satisfaction of basic human needs such as food, safety, belonging, and security is prerequisite for appropriate classroom behavior.
3. The need for a sense of significance, competence, virtue, and power influences student behavior.
4. Changes in cognitive and moral development result in normal student behavior that often is disruptive in learning environments.
5. Teaching competence can reduce the effects of negative outside influences and prevent the misbehavior that occurs as a result of poor instruction.

Effective teachers have their own individual plans for addressing management problems designed for their own specific classrooms. Not having a well-conceived and workable plan will stymie the teacher in reaching the primary goal in teaching, i.e., assisting and guiding students as they advance in the learning process. When management problems develop, such problems stand in the way of the teacher being successful in meeting this goal. Characteristics 2, 3, and 4 of the suggested management plan that follows specifically address motivating students (Koenig, 2000). The overall characteristics are that the plan should be:

1. individualized to fit each teacher's teaching style and personality,
2. designed to prevent misbehaviors and encourage cooperation,
3. able to motivate a student to stop disruptive behaviors,
4. effective in motivating a student to want to learn, and
5. quick and easy to use.

It is important that teachers carefully analyze the characteristics of student motivation, classroom management, and discipline as they prepare to be effective teachers and problem solvers in their classrooms. Effective behavior management is ultimately characterized by teachers understanding and appropriately selecting from an array of possible interventions that will help them influence the behavior of their students and teach them to behave in positive and safe ways (Danforth & Boyle, 2000). In the end, it is the teacher's ability to resolve instructional, motivational, and managerial problems that determines the true measure of the teacher's effectiveness, in particular as successful resolutions to problems inform the teacher's practice, thus reducing the likelihood of similar problems being repeated in the future.

THE TEACHER AS A REFLECTIVE PRACTITIONER

Teachers make assumptions and develop beliefs about teaching and learning and act on what they know and believe as they carry out their daily teaching activities (Wilen, Ishler, Hutchison, & Kindsvatter, 2000). Assumptions tend to be more informal where beliefs are more structured; both develop from one's experiences. The more that teachers have learned from their experiences, the better grounded their assumptions and beliefs will be. As professionals, effective teachers make decisions and take action based on the most current information that is available to them and continually seek to add to their information base. For teaching to be viewed as a profession, teachers must look upon their work as knowledge- or information-based and develop habits of deep, substantive thinking and reflection (Darling-Hammond & Goodwin, 1993). Of the many important teaching skills, decision making is the most significant of all (Shavelson, 1973). Given the challenges of instructing, motivating, and managing children in today's schooling environments, it is difficult to argue that this is not the case.

Teaching involves many highly complex processes and effective teachers must be well informed on the current research on teacher effectiveness and be able to make use of this information to strengthen and advance their practice. Teachers need to be able to make sound decisions on a daily basis, and, in fact, many times each day. Reasoned, reflective decision making is at the heart of good teaching and helps ensure the highest possible levels of effective practice (Wilen et al., 2000).

Reflection is considered a cornerstone of professional competence, especially as making appropriate change requires that a person objectively reflect on past practice (York-Barr, Sommers, Ghere, & Montie, 2005). **Reflection** is *a way of thinking that involves the ability to use information to make rational choices and to assume responsibility for those choices; it requires that the teacher be introspective, open-minded, and willing to accept responsibility for decisions and actions.* Reflection facilitates learning and continued professional growth and is a key factor in the ability of teachers to be effective throughout their careers (Burden & Byrd, 2013).

Even if a teacher has a deep understanding of the principles of motivation and management and plans for each, this understanding alone will not ensure that students will always be well motivated and that the classroom will always be well managed. In addition to this deep understanding, the teacher must know how to make use of this knowledge and utilize sound decision-making skills in applying them in whatever context it is needed. While teachers need to know how to establish positive learning environments, they also need to be able to make appropriate adjustments to these environments as necessary, in particular when student behavior problems arise. These moments reinforce the importance of the teacher's ability to reflect and be an informed decision-maker. Whether a classroom problem is one of motivation, management, teaching, or a combination of all three together, it is essential that the teacher has the ability to make sound decisions based on relevant and accurate information. As this is the case, when made, effective classroom instruction, motivated students, and a safe, well-managed environment will more likely be the end result. If effective instruction is not occurring, and if student motivation and management are not as they are desired, the teacher must be able to alter what is taking place in the classroom in some meaningful way so that motivated students and a managed classroom environment will be the end result.

A one-size-fits-all approach to classroom management will not appropriately serve teachers who seek to create calm and safe learning environments in their classrooms and, in so doing, meet the needs of all of their students (McEwan, 2000). Establishing positive classroom behavior necessitates determining exactly what students expect from teachers and what teachers expect from students. When students elect to relate to the learning environment through misbehavior, their teachers need to be able to recognize the purpose or the goal of the students' misbehavior and know how to respond to it immediately and in the long term. Teachers have enormous power in influencing student behavior. The *Cooperative Discipline* system by Albert (1996), for example, represents an approach to student behavior management designed to bring about the type of learning environment that both teachers and students need and desire. In this system, emphasis is placed on cooperation and, through it, two important achievements are possible. First, the classroom environment is made a safe, orderly, and inviting place where teachers can teach and students can learn. Second, student self-esteem increases. Increased student self-esteem is necessary if teachers desire for their students to behave responsibly and achieve academically. The system offers a process for management that is corrective, supportive, and preventive. Regardless of the management approach used, key to the teacher when dealing effectively with instances of student misbehavior is determining the cause of the misbehavior, deciding thoughtfully and knowledgeably what to do about it, and then taking appropriate action.

The following case studies are of first-year teachers who are facing decisions to make as a result of student behavior problems that have occurred in their classrooms (Brubaker, Case, & Reagan, 1994).

Seth's Confidence

Seth is a first-year teacher in a first-grade classroom. He completed his student teaching last year in a neighboring school with an experienced teacher near the end of a long, excellent career. Although Seth respected her, he often felt she was rather old-fashioned and knew less about modern techniques than he himself knew. By the end of his student teaching experience, Seth rarely took advice from anyone; he was confident that he knew what there was to know about teaching first-graders. He found, though, that he still had much to learn. On one particular day early in the year, the children were especially disruptive, and in spite of his many efforts, the noise level in the classroom continued to grow. It seemed as though the children were consistently out of their seats and doing things that were inappropriate.

This type of behavior frustrated Seth and he began making mistakes as a result. At one point, the students even teased him and laughed at his clumsy errors. After school he went home and shared his day with his wife who was sympathetic and soothing. Seth began to feel better about things and even laughed at his own silly mistakes. He felt sure that he would do better the next day and that the children would settle down more as the school year progressed. He felt it would help if he tried to be more humorous while teaching. Seth decided that the best thing for him to do was to take each day as it came because worrying about it would only be extra stressful on him and take away from his ability to do his best.

Susan's Problem Ownership

Susan did her student teaching last year in a ninth grade setting where she taught pre-algebra and algebra I. However, this year she was hired in the same school system but was assigned to teach sixth grade in a middle school on the other side of the district. Susan liked the area so she took the new position thinking that she could soon transfer to another school with more mature students when such a position came open. Susan had had a few difficult days early on, but today was an absolute disaster. Students were talking out of turn and not cooperating as she taught. Soon the conditions in the classroom deteriorated to the point where some students were actually arguing with one another across the room and in one case, a student even showed defiance to Susan. Susan lost control of herself as a result of what she considered her students' petty, childish behavior. She made several threats about after school detention and parent conferences, but, by the day's end, had failed to follow through on any of them. As she drove home in her car, she thought about her unfortunate circumstances during the day. It was obvious that her mentor teacher and her principal were not helping her enough. The parents of her students were, in her opinion, not doing their jobs either. The school district itself had made a mistake, she felt, in even assigning her to a position teaching such immature students. By the time she arrived home, she had begun to feel better. She believed that things would work themselves out and, if they didn't, she would find a position elsewhere next year where the students behaved as they should and really wanted to learn mathematics.

Tameka's Planning and Analysis

Tameka is a first-year art teacher in the same high school where she had completed her student teaching the year before; in fact, she was hired to replace her former cooperating teacher, Ms. Smith, who moved with her family to another state. Ms. Smith and Tameka had become very close, yet Ms. Smith was a very strong individual who made most of the decisions in the classroom unilaterally. Ms. Smith, who had excellent control of her classroom, was almost more like a mother to Tameka than a mentor. On this particular day, Tameka had set up sixteen work stations in her classroom complete with easels, paint, and other necessary materials. She had arranged the stations neatly giving each student adequate space to prevent students from interfering with one another while working. Ms. Smith had correctly taught her the importance of having everything prepared before the students' arrival in order to not waste valuable instructional time. When the first class began, Tameka was ready to teach; however, some problems arose almost immediately. Ray and Becky had been feuding all week, and Ray came into the classroom and selected the workstation closest to the one where Becky was working. Very soon Ray and Becky were arguing and everyone was watching them instead of working on their projects. Bill, who liked Becky, walked past Ray's station and bumped into it knocking Ray's supplies on the floor. Two of the other boys in the classroom had to separate Ray and Bill to prevent a fight. Sally, another student, began laughing and making loud remarks. This was too much for Tameka who raised her voice and scolded Sally in front of the entire class. Finally, the bell rang and the students left; Tameka was totally depressed. During her planning session she got out her lesson plans and made some diagnostic notes which was one of the techniques that she had learned from Ms. Smith. As she reflected on the class that had just finished, Tameka realized she had made some mistakes that needed correcting. She listed each mistake she could think of and then wrote beside each error what she could do to correct it in the future. For example, when you know certain students do not get along well together, you should assign their workstations in a way as to avoid the kind of problem she had had with Ray and Becky. She felt that she needed to have a conference with her first-year mentor who might have additional ideas to help her avoid some other problems she noted in terms of motivating her students to stay on task. She wondered if some type of a reward system might help. Finally, she was concerned that she had mishandled the situation with Sally in front of the class. The next day she would make a point of interacting positively with Sally where all other students could see.

These three case studies provide real-life situations for analysis and represent three different ways that the teachers involved chose to approach their student behavior problems. Each took a different approach with only one, Tameka, selecting a systematic approach of breaking down the events of the day for specific review, acknowledging ownership of both the problem and the responsibility for seeking a solution, and preparing a strategy or plan to follow when the class next met. Seth took a general and less thorough approach to analyzing the problems he encountered by talking to only one other individual about them (his wife) and concluding that he should try to be more humorous in the classroom and not worry but take each day as it came. A plan for problem resolution was not developed. Susan appeared to feel no responsibility whatsoever for the problems in her classroom and was prepared to return to school the next day without acknowledging the need for any specific adjustments in her approach to teaching her students or managing her classroom. She held others responsible for the problems that she was having, e.g., the students, their parents, her principal, her mentor. Like Seth, she also did not develop a plan for problem resolution nor saw a need to do so. Tameka was the only one of the three teachers who accepted responsibility for the problems that had occurred, systematically analyzed them, and formed a plan to deal with them.

Effective instruction is contingent on the teacher's use of reflective practice. Reflective practice is the culmination of various forms of reflection, e.g., reflective teaching, reflective thinking, reflective inquiry. The purpose of reflective practice is to think critically about oneself, the assumptions that one holds, and the teaching choices and actions that one takes (Cole & Knowles, 2000). The teacher who regularly reflects on his or her professional practice is considered to be a reflective practitioner; the following behaviors/attributes are characteristic of a reflective practitioner (Larrivee, 2009).

- Reflects on and learns from experience.
- Engages in ongoing inquiry.
- Solicits feedback.
- Remains open to alternative perspectives.
- Assumes responsibility for own learning.
- Takes action to align with new knowledge and understandings.
- Observes self in the process of thinking.
- Is committed to continuous improvement in practice.
- Strives to align behaviors with values and beliefs.
- Seeks to discover what is true.

The Model for Reflection and Inquiry

The Model for Reflection and Inquiry in Figure 1.1 is provided as a guide for teachers to formally analyze both motivation and management problems in the classroom. The teachers identified in the three case studies just presented would find using the model beneficial as a strategy to improve their respective classroom situations. Used systematically, the model can play an important role in helping teachers organize pertinent information and make decisions regarding the use of initial strategies and plans to motivate students and manage their classrooms. It can also be beneficial in analyzing problems related to motivation and management once they have occurred. The model presents a logical problem solving process for reflecting on and making decisions in a variety of areas regarding student motivation, classroom management, and instruction. While use of the model cannot guaran-

---

Model for Reflection and Inquiry

1. **Statement of the Problem**

   The problem is identified and clarified; the problem should be meaningful and manageable.

2. **Development of a Hypothesis(es)**

   A hypothesis, i.e., educated guess, regarding a solution to the problem is formulated; there may be more than one hypothesis.

3. **Collection of Relevant Data**

   Data or pertinent information relevant to the problem is collected and/or identified; references or sources of information are considered and reviewed.

4. **Analysis of Data**

   Clarifications are made as to information collected; sources of data are considered and perhaps reconsidered. Relationships should be identified among data collected and data should be clearly organized and analyzed as to how this information relates to the problem.

5. **Interpretation and Reporting of Results, Drawing Conclusions and Making Generalizations**

   Conclusions should be drawn and relevant generalizations made related to the accuracy of the original hypothesis.

Figure 1.1. Model for Reflection and Inquiry.

tee motivated students or well-managed classrooms, its use will ensure that the teacher is approaching issues in these areas in a logical and reasoned way. In turn, this will enhance the likelihood of a higher level of student motivation and a better managed classroom in the future.

Many see solving student behavior problems in the classroom as a process of trial and error decision making. While to some degree when dealing with human beings it is, the use of an approach such as the Model for Reflection and Inquiry can be especially important. The model will guide the teacher's thinking processes and problem-solving efforts by focusing on the use of systematic decision making with respect to what problem solving strategies are used and how they are evaluated. Over time, a better match will develop between typical classroom problems and effective solutions. This will then reduce the "starting from the beginning" approach that many teachers follow when they have not systematically observed and learned from their past efforts. In becoming more knowledgeable about what problem solving strategies to use in certain situations, the teacher will be able to solve problems of student motivation and classroom management more efficiently and effectively when called upon to do so. Classrooms will run more smoothly and productively, students will see themselves more positively as learners, and teachers will see themselves as working more effectively as teachers. All of this will result in greater attention given to the instructional program that the teacher has established and higher levels of student learning.

CLASSROOM PROBLEMS ANALYSIS

Read through the following classroom situations and: (1) identify the problem; (2) decide whether the problem is one of student management or motivation, or both; and (3) formulate a hypothesis that could apply to successful problem resolution.

1. Bailey and Jadon are students in the third grade who sit next to each other at the back of the classroom. Day after day they continually talk to each other when the teacher is teaching. Neither becomes involved in small group activities or in individual seat work when these strategies are used.

2. Alexis is an eighth grade student who frequently appears uninterested in becoming involved in classroom activities. During the teacher's lessons, she frequently stares out the window or draws in her notebook. She seldom turns assigned homework in to her teacher and often seems to be mentally far away and daydreaming.

3. Carson is in the eleventh grade for the second year and seems to have all but given up on graduating from high school. He rarely brings books or writing utensils to class. When the teacher is teaching, he often speaks out to those around him or directly interrupts the teacher during the lesson. The teacher seldom calls on him for fear of what he might say or how he might say it.

4. Devlin is a fifth grade student who has been identified as very capable academically. However, he seldom answers the teacher's questions when they are asked. When he is returning from lunch, sharpening a pencil, or going back to his seat from the teacher's desk, he often punches students as he walks by them or even marks on their papers or desks. He does not associate with any particular student in the class and keeps to himself most of the time.

5. Koby is in the ninth grade and has been in the school for only a few weeks. When the teacher is teaching, he sometimes calls out answers to questions without being called on or makes comments about what the teacher has said. When he does this, other students turn to him and make derogatory remarks. This results in Koby making derogatory statements back to them. He seems to have no friends.

Whether classified as representing a motivation or management problem, or both, each of these situations represents problems that can often be found in schools today. Each also illustrates the difficulty in identifying situations as being grounded in only student motivation or classroom management issues. The Model for Reflection and Inquiry can help direct the teacher to more immediate and effective solutions to problems such as these through a systematic approach to analyzing each situation. The first step in using the model involves clearly identifying and understanding the nature of the problem. Consider each situation just presented and identify the basic problem with which the teacher is dealing. Then, go to the second step of the model and hypothesize what the teacher might do about it. The purpose here is not to "solve" any individual problem at this point, but to logically explore the interplay between motivation and management and accurately identify and classify the problem and a possible approach to its resolution.

In the first situation, Bailey and Jadon obviously represent a management problem for their teacher. They are inattentive as they continually talk to one another while the teacher is teaching and do not become involved in the teacher's planned activities. It also can be said that neither student is motivated by the learning activities that the teacher is using. Both are more motivated by their desire to interact with each other than they are to engage in the teacher's activities. Recognizing this, the teacher might first try to solve the problem by no longer allowing them to be seated next to each other and begin working with them individually to get them involved in the classroom lessons. The teacher might also use the management strategy of proximity control and move around the room more frequently when teaching and stand closer to them whenever possible. Both of these strategies are reasonable for the teacher to use and are likely to produce positive results.

In the second situation, Alexis's behavior initially appears to represent more of a motivation problem than a problem of management. She does not participate in the classroom activities, but she does not outwardly cause trouble either. The teacher, however, should not conclude that Alexis's behavior is not also a problem of management just because she is not outwardly misbehaving. Alexis's situation is a motivation problem as she is not engaged in the academic program that the teacher has established but also a management problem for this same reason. It is recommended that the teacher set up a time to personally meet with Alexis and explore what interests her and what she likes to do when not in school. The teacher needs to understand Alexis better and should take the time to ask her how she thinks the class is progressing and what she thinks about the activities that are being used. The teacher can work much more effectively with Alexis by knowing more about her, and, with this information, the teacher's instruction can become much more personalized.

In the third situation, Carson's behavior reflects a management problem for the teacher in that he talks out and is not engaged in the teacher's instructional activities. Given that he is repeating the eleventh grade, he also represents a motivational challenge. Carson may have concluded that he will never graduate from high school. If this is the case, the classic strategy used by many teachers to motivate students, using good grades as rewards, may be less effective. The teacher should be mindful of the theories of William Glasser (1997) and take time to establish a personal relationship with Carson. Many students have problems because they feel that no one cares about them personally. The teacher needs to find out what Carson hopes to do after he finishes high school and what his long-term plans are for the future. In doing this, the teacher will let Carson know that he cares about him. It will also allow the teacher to learn more about Carson's interests and the problems that he has encountered in his high school career.

In the fourth situation, while Devlin's classroom misbehavior is obvious, it may reflect that the teacher's primary difficulty is an inability to motivate him. Devlin's lack of involvement and disinterest in the teacher's activities has led to management problems. Although Devlin is identified as being academically able, he has not become involved in the lessons and activities that the teacher has presented and, because of this, his behavior has become a disruption and a management problem. The teacher should recognize that a part of the problem could be that Devlin does not find what goes on in the classroom challenging, interesting, or meaningful. The teacher needs to know how Devlin views what is taking place in the classroom in terms of what and how the teacher teaches. This might result in the teacher revisiting the instructional program and individualizing the program in a way or ways that are more relevant to Devlin's needs and interests, and possibly the needs and interests of other students as well.

In the final situation, Koby exhibits the typical management problem of a student who does not feel connected to the classroom or the student group. Because he is new to the school and has not established any meaningful friendships, he has selected attention-getting behaviors to be recognized. Koby has created management problems for the teacher as a result of his inappropriate behaviors. The teacher should review the instructional activities that have been used and consider the possibility of using cooperative learning or group activities if they have not been used up to this point. To some degree, Koby's problems rest on an absence of positive relationships with his classmates. These problems could partly be addressed by making sure that, through the use of cooperative or group instructional strategies, he gets to know more students and works with them in a mutually reliant way.

Specific plans can and should be developed to address each of the situations described here. After clearly identifying the problem, the teacher must formulate an idea or a plan with strategies for problem resolution. Some initial ideas (hypotheses) have been offered for consideration. As a part of this process, the teacher needs to learn more about the individual students involved, their interests, their styles of learning, their strengths, what distracts them, what successes they value, etc. With this knowledge and having a clear understanding of the problem, the teacher can develop a workable plan for each situation so that each student becomes more motivated, meaningfully connected to, and successful in the learning experiences in the classroom.

Problem solving to improve student motivation and classroom management can be difficult and uncertain work. Without using a systematic approach to it, however, the potential for success in meeting individual student needs will be even more uncertain. The Model for Reflection and Inquiry is a system that can be used to reflect on, logically analyze, evaluate, and develop solutions for problems of student motivation and classroom management. If applied consistently, use of the model will result in improved learning conditions for students and improved teaching conditions for teachers.

CONCLUSION

Chapter 1 has stressed that problems of student motivation and classroom management should be considered together rather than as separate and isolated issues. The chapter provided a number of definitions popularly used for both classroom management and student motivation. The concept of discipline was also introduced and defined as what the teacher is engaged in when efforts at management and motivation have not been successful.

The chapter emphasized that teachers need to be well prepared by having well-thought-out plans for instruction, management, and motivation. Teachers also need to have discipline plans in place and be comfortable and confident in their use should student behavior problems arise. No pilot would leave an airport without a flight plan nor would a coach enter an athletic contest without a game plan. Likewise, no teacher should enter the classroom without having plans to instruct, motivate, manage, and deal with student problem situations should they occur.

Finally, the chapter emphasized the necessity of the teacher being a logical decision-maker or reflective practitioner in addressing problems of student motivation and classroom management. The Model for Reflection and Inquiry was introduced to guide the teacher in the decision-making process. Without a logical approach to making decisions, the teacher will not be able to establish and then maintain a well-managed classroom with motivated students. Neither will the teacher be able to effectively solve problems after they have occurred or fully understand how problems were solved after conditions have improved.

QUESTIONS/ACTIVITIES FOR REFLECTION

1. If a student consistently fails to complete homework assignments, how might you address the problem as a management concern as well as a motivation concern? What steps would you take in dealing with the problem?
2. Kounin (1970) found effective teachers to be no better than ineffective teachers when responding to student misbehavior after it had occurred. Analyze Kounin's finding. Why do you think that he drew this conclusion? Based on your observations of teachers, do you agree? Explain.
3. In Seth's case study, it was stressed that Seth was highly confident but that his confidence may actually be overconfidence resulting in a problem in the classroom. In being a manager and motivator of students, what are some of the reasons for and ways to show confidence? What are some of the pitfalls associated with being or appearing to be overconfident?
4. It is observed that to be an effective manager and motivator a teacher must be a reflective practitioner. Explain what it means to be a reflective practitioner. Describe a classroom situation illustrating how a teacher who is a reflective practitioner might handle a behavior problem associated with students continually calling out in class when the teacher is teaching a lesson.
5. Develop a list of five management rules for the classroom with related consequences for students when the rules are broken. Identi-

fy what classroom purpose each rule serves. How would you proceed to develop and then implement your list of management rules in your own classroom?

Chapter 2

UNDERSTANDING MOTIVATION AND MOTIVATING ENVIRONMENTS

People, more often than not, do what is expected of them. Much of our behavior is governed by widely shared norms or expectations that make it possible to prophesy how a person will behave in a given situation, even if we have never met that person and know little of how he differs from others. At the same time, however, there is considerable variability of behavior so that often we can more accurately prophesy the behavior of a person we know well than we can prophesy the behavior of a stranger. (Rosenthal & Jacobson, 1968, p. vii)

MOTIVATION

Motivation is an internal state that arouses students to action, directs them to certain behaviors, and assists them in maintaining this action and direction with regard to behaviors important and appropriate to the learning environment. Chapter 1 provided an overview of motivation and management as these concepts apply to students and classrooms. It was emphasized that motivation and management are closely related to effective teaching in terms of their relationship to the behaviors that students exhibit in classrooms today. Definitions were given for both concepts with the above definition being given for motivation. Three key elements comprise this definition. Motivation is an internal state that:

1. arouses students to action,
2. directs them to certain behaviors, and

3. assists them in maintaining that arousal and action.

However, many teachers who understand the meaning of motivation are unable to motivate students or establish truly motivating environments in their classrooms. Knowing is one thing, and doing is another. The definition provided here represents an important foundation for understanding motivation as it relates to students and a natural starting point from which to develop the ability needed to motivate students in schooling settings. Teachers have at least three important questions to answer when dealing with challenges of student motivation. First, *What can I do to arouse my students so that they will be engaged in the learning activities that I have planned and stimulated to learn the subject matter that I am teaching?* Second, *What can I do to help my students become focused on and show the learning behaviors that I desire?* Third, *What can I do to assist my students in maintaining their arousal and action related to the learning activities of the classroom?* The Model for Reflection and Inquiry, introduced in Chapter 1, can guide teachers as they seek answers to these questions.

Part of the answer to these important questions lies in the knowledge that teachers have of their students. *What interests do the students bring with them to the classroom? What issues do they have as they enter the school each day? What are their lives like at home and away from school in general? How do they learn best in terms of their learning styles? What are their aspirations? What have their past records of academic performance been like?* The list of questions and needed answers reflecting knowledge of students can be lengthy. Questions such as these must be asked and answered if teachers desire to establish high levels of student motivation in their classrooms.

Beyond their knowledge of their students, it is also critical that teachers have a good understanding of motivation itself. *What is motivation? What causes it? How can it be established and then maintained?* Students choose to do many different things every day in many different situations and for many different reasons. In exploring motivation in the context of influencing student behavior, it is helpful to break the concept down into its component parts and systematically look at the *motives* behind the actions that students take. To be able to motivate them, teachers need to know why their students display or do not display certain behaviors, or become or do not become involved in the learning activities of the classroom.

Consider the following comments made by students regarding their learning experiences and analyze them against what has been presented so far about the concept of motivation. Continue to think about them as important points of reference throughout the rest of the chapter.

Joey (fifth grade):	"That activity was really fun. I didn't think that we had spent so much time on it, and it's already time to stop."
Sarah (ninth grade):	"I've tried it and tried it and I just can't get it. I don't see the point in trying again."
Hannah (seventh grade):	"I thought I understood it, but I guess I didn't. I'm really not very good in that area. I don't like doing this."
Matt (second grade):	"My teacher spent a lot of time with me today. Maybe she thinks that I can't get it on my own."
Sam (eleventh grade):	"If my friends wouldn't talk so much when I am trying to listen, I would understand things better. I don't know why the teacher can't explain things more clearly."

Effective teachers not only understand what motivation is, they also know how to apply this understanding to motivate their students. Table 2.1 identifies four key dimensions of motivation for consideration: *interest, relevance, expectancy,* and *satisfaction.* Understanding these dimensions is directly related to understanding and then motivating students in the classroom.

It is essential that teachers understand the impact motivation has on student learning and behavior as well as the degree to which motivation and achievement are linked to addressing student academic needs. When academic needs are met, student motivation and achievement are enhanced. Following are twelve academic needs of students that are closely related to student motivation and achievement (Jones & Jones, 2013). Students have a need to:

1. understand and value learning goals,
2. understand the learning process,
3. be actively involved in the learning process,

Table 2.1

Four Dimensions of Motivation

Dimensions of Motivation	*Relevant Questions in Understanding the Dimensions of Motivation*
Interest	Is the student's curiosity aroused and sustained over time?
Relevance	Does the student see the teacher's instruction as satisfying his or her personal needs or goals?
Expectancy	Does the student believe that it is within his or her control to be successful in the lesson?
Satisfaction	Is there a positive balance between the student's intrinsic motivation and his or her responses to extrinsic rewards?

Source: From Gagne, R., Wagner, W., Golas, K., & Keller, J. (2005). *Principles of instructional design* (5th ed.). Independence, KY: Cengage Learning.

4. have learning goals related to their own interests and choices,
5. receive instruction matched to their learning styles and strengths,
6. see learning modeled by adults as an exciting and rewarding process,
7. experience success,
8. have time to integrate learning,
9. receive realistic and immediate feedback that enhances self-efficacy,
10. be involved in self-evaluating their learning and effort,
11. receive appropriate rewards for performance gains, and
12. experience a supportive, safe, well-managed learning environment.

Effective teachers recognize how motivation relates to successful learning for their students as well as how it relates to their own behaviors as individuals charged with the responsibility of guiding this learning. Ormrod (2011) described five specific effects that motivation has on students in their learning. Understanding these effects can assist teachers in establishing classroom environments that help motivate students to learn.

1. **Motivation directs behavior toward particular goals**: Motivation helps to determine the specific goals toward which students will work and affects the choices that they make.
2. **Motivation leads to increased effort and energy in pursuit of these goals**: Motivation helps determine the extent to which

students pursue tasks enthusiastically and wholeheartedly or apathetically and reluctantly.

3. **Motivation increases initiation of, and persistence in, certain activities, even in the face of occasional interruptions and frustrations**: Motivation helps determine the level at which students will, on their own, initiate and stay involved in activities.

4. **Motivation affects cognitive processes, such as what students pay attention to and how much they think about and elaborate on it**: Motivation influences what and how information is processed, e.g., motivated students are more likely to pay attention, try to understand material, and seek help on a task when they need it.

5. **Motivation determines which consequences are reinforcing and which are punishing**: The more motivated students are to achieve in certain areas, e.g., academics, athletics, and social interactions, the more they value the rewards that come from their success in these areas.

As a result of these effects, higher levels of student motivation are believed to lead to higher levels of student performance; students who are motivated to learn tend to be the highest achievers in the school. Even with all of the studies that have been conducted over the years, myths about motivation do exist. For example, though not the case for most students, some teachers believe that failure is a good motivator. While it is popularly thought that experience can be a valuable teacher and that all students can learn from their mistakes, a student who experiences chronic or persistent failure can become trapped in a failure cycle from which he or she may not be able to escape. Too frequently, some failure leads to more failure, and more and more failure can lead to helplessness. Feeling that success simply is not possible may be the ultimate end result (Seligman, 1975). **Learned helplessness** is *the belief held by students that no amount of effort on their part will produce success and that events and outcomes in their lives are beyond their control.* Learned helplessness has been related to cognitive, affective and motivational problems in students (Woolfolk, 2013).

Learned helplessness in school occurs when students, usually students who have experienced a great deal of failure, believe that there is nothing they can do for failure to be avoided. When they fail, students experiencing learned helplessness typically attribute their failure to their low ability, which they believe is not alterable and not within their control. The following student behaviors or characteristics are often considered to suggest learned helplessness (Stipek, 2002). The student:

- says "I can't,"
- doesn't pay attention to the teacher's instructions,
- doesn't ask for help, even when it is needed,
- does nothing (e.g., stares out the window),
- guesses or answers randomly without really trying,
- doesn't show pride in successes,
- appears bored, uninterested,
- is unresponsive to the teacher's exhortations to try,
- is easily discouraged,
- doesn't volunteer answers to the teacher's questions, and
- maneuvers to get out of or to avoid work (e.g., has to go to the nurse's office).

While learned helplessness is a maladaptive behavior, teachers can have a positive impact on students in such situations. For example, it is important to recognize that learned helplessness is less common in classrooms where teachers focus on understanding, stimulate creative thinking, and ask students their opinions. Unfortunately, chronic failure leads to more failure unless a better pathway to success is found. Even in small amounts, success is a more potent motivator for most students than failure; this is especially true when working with students who have had any pattern of repeated failure.

A second myth about motivation is that threats or coercion can increase student motivation. Teachers threaten students with detention, retention, low grades, or calling their parents in anticipation that these actions will "get the student's attention" and that improved motivation will be the end result. (See Chapter 6 for an in-depth discussion of teacher responses to student misconduct.) While the use of such strategies may result in a short-term positive change in behavior with some students, they generally are not productive in the long-term. If used at all, punishment as a motivator should be considered to be a part of the later steps of the principle of least intervention. The **principle of least intervention** states that, *when dealing with routine classroom behavior, misbehaviors should be corrected with the simplest, least intrusive intervention that will work* (Slavin, 2000). The main goal in using any intervention is to successfully address the misbehavior in a manner that avoids unnecessarily disrupting the teacher's ongoing lesson. Punishment should only be used after other behavior-changing interventions have been tried. A coercive strategy, the use of punishment is characterized by imposing a penalty with the intention of suppressing undesirable behavior. There are two procedures for achieving this purpose: (1) withholding positive reinforcers or desirable stimuli through techniques such as logical consequences and a behavior modification approach like time-out or loss of privileges, and (2) adding aversive, unpleasant stimuli through actions by which students receive a penalty for their behavior. Withholding positive reinforcers is considered to be less harmful than adding aversive stimuli. Table 2.2 includes ten factors that should be considered for punishment to be used effectively.

Including the use of punishment, the following practices should be avoided in any effort to change student behavior:

- harsh and humiliating reprimands
- threats
- nagging
- forced apologies
- sarcastic remarks
- group punishment
- assigning extra academic work
- reducing grades
- writing as punishment
- physical labor or exercise
- corporal punishment

The continued use of punishment may reveal how little a teacher knows about his or her students, what interests them, what they enjoy and do not enjoy, and, basically, what motivates them. It also may reflect a lack of understanding about motivation itself. A student who has grown accustomed to receiving low grades, for example, generally will not be motivated by the threat of receiving more low grades. Likewise, a student who has often been made to stay after school for detention or has had his or her parents previously called by the teacher for misbehavior typically will not see the continuation of such actions on the part of the teacher as motivating.

Actions that teachers take or behaviors that teachers exhibit that motivate some students may not motivate others. This is to say that some actions and behaviors will have *potency* for some students and not for

Table 2.2

Guidelines for the Use of Punishment

Guideline	Guideline Elaboration
1. Discuss and reward acceptable behaviors.	Acceptable behaviors should be emphasized when classroom rules are first discussed; it should be made clear to students why the rules exist.
2. Clearly specify the behaviors that will lead to punishment.	Clarifying acceptable behaviors may not be enough. It is helpful to identify and discuss examples of behaviors that break the rules and result in punishment.
3. Use punishment only when rewards or nonpunitive interventions have not worked or if the behavior must be decreased quickly because it is dangerous.	Punishment should be used as a last resort when other techniques have not proven to be successful. If there is a dangerous situation in the classroom, action must be taken.
4. Administer punishment in a calm, unemotional manner.	Punishment should not be an emotional response, a way to get revenge, or a spontaneous response to provocation. It should not be given out when emotionally upset.
5. Deliver a warning before punishment is applied to any behavior.	The warning itself could reduce the need for the punishment; if the student does not correct the behavior after the warning, punishment should be delivered at the next occurrence.
6. Apply punishment fairly with everyone who exhibits the targeted behaviors.	Treat students from both genders and low-achieving students and high-achieving students the same way.
7. Apply punishment consistently after every occurrence of the targeted misbehavior.	Behaviors that reliably receive punishment are less likely to be tried by students than behaviors that occasionally go uncorrected.
8. Use punishment of sufficient intensity to suppress the unwanted behaviors.	Generally, the greater the intensity, the longer lasting the effect. However, this does not call for the use of extreme or harsh measures.
9. Select a punishment that is effective, that is not associated with a positive or rewarding experience, and that fits the situation.	Not all aversive consequences may be seen as punishment. For example, some students might think that it is a reward to be placed in a time-out area. Too, teachers should not overreact to mild misbehavior or underreact to serious misbehavior. The seriousness of the misbehavior, the student, and the context of the situation need to be taken into consideration.
10. Avoid extended periods of punishment.	Lengthy, mild punishment, such as missing open study time for a week, may have an unintended consequence effect. Punishment with a short duration is typically more effective.

Source: From Burden, P., & Byrd, D. (2013). *Methods for effective teaching: Meeting the needs of all students* (6th ed.). Boston: Pearson, pp. 270–271.

others. **Potency** is *the strength or the power of a reinforcer, reward, praise or criticism, to change behavior.* The most effective teachers are those who have learned what reinforcers work with what students and who have knowledge of each student's past history of success and failure. Using this knowledge, such teachers are able to select those reinforcers that have the greatest likelihood of bringing about the desired behavior change. They tailor their use of reinforcers in a way that is determined by what they know about motivation and reinforcement as well as what they know about their students.

INTRINSIC AND EXTRINSIC MOTIVATION

In a perfect world, students are eagerly involved in all of the activities planned by their teachers simply because they find enjoyment in learning. Observation shows, however, that there is no perfect world. And yet, many students do seem to enjoy learning and want to experience more of it. Others seem to not enjoy learning at all and are disinterested in their teachers' efforts to get them engaged. Still others only seem to do what their teachers ask of them after considering what they will receive if they complete the task or what will happen to them if they do not. These different observations of motivation are applicable to the concepts *intrinsic* and *extrinsic motivation.* **Intrinsic motivation** is *motivation to become involved in an activity for its own sake.* **Extrinsic motivation** is *motivation to become involved in an activity as a means to an end.* Intrinsically motivated students become active in their learning because they see the task as important and/or enjoyable. They do not engage in learning activities for concrete rewards or incentives, but because they find the activities themselves rewarding and pleasurable. Students who are intrinsically motivated do not need incentives or punishments because the teacher's learning activities themselves are satisfying and rewarding to them (Anderman & Anderman, 2010). Intrinsic motivation is linked to many positive school outcomes such as academic achievement, creativity, reading comprehension and enjoyment, and using deep learning strategies (Corpus, McClintic-Gilbert, & Hayenga, 2009). Extrinsically motivated students, on the other hand, become active in their learning because they understand that they will receive something of value if they do what the teacher desires or something that they dislike if they do not. They represent a significant part of today's student population that wants to know *What's in it for me?* when deciding whether or not to be involved in or to complete or not complete a particular learning task. This *What's in it for me?* outlook seems to represent a large part of the societal population as well. Extrinsic motivation has been linked to negative outcomes such as negative emotions, lack of academic achievement, and maladaptive learning strategies (Corpus et al., 2009).

Many activities or tasks that characterize school environments are not intrinsically motivating to students, and many students do not find them naturally enjoyable, personally rewarding, or even see the point in them (Brophy, 1983). As a response to this, many teachers approach the challenges of student motivation by relying on extrinsic incentives such as praise, tokens, prizes, and special recognitions (e.g., Student of the Month) to get students to do what they want them to do (Alderman, 2008). In many cases, students become accustomed to this reward-giving approach to learning and conditioned to receive rewards as a natural part of the schooling process. They make the association that completing schoolwork on their part produces the giving of rewards on the part of their teachers. Once this cycle begins, and students learn to anticipate some type of reward for the completion of their assignments, it becomes a difficult pattern of behavior to break.

While intrinsic motivation does exist, teachers cannot count on students being intrinsically motivated on every task presented before them. It is unrealistic for teachers to expect what might be considered as ideal motivation in the classroom with each and every lesson taught (Brophy, 1998). Working to produce a state of *motivation to learn* is a more realistic and reachable goal. Motivation to learn differs from extrinsic or reinforcement-oriented motivation and intrinsic or pleasure-oriented motivation. **Motivation to learn** is *motivation represented by the quality of a student's cognitive engagement in a learning task or activity.* It is a realistic goal for teachers to develop and then sustain their students' motivation to learn from academic activities. This will be based on students finding the academic activities in the classroom meaningful and worthwhile, their ability to be successful with them, and valuing the benefits derived from them. Table 2.3 provides a comparison of how different factors contribute to student motivation to learn. Motivation to learn is enhanced when the student is focused on the task, has a mastery orientation, attributes success and failure to controllable causes, believes his or her ability can be improved, and the sources of motivation are intrinsic and the goals are personally challenging. Lack of motivation to learn often leads to student time-off-task which can lead to behavior problems.

Table 2.3

Factors That Enhance Motivation to Learn

Source of Motivation	Factors that Enhance Motivation to Learn	Factors that Diminish Motivation to Learn
Type of Goal Set	Intrinsic: Personal factors such as needs, interests, curiosity, enjoyment.	Extrinsic: Environmental factors such as rewards, social pressures, punishment.
Type of Involvement	Learning Goal: Personal satisfaction in meeting challenges and improving; tendency to choose moderately difficult and challenging goals. Task-Involved: Concerned with mastering the task.	Performance Goal: Desire for approval of performance in others' eyes; tendency to choose very easy or very difficult goals. Ego-Involved: Concerned with self in others' eyes.
Achievement Motivation	Motivation to Achieve: Mastery orientation.	Motivation to Avoid Failure: Prone to anxiety.
Likely Attributions	Successes and failures attributed to controllable effort and ability.	Successes and failures attributed to uncontrollable causes.
Beliefs About Ability	Incremental View: Belief that ability can be improved through hard work and added knowledge and skills.	Entity View: Belief that ability is a stable, uncontrollable trait.

Source: From Woolfolk, A. (2013). *Educational psychology* (12th ed.). Boston: Pearson, p. 456.

An important question for teachers to ask in developing motivation to learn environments in their classrooms is, *What will arouse students to action, direct them to engage in or exhibit certain behaviors, and assist them in maintaining this arousal and direction?* While some instructional strategies contribute better than others to increased motivation in the classroom, some strategies actually seem to work against such student motivation. For example, motivation in the classroom is increased when the teacher: (1) directly communicates the importance of the assigned work, (2) makes connections across the curriculum, and (3) makes home-to-school connections with assignments that are given. Motivation in the classroom is not being supported when the teacher: (1) attributes student success to intellect rather than effort, (2) emphasizes competition rather than cooperation, and (3) gives ineffective and/or negative feedback to students.

Adding to its complexity, there are a number of different theoretical approaches to the study of motivation. Table 2.4 provides an overview six of these theoretical approaches: *trait theories, behaviorist theories, humanism, social cognitive theories, cognitive theories,* and *sociocultural theories.*

Table 2.4

Theoretical Approaches to the Study of Motivation

Theoretical Perspective	*Theoretical Approaches to the Study of Motivation*
Trait theories	Relatively enduring characteristics and personality traits play a significant role in motivation. For example, learners have different temperaments that predispose them to seek or avoid novel experiences and social situations. Significant individual differences exist in learners' motives – e.g., in their desires to achieve at high levels, to interact frequently with other people, and to obtain other people's approval for their achievements and behaviors.
Behaviorist theories	Motivation is often the result of drives, internal states caused by a lack of something necessary for optimal functioning. Consequences of behavior (reinforcement, punishment) are effective to the extent that they either decrease or increase these drive states.
Humanism	Learners have within themselves a tremendous potential for psychological growth and continually strive to fulfill this potential. When given a caring and supportive environment, they strive to understand themselves, to enhance their abilities, and to behave in ways that benefit both themselves and others.
Social Cognitive theories	In the first few years of life, learners are motivated largely by the consequences that follow either their own behaviors or the behaviors of other people. With age and experience, they acquire self-efficacy beliefs – that is, beliefs about their ability to achieve desired results in different domains. As many learners become increasingly self-regulating over time, they begin to set goals for themselves, and much of their motivation comes from within, rather than from external consequences.
Cognitive theories	A variety of cognitive factors – sometimes in combination with emotional factors – affect learners' perceptions of themselves, of various topics, and of the world at large. Such perceptions, in turn, influence learners' inclinations to engage or not engage in particular tasks and activities. For example, learners tend to be more intrinsically motivated when they believe they have some control and choice in their activities. Learners also identify what are, in their minds, the likely causes of their successes and failures, and these attributions influence their subsequent behaviors.
Sociocultural theories	Many aspects of motivation are the result of social and cultural factors, such as the norms for behavior that parents, peers, and others communicate and encourage. For example, children may initially engage in certain behaviors to get parental approval, but many gradually internalize the importance of these behaviors and engage in them even in the absence of external pressure and reinforcement.

Source: From Ormrod, J. (2011). *Educational psychology: Developing learners* (7th ed.). Boston: Pearson.

Theories of student motivation can also be categorized much like theories of learning: *behaviorist, cognitive,* or *humanist.* An understanding of these theories in the context of student learning can be beneficial to the teacher in knowing how to increase student motivation in the classroom. Table 2.5 provides brief definitions of these three theories.

Table 2.5
Theories of Student Motivation

Theory	*Definition*
Behaviorism	Motivation is the result of responses to reinforcement. The effective use of reinforcers, either present internally within the student or externally as influenced by the teacher, is critical to behaviorist approaches to motivation.
Cognitive theories	Motivation results from students attempting to find order or balance, i.e., predictability, and an understanding of the world. Students have a natural motivation to understand their world and bring into balance irregularities that they may experience. These are needs that students have, and they are motivated to satisfy them.
Humanism	Motivation results from students attempting to fulfill their full potential as human beings. Individuals have an innate tendency to develop their talents and to grow and enhance themselves. There is no such thing as an unmotivated student.

Source: From Lefrancois, G. (2000). *Psychology for teaching* (10th ed.). Belmont, CA: Wadsworth/ Thompson Learning.

BEHAVIORISM AND MOTIVATION

The behaviorist theory of learning emphasizes observable behavior changes that take place as a result of experience. The behaviorist perspective emphasizes external rewards and punishments or consequences as keys in determining a student's motivation (Santrock, 2008). Behaviorism does not focus on what necessarily may have changed in the student's mind, but on that which can be seen.

Behaviorism is popularly associated with giving reinforcement or the use of reinforcers to motivate. A **reinforcer** is *something given or a consequence that, depending on whether it is positive or negative, either adds to or reduces the frequency or length of a behavior.* An important question to be answered in the behaviorist theory of motivation is, *What are the best reinforcers, and when should they be used?* The answer to this question is actually quite complex and not without some controversy and criticism (Harter & Jackson, 1992; Kohn, 1992). In spite of this, the use of reinforcers (e.g., popcorn, soft drinks, watching favorite videos, free time, teacher praise, grades, class positions and responsibilities, etc.), is common in schools today, especially in elementary classrooms.

The concept of punishment was introduced earlier as an example of a coercive strategy to modify student behavior and increase motivation. Positive and negative reinforcers are consequences that are used to increase or decrease behavior. Punishers are consequences that are intended to weaken behaviors or decrease the likelihood of them recurring. **Punishment** is *the process of using punishers to decrease behavior.* Punishment is often a part of the teacher's discipline process and overall management system. When punishers are used as reinforcers to extinguish a behavior, the teacher must be mindful of both the short-term and long-term impact of their use. Punishers such as **desists**, *the use of verbal or nonverbal communications by teachers for the purpose of stopping student misconduct or misbehavior* (Kounin, 1970), time-out, and detention are commonly used by teachers and can be effective in modifying student behavior. Punishers in the form of physical punishment, embarrassment, and humiliation, or the completion of additional class work with the intent of changing student behavior, are not considered effective and should be avoided.

Teaching activities themselves are some of the most common reinforcers that teachers have available. A helpful guide for choosing the most effective reinforcers is the Premack principle (Santrock, 2008). Named after psychologist David Premack, the **Premack Principle** is the *principle that a high-probability or desired activity or behavior can serve as a reinforcer for a low-probability or perhaps less desired activity or behavior.* The principle can be a useful guide in choosing the most effective reinforcers. For example, the Premack principle is being applied when the teacher tells a student, *When you complete your writing assignment, you can play a game on the computer.* This approach to motivating students, however, is only effective if playing games on a computer (the high-probability activity) is more desirable for the student than writing (the low-probability activity). The Premack principle can also be used with the entire class. For example, the teacher might tell the class, "If everyone in the class gets their homework done by Friday, we will take a field trip next week." For the Premack principle to be effective, the low-frequency (less preferred) behavior must happen first. Just as with praise, by making privileges and rewards directly contingent on learning and positive behavior, the teacher can significantly increase both learning and desired behavior. While reinforcers are considered valuable tools by many, the use of reinforcers has been found to be less effective for middle or high school students and underachieving students in general.

It should be remembered that some reinforcers are more potent or have greater impact than others and that a reinforcer that may have potency for one student in one situation may not have such potency for another student, in even a similar or comparable situation. Too, a reinforcer that may be potent for a student at one point may be less potent or not potent at all for the same student at a later point. This change of influence could be brought about by the inappropriate or overuse of the reinforcer. In spite of their popular use, the following criticisms have been identified with respect to the use of reinforcers.

1. **The use of reinforcers may decrease intrinsic motivation.** Offering reinforcers for engaging in intrinsically motivating tasks can decrease student interest in such tasks. The problem with reinforcers can be related to how a behavior is rewarded. Rewarding students for simply completing tasks, rather than for making progress in learning, may ultimately detract from motivation.

2. **The use of reinforcers can narrow the student's focus.** In some cases, reinforcers can become the goals of learning rather than the academic content or the beauty of or interest in learning itself. Rather than adding to the breadth of the learning experience, reinforcers can have the impact of narrowing that experience. A reinforcer can become the reason for the student's motivation to learn, i.e., so the reward can be received. In such a case, the student is really learning for the reward, not because of it.

3. **The use of reinforcers can create logistical problems.** Using reinforcers demands time, energy, and sometimes money; additionally, rewards given to some students may cause resentment in other students who do not receive them. This can bring about an inconsistent use of rewards with the end result actually being a lower level of student motivation.

4. **The use of rewards ignores student cognitions.** The use of behaviorism as an approach to motivate students is sometimes criticized from the view that it focuses on the use of reinforcers (rewards) and ignores learners' perceptions and beliefs about

themselves and about learning. For example, while praise is a common reinforcer and its use can be misunderstood. Older students may see praise as reward for effort as opposed to an accomplishment. Such students may interpret praise for performance on easy tasks as indicating that the teacher sees them as having low ability. Although intended as a reinforcer, the praise may be perceived negatively.

Behavioristic approaches to motivation emphasize the teacher's use of extrinsic reinforcers (e.g., reward and praise) rather than relying on the student being intrinsically motivated. Using grades, stars, stickers, or other reinforcers for learning, or demerits or time-out for misbehavior, are examples of attempts to motivate students by extrinsic means. Such extrinsic reinforcers may be considered as being either primary or secondary in nature, although both can be used to influence behavior. Examples of **primary reinforcers** are *food, water, and safety that meet basic physiological needs.* Examples of **secondary reinforcers** are *praise, grades, and money that may address a student's psychological needs.* The behaviorist theory of motivation rests on the belief that individuals are motivated through the desire to receive something for their actions. Interestingly enough, for some students, this can include love of learning (Henson & Eller, 1999). While many are not supportive of their use, research suggests that the appropriate use of rewards can motivate some students and bring about change in behavior. The use of praise for genuine achievement and rewards that acknowledge increasing competence can result in increased intrinsic motivation (Cameron, Pierce, & Banko, 2005).

COGNITIVE THEORIES OF MOTIVATION

Cognitive theories of motivation are grounded in the belief that individual behavior is influenced by the way people see themselves and their environment (Snowman, McCown, & Biehler, 2012). According to this perspective, students' thoughts guide their motivation. Students have a need for order and predictability and an understanding of things around them. When order and understanding are present, they seek to maintain it. When order and understanding are absent or lost, they seek to gain or regain it. Order and understanding represent an important

balance for students and, therefore, predictability. Students are naturally motivated to learn when they encounter experiences that are inconsistent with their current understandings (Greeno, Collins, & Resnick,
1996); they seek to establish, or perhaps re-establish, consistency when
it is absent. Students also are naturally motivated when they encounter
information that is not yet found in their already-held definitions and
ideas of the world. When this type of situation occurs, they seek to acquire an understanding of this information and incorporate it into their
individual ways of seeing the world.

The work of Piaget (1952) is applicable to the discussion of motivation and a student's need for order and understanding. Well known in
the study of learning processes, Piaget's concept of equilibrium is applicable here in that it represents a need that all individuals possess.
Equilibrium is defined as *a state of balance.* When students experience
disequilibrium, *a state of being out-of-balance,* they seek to regain their
balance. *The process of searching for order or balance and, in so doing, testing
one's understanding against the real world* is referred to as **equilibration**.
What might be thought of as a need for understanding and a drive for
equilibrium is a part of the cognitive theory of motivation where new
experiences are better understood because students are able to explain
them using their existing understanding (Berk, 2010). Certain amounts
of disequilibrium, however, can be desirable and teachers can carefully create situations of disequilibrium and use them to their teaching advantage to motivate their students. As students encounter out-of-balance situations, they are motivated to regain their balance, and they
grow in their learning through the process of striving to re-establish a
state of equilibrium. While this can be the case, extreme disequilibrium
can be counterproductive, creating too much frustration and anxiety
for students. When learning activities or teacher actions create out-of-
balance situations that are too severe, students may perceive that no
amount of effort on their part can bring about a return to balance and
that success cannot be achieved. A result of this perception can be the
student pulling away from or displaying misconduct toward the learning task, the teacher, or both.

Most teachers have seen students who appear quite motivated as well
as those who seem virtually impossible to motivate. A close observation of these two types of students can reveal many things. One thing
that observation can show is how differently the two types of students
may view themselves. Cognitive theories of motivation consider beliefs

and expectations as two important personal factors in the role of expectations in the *expectation X value theory* of motivation (Atkinson, 1964; Feather, 1982). The **expectation X value theory** is *the theory of motivation that suggests that students are motivated to engage in learning tasks to the extent that they expect to succeed on the tasks and the degree to which they value achievement on the tasks or other potential outcomes that may come as a result of task achievement.* The theory takes into account both the behaviorist's concern with the effects or outcomes of behavior and the cognitivist's interest in the impact of individual thinking. If either factor is absent or low, motivation itself will be absent or low (Tollefson, 2000).

More contemporary motivation theorists have based their research on the early expectancy X value model developed by Atkinson. Atkinson (1964) identified incentive values in terms of the pride or shame a task was expected to generate. This has been viewed as a narrow conceptualization of values, especially in that levels of pride and shame are determined, in theory, by an individual's perception of the probability of success or failure (Stipek, 2002). More recent theorists have suggested broader conceptualizations of the value component of expectancy X value theory, i.e., attainment value, utility value and intrinsic value, which are felt to have greater application to classroom practice and student achievement (Eccles, Adler, Futterman, Goff, Kaczala, Meece, & Midgley, 1983).

1. **Attainment value**: value determined by how the task or the domain fulfills a person's needs; it concerns the relevance of an activity to a person's actual or ideal self-concept. People engage in activities and develop competencies that are consistent with their real and desired concept of themselves.
2. **Utility value**: value that focuses on the usefulness of a task as a means to achieve goals that might not be related to the task itself. For example, understanding chemistry and biology would have utility value for students planning to attend medical school.
3. **Intrinsic value**: value as the immediate enjoyment one gets from doing a task. When a task has intrinsic value it is engaged in for its own sake, rather than for some other purpose.

In a further consideration of the expectancy X value theory, Jones and Jones (2013) identify the addition of climate as a third variable of the theory. Climate is explained as the quality of relationships within the task setting during the time students are engaged in the task. This theory might be viewed as *motivation = expectation X value X climate.* It suggests that students will not be motivated to complete a task until all three components or variables are present, i.e., when students expect that they can achieve on the task, see value in the task, and are able to complete the task in an environment supportive of their personal needs.

The challenge to the teacher in applying the expectation X value theory is twofold, or threefold if one subscribes to the model offered by Jones and Jones. The teacher must create legitimate learning experiences where students can find success, and the success that they achieve must be on activities that they see as being of value. If students do not necessarily see a task as being of value, it is important that they see value in other outcomes associated with successful task attainment. The expectation X value theory of motivation creates a new way of looking at motivation for some teachers in that many teachers have the belief that student success is the overriding factor in motivation. In the expectation X value theory, success is necessary but not sufficient to motivate students. Ratcliff, Jones, Costner, Knight, Disney, Savage-Davis, Sheehan, and Hunt (2012) reported that success, coupled with seeing value in what is attained, or at least in some other outcome that will be forthcoming, are key to student motivation. Being successful at a task that holds little value will have limited positive motivational impact, at least in the long run.

Self-Efficacy

When students are successful on tasks that they value, they develop higher *self-efficacy* (Schunk, 1994). **Self-efficacy** is *one's beliefs about the capability of succeeding on specific tasks.* Students who have high self-efficacy believe in their abilities and see themselves as capable of making genuine progress toward worthwhile goals. Such students are able to sustain their work effort longer as they anticipate that they will be successful at the end of the task (Bandura, 1997). Students who have low self-efficacy see themselves as having limited ability and unlikely to be successful in the teacher's learning activities. Students with high self-efficacy try hard while holding on to the belief that they can succeed; students with low self-efficacy tend to put forth little effort. Table 2.6 provides an analysis of some of the characteristics of students with high and low self-efficacy.

Table 2.6

Characteristics of Students with High and Low Self-efficacy

Characteristics	High Self-efficacy	Low Self-efficacy
Task Orientation	Accepts challenging tasks.	Avoids challenging tasks.
Effort	Expends high effort when faced with challenging tasks.	Expends low effort when faced with challenging tasks.
Persistence	Persists when goals are not initially reached.	Gives up when goals are not initially reached.
Beliefs	Believes that success will be forthcoming	Focuses on feelings of incompetence and the absence of future success.
	Controls stress and anxiety when goals are not met.	Experiences anxiety and depression when goals are not met.
	Believes they are in control of their environment.	Believes they are not in control of their environment.
Strategy Use	Discards strategies when they are seen as unproductive.	Continues the use of strategies even when they are unproductive.
Performance	Performs better than low-efficacy students who are of equal ability.	Performs more poorly than high-efficacy students of equal ability.

Source: From Bandura, A. (1993). Perceived self-efficacy in cognitive development and functioning. *Educational Psychologist, 28*(2), 117–148; Eggen, P., & Kauchak, D. (2007). *Educational psychology: Windows on classrooms* (7th ed.). Upper Saddle River, NJ: Pearson Education, Inc; Schunk, D. (1994, April). *Goal and self-evaluative influences during children's mathematical skill acquisition.* Paper presented at the Annual Meeting of the American Educational Research Association, New Orleans.

An understanding of self-efficacy is important to an understanding of the potential for student motivation. It is also important to an understanding of a student's motivational state as related to any given learning task. While having an understanding of self-efficacy is important, being able to recognize a particular student's level of self-efficacy is more important. What is of even greater value is being able to influence students with low self-efficacy to increase their self-efficacy and to influence students with high self-efficacy to maintain or increase their self-efficacy. The teacher's role here is twofold. First, the teacher must be able to understand the individual levels of self-efficacy of his or her students. Second, the teacher must take appropriate action with this knowledge to motivate his or her students in their learning and, in so doing, increase their levels of self-efficacy. Many struggling students resist academic activities, believing that they lack the ability to succeed, even if they expend great effort (Margolis & McCabe, 2004). A key to reversing this outlook and getting struggling students with low self-efficacy to expend sufficient effort to persist on tasks, to work to overcome difficulties, to take on increasingly challenging tasks, and to develop interest in academics, is for teachers to systematically focus on the development of high self-efficacy. Research suggests that teachers can often strengthen struggling learners' self-efficacy by linking new work to recent successes, teaching needed learning strategies, reinforcing effort and persistence, stressing peer modeling, teaching students who are struggling to make facilitative attributions, and helping them identify or create personally important goals. Self-efficacy has a strong influence on motivation to learn. Students with high self-efficacy take on more challenging tasks, exert more effort, stay with tasks longer, use more effective learning strategies, and perform better overall. Factors that influence students' beliefs about their ability to perform include the following (Bandura, 1986).

1. **Past performance**: how a student has done in the past on a particular task provides evidence that the student is capable of completing the task.
2. **Modeling**: being able to see someone else perform a task successfully raises expectations and provides information about how a task should be performed.
3. **Verbal persuasion**: persuasion provides encouragement to students to try challenging tasks; their success then increases their self-efficacy.
4. **Emotional state**: negative emotional states can reduce self-efficacy by filling a student's working memory with thoughts of failure.

Research on students, in particular at-risk students, has increasingly focused on the concept of resilience. **Resilience** is *the ability to recover quickly from some type of misfortune or adversity; resilience results in a heightened likelihood of success in school and in other aspects of life, despite environmental adversities* (Wang, Haertel, & Walberg, 1995). Students with low self-efficacy are characterized by having little resilience. Students with high self-efficacy are considered to be resilient in that they have developed characteristics and coping skills that help them rise above adverse circumstances. Once students have developed a high sense of self-efficacy, failure on an occasional basis is unlikely to dampen their optimism for the future. When these students encounter small setbacks on the way to achieving success, they learn that sustained effort and perseverance are key ingredients of their success and they persevere. Such students have developed resilient self-efficacy (Bandura, 1989). **Resil-**

ient self-efficacy is *the belief that one can perform a task successfully even after experiencing setbacks with the recognition that effort and perseverance are essential for success.*

Just as teachers and schools can have a positive impact on the development of self-efficacy, so too can they have a positive impact on the promotion of resilience. Research reinforces the following school practices that promote resilience in students (Eggen & Kauchak, 2013).

1. **High and Uncompromising Academic Standards**: teachers emphasize mastery of content and do not accept passive attendance and mere completion of assignments.
2. **Strong Personal Bonds**: teachers become the adults who refuse to let students fail, and students feel connected to the schools.
3. **High Structure**: the school and classes are orderly and highly structured; teachers emphasize reasons for rules, consistently enforce rules and procedures and explain reasons for rules.
4. **Participation in After-School Activities**: activities such as clubs and athletics give students additional chances to interact with caring adults and bond with school.

Teachers who talk more frequently with their students, learn about their families, share their own lives, maintain high expectations, use interactive teaching strategies, and emphasize success and mastery of content promote resilience in students. Such teachers motivate students through personal contacts, instructional support, and attempts to link school to their students' lives. Teachers who are less effective in promoting resilience are more authoritarian and less accessible, distance themselves from their students, and place primary responsibility for learning on them. Students often view such teachers as adversaries to be avoided if possible. In the end, promoting resilience lies in the teacher's attitude, instructional practice, and commitment to students (Doll, Zucker, & Brehm, 2004; Gschwend & Dembo, 2001).

HUMANISTIC VIEWS OF MOTIVATION

As with cognitive theories, intrinsic motivation of students is also important to humanistic views of motivation. Humanists see motivation as an attempt to fulfill the total potential of a human being (Hamachek, 1987). The humanistic perspective stresses students' capacity for personal growth, freedom to choose their destiny, and positive qualities such as being sensitive to others (Santrock, 2008). The humanistic theory of motivation represents a position contrary to the belief that human behavior is either a response to the environment or internal instincts. The humanist view focuses on the entire physical, emotional, interpersonal, and intellectual qualities of an individual as they impact what that person chooses to do. From the humanistic perspective, to motivate means to encourage the student's inner resources, i.e., their sense of competence, self-esteem, autonomy, and self-actualization. According to the humanist, there is no such thing as an unmotivated student; all students are motivated. Some students simply may be motivated to do things other than that which the teacher desires for them to do.

The now-classic Hierarchy of Needs theory of Abraham Maslow (1970), called the father of the humanistic movement, is frequently discussed when exploring the question of student motivation as influenced by need. Maslow identified student needs as being in one of two categories: *deficiency needs* and *growth needs.* **Deficiency needs** are *needs at the lower levels of the hierarchy including survival, safety, belonging, and self-esteem.* These are needs that must be met for the student to move to the higher levels of the hierarchy. **Growth needs** are *needs at the higher levels of the hierarchy and include intellectual achievement, aesthetic appreciation, and self-actualization.* Growth needs expand and evolve as individuals have experience with them. Efforts to satisfy growth needs lead to further development within them. Students who are intellectually stimulated, for example, will seek additional intellectual stimulation. Students who engage in the pursuit of beauty, through art, music, etc., will seek to continue in this pursuit. The highest level of the hierarchy is *self-actualization.* **Self-actualization** is *the full development or use of one's potential.* Achieving self-actualization represents an ongoing evolution and is never fully reached.

Applications of the hierarchy to the work of the classroom teacher are obvious. Students who are hungry and tired do not learn and develop to their fullest potentials as long as these conditions are present. Students who do not feel safe and accepted in the learning environment do not reach their fullest potentials until they feel safe and accepted. Students who have low self-esteem will not move forward at an optimum rate in terms of either their intellectual achievement or their full understanding of themselves until their self-esteem is strengthened. Figure 2.1 offers a representation of Abraham Maslow's Hierarchy of Needs.

Abraham Maslow's Hierarchy of Needs	
GROWTH NEEDS	**Self-Actualization**: meets and uses one's full potential
	Aesthetic: goodness, beauty, truth, justice, order
	Intellectual (cognitive) achievement: knowledge, understanding, symmetry
DEFICIENCY NEEDS	**Self-esteem**: recognition, respect, approval, feeling of adequacy
	Belongingness and Love: affection, acceptance from family and peers
	Safety: security, absence of physical and emotional threat, psychological safety
	Physiological: food, sleep, drink, shelter, warmth

Figure 2.1. Abraham Maslow's Hierarchy of Needs.

While the idea of arranging human needs in a hierarchy may be appealing to many, there is not universal agreement with Maslow's ordering of human motives. For some students, cognitive needs might be more fundamental than esteem needs. Other students might meet their cognitive needs while not having experienced acceptance and belonging. Though thought-provoking and perhaps helpful conceptually, such a hierarchy may not be absolute. The appeal of the concept of the hierarchy notwithstanding, the challenge of identifying where any particular student is at any given point in time on the hierarchy would be quite complex.

FACTORS THAT AFFECT STUDENT MOTIVATION

Having a sound theoretical base in understanding motivation is critical for teachers to be able to motivate their students. Additionally, factors such as *attribution, locus of control, teacher expectations, goals (performance* and *learning), anxiety,* and *environment* also affect the teacher's understanding of and ability to establish high levels of student motivation.

Attribution

Attribution is *a cognitive theory that represents a student's view of the causes of outcomes or of an event and how this view influences his or her future expectations and behavior* (Alderman, 2008). In looking at why he or she was or was not successful, the student may pose the question, *To what may I attribute my success or failure?* The answer that the student gives to this question has bearing on how the student approaches, or may choose to not approach, a learning task. It is suggested that there are two primary reasons that people use to explain their performance: *can* and *try* (Heider, 1958). *Can* speaks to whether an individual has the ability to do a task and *try* speaks to how much effort an individual puts forth. If a student fails at a task, the student's expectations for future success will differ depending on whether the student attributes the failure as being a lack of effort (*try*) or to not having the ability (*can*) to succeed on the task.

One of four reasons is generally given by students as their cause of success or failure in school (Weiner, 1990, 1992, 1994a, 1994b):

1. **Ability**: the student might say, "I was successful because I am just good at that," or the student might say, "I was not successful because I just don't have enough ability to be successful."
2. **Effort**: the student might say, "I was successful because I really tried hard," or the student might say, "I know that I could have been successful if I had tried harder and put more time into it."
3. **Task Difficulty**: the student might say, "I was successful because the assignment was really easy," or the student might say, "I was not successful because what the teacher wanted was just too hard."
4. **Luck**: the student might say, "I don't know why I was successful. It must have just been my good luck," or the student might say, "I don't know why I couldn't get it right. It must not have been my lucky day."

Ability and effort have been found to be the most frequent reasons given by students for their success or failure in school.

The causes of success or failure have also been classified into three different dimensions:

1. internal versus external,
2. stable versus unstable, and
3. controllable versus uncontrollable.

The internal versus external and controllable versus uncontrollable dimensions are especially important to teachers as they provide ways to motivate their students. Teachers need to be able to identify how their students see themselves and how they perceive the reasons for their success or lack of success. Having this information will enable teachers to address the learning needs of their students more completely and, in so doing, better motivate them.

Though many teachers may not realize it, most students do think about and try to understand the reasons for their failures. When students who are usually successful are unsuccessful, they typically identify internal and controllable reasons (attributions) for their lack of success. Such students may recognize that they did not study hard enough, did not understand a particular assignment, or did not prepare correctly for what was expected of them. They generally attribute the reason for their lack of success to controllable causes and, because of this, believe that they will be successful the next time they attempt the task. Students who perceive themselves as having sufficient ability and being in control of the situation usually do not pose motivation problems for teachers. When students attribute their learning outcomes to controllable causes, their motivation to learn remains encouraged, regardless of whether they have histories of failure or success.

Students with a history of repeated failure, and who attribute their learning difficulties or lack of success on learning tasks to uncontrollable, external forces, represent the teacher's greater motivational challenges. When these students attribute the outcomes or results to uncontrollable causes, their motivation to learn tends to lessen. Students of this type often see themselves as inadequate in learning situations and can represent difficult motivation (and frequently behavior) problems for teachers. They often see themselves as helpless and can be depressed and/or anxious about their learning and doubtful of their abilities. They characterize themselves as more unsuccessful than successful and concentrate more on what they see as their own inadequacies. Lack of future effort is a common reaction to failure for such students as they believe that their situation is not likely to change. Success is not in their control; for many, the view is that success simply is not achievable. They also are less likely to seek help because they do not believe that they can be helped (Ames & Lau, 1982).

In addition to the area of student motivation, attribution theory has provided important observations regarding culture, ethnicity, and gender (Alderman, 2008). The following recommendations are of special importance with respect to implications for teachers in these areas.

1. Listen carefully to student expectations and attributions for performance to identify patterns of attributions that might be gender-related or culture-related.
2. Examine your own beliefs about competence for subjects like math and science that have been traditionally gender-typed. If you are an elementary school teacher, do you think of yourself as a math teacher? As a science teacher?
3. Provide feedback that helps both male and female students make more realistic estimates of their ability.
4. Become familiar with cultural values for ability and effort. What is the relative value placed on effort and ability?
5. Be prepared to discuss attributional beliefs and their implications with parents.
6. Be especially sensitive to giving feedback that might be seen by students as sympathy and thus be interpreted as their having low ability.

Locus of Control

Locus of control refers to *the degree to which students perceive that both positive and negative events that impact their lives are under their control* (Bernhard & Siegel, 1994). The study of attribution theory has implications for the understanding of locus of control. Locus of control, i.e., place of control, is an important aspect of attribution theory and the reasons for or causes of student motivation described earlier. Some students have an **internal locus of control** which is indicated *when students feel that they are responsible for what happens to them.* Others have more of an **external locus of control** which is indicated *when students feel that forces external to or outside themselves control their lives.* Students who hold the view that success comes as a result of skill and not luck or chance believe that they have control over their own destinies. Students who have the view that success comes as a result of luck or chance or something external to them and not skill or their own ability believe that they have little control over their destinies. How students see themselves as being successful or unsuccessful learners has bearing on whether they will be successful or unsuccessful. It is important for teachers to know how their students see themselves to be successful in motivating them to higher levels.

A great deal of research has been conducted on the concept of locus of control as it affects students and their learning as well as teachers' attitudes toward students. The following four factors are related to locus of control and are relevant to the work of teachers in motivating their students (Dacey, 1989).

1. Teachers often look upon students who have an external locus of control more negatively than those who have an internal locus of control; interestingly, students who have an external locus of control frequently look upon their teachers more negatively than do students who have an internal locus of control.
2. Students who have an external locus of control perform better when they receive specific comments concerning their teachers' expectations.
3. Students with an internal locus of control are more effective than those with an external locus of control in recognizing and using available information.
4. Students with an external locus of control are less successful in competitive situations than are students with an internal locus of control.

A student's view regarding what causes him or her to be successful or not successful influences the student's motivation in different situations. If students believe that they are responsible for their own successes, they are referred to as *internals*; if they believe that something or somebody other than themselves is responsible, they are referred to as *externals.* External students often have higher levels of anxiety than internal students as they see themselves as having less power over their surroundings (in this case their classroom and their learning). Internal students generally have more self-confidence, are greater risk-takers, are more curious, and anticipate success rather than failure when they enter into learning activities.

Locus of control, however, can change. When teachers help their students gain greater confidence, their sense of internal control increases.

Their anxiety in learning situations decreases and their performance improves. As students become older and more mature, and as they experience more success in their learning, their beliefs about the causes of their success become more internal (Wigfield, 1994). Teachers can enhance this change through the appropriate use of different learning activities (e.g., active learning and cooperative learning are preferred over passive learning and individual and isolated learning), rewards, and approaches to instruction that ensure that students are able to achieve higher levels of success.

Teacher Expectations

While students at times may not be certain as to what teachers expect of them in the completion of particular learning tasks, they frequently do understand, or at least think they understand, what their teachers' views are in terms of their ability to be successful in completing these tasks. Two concepts important to this dynamic are *teacher expectation* and *teacher efficacy*. **Teacher expectation** refers to *what teachers expect or think students will be able to accomplish*. **Teacher efficacy** refers to *the teacher's belief in his or her ability to be successful in getting students to learn*. Teacher expectations and teacher efficacy are closely related. When teachers have high expectations for their students' learning potential, they have a greater belief that they will be successful with them. When they have low expectations of their students' abilities, they have greater doubt (lower teacher efficacy) that they can be successful with them. Students themselves have their own views about how their teachers see them as being successful or not successful, and these student views are related to the levels of motivation that the students exhibit.

Table 2.7 provides an analysis of attitudes of teachers with high and low efficacy. The analysis can be helpful in assisting teachers in preparing for their teaching and in their self-reflection after their lessons have concluded.

Teacher expectations influence how teachers treat students, tend to perpetuate themselves, and affect students' self-concepts (Ormrod, 2011). Teachers generally treat students in ways consistent with the expectations they hold for them. This point can become a serious concern when teachers believe that certain students are destined to have problems or even fail to learn altogether. When teachers expect students to

Table 2.7

Attitudes of Teachers with High and Low Efficacy

Teacher Attitude	High Efficacy	Low Efficacy
A sense of personal accomplishment	Feel their work with students is important and meaningful and that they have a positive impact on student learning	Feel frustrated and discouraged about teaching
Positive expectations for student behavior and achievement	Expect students to progress and, for the most part, find that students fulfill their expectations	Expect students to fail, react negatively to their teaching efforts, and misbehave
Personal responsibility for student learning	Believe it's their responsibility to see their students learn and, when students experience failure, look to their own performance for ways they might be more helpful	Place responsibility for learning on students and, when students fail, look for explanations in terms of family background, motivation, or attitude
Strategies for achieving objectives	Plan for student learning, set goals for themselves and their students, and identify strategies to achieve them	Lack specific goals for their students, are uncertain about what they want their students to achieve, and do not plan strategies according to goals
Positive affect	Feel good about teaching, themselves, and their students	Feel frustrated with teaching and often express negative feelings and discouragement about their work with students
Sense of control	Confident they can influence student learning	Experience a sense of futility in working with students
Sense of common teacher-student goals	Feel they are involved in a joint venture with students to achieve goals they have in common	Feel they are pitted in a struggle with students with goals and strategies in opposition to their own
Democratic decision-making	Involve students in decision-making regarding goals and strategies for achieving them	Impose decisions regarding goals and learning strategies on students without involving them in the process

Source: From Alderman, M. (2008). *Motivation for achievement: Possibilities for teaching and learning* (3rd ed.). New York: Routledge, p. 194.

achieve at higher levels, they typically do. Conversely, when they expect them to not achieve at higher levels, they often do not (Rosenthal & Jacobson, 1968). Even before a teacher has seen a student deal with an academic task, he or she is likely to have some expectation for the student's behavior and potential achievement on the task. This has been referred to as the **self-fulfilling prophecy** or *the phenomenon that a student's performance is greatly influenced when a teacher holds certain beliefs* *about the student's ability to perform.* When teachers anticipate a higher level of student performance, they will generally get it, and when they predict a lower level of student performance, this is what is usually found. As a correlate to this, a student's level of motivation is influenced by what the student perceives as being the prophecy held by the teacher. A student's behavior in both motivation and learning responds to what the student perceives as being the belief held by his or her teacher. The following teacher behaviors may indicate differential teacher treatment of high and low achieving students (Good & Brophy, 2003).

1. Waiting less time for lows to answer a question (before giving the answer or calling on someone else).
2. Giving lows answers or calling on someone else rather than trying to improve their responses by giving clues or repeating or rephrasing questions.
3. Using inappropriate reinforcement such as rewarding inappropriate behavior or incorrect answers by lows.
4. Criticizing lows more often for their failures.
5. Praising lows less often for their successes.
6. Failing to give feedback in a public response of lows.
7. Generally paying less attention to lows or interacting with them less frequently.
8. Calling on lows less frequently to respond to questions, or asking them only easier, nonanalytic questions.
9. Seating lows farther away from the teacher.
10. Demanding less from lows (e.g., teach them less, use gratuitous praise, give excessive offers of help).
11. Interacting with lows more privately than publicly and monitoring and structuring their activities more closely.
12. Differential administration or grading of tests or assignments in which highs but not lows are given the benefit of the doubt in borderline cases.
13. Less friendly interactions with lows, including less smiling and fewer other nonverbal indicators of support.
14. Briefer and less informative feedback to questions of lows.
15. Less eye contact and other nonverbal communication of attention and responsiveness (forward lean, positive head nodding) in interactions with lows.

16. Less use of effective but time-consuming teaching methods with lows when time is limited.
17. Less acceptance and use of lows' ideas.
18. Exposing lows to an impoverished curriculum (overly limited and repetitive content, emphasis on factual recitation rather than on lesson-extending discussion, emphasis on drill and practice tasks rather than application and higher-level thinking tasks).

The relationship between expectation and performance is now a part of the supporting argument on a national scale (e.g., No Child Left Behind legislation) that teachers need to have overall higher expectations for their students. When teachers expect more, they typically receive more. Once formed, teachers are likely to maintain their expectations about their students and this can be positive or negative for a student depending on how he or she is viewed. Positive views normally result in higher levels of student performance while negative views often result in lower levels of performance. Some teachers, for example, underestimate the capabilities of students from minority and low-income backgrounds and maintain these expectations in their teaching (Garcia, 1994; Knapp & Woolverton, 1995). This can be devastating in terms of the impact on the achievement levels of such students.

A key part of the perspective on how students are viewed that also must be addressed is how students view themselves as influenced by how they feel their teachers view them. If students believe their teachers see them as capable of only low achievement, they often will perceive themselves of being capable only of low achievement and their individual self-concepts and performances will respond in a like manner. In the end, their level of motivation will frequently be lower as it has been negatively influenced by what their teachers believe about and expect of them. On the other hand, if students feel as though their teachers have confidence in them and that they can succeed on the assignments given, this influences them to be motivated to persevere on these tasks and will have a positive impact on their achievement. The following six-step process describes the effect of the self-fulfilling prophecy (Good & Brophy, 2003).

1. Early in the year, the teacher forms differential expectations for student behavior and achievement.
2. Consistent with these differential expectations, the teacher behaves differently toward different students.

3. This treatment tells students something about how they are expected to behave in the classroom and perform on academic tasks.

4. If the teacher's treatment is consistent over time, and if students do not actively resist or change it, it will likely affect their self-concepts, achievement, motivation, levels of aspiration, classroom conduct, and interactions with the teacher.

5. These effects generally will complement and reinforce the teacher's expectations, so that students will come to conform to these expectations more than they might have otherwise.

6. Ultimately, this will affect student achievement and other outcome measures. High-expectation students will be led to achieve at or near their potential, but low-expectation students will not gain as much as they could have gained if taught differently.

Each student is different and although all teachers know this, they often overlook the differences and focus on the similarities. While young people may share a common ethnic background, speak a common language, or share a particular religious upbringing, despite these similarities, each is unique. Both teachers and students can at times feel isolated. For students and parents not socialized in the ways of schools, it is difficult to determine that something is amiss. The raw power of education is so strong that many children and their families often feel left out and inadequate (Strother, 1991). These feelings manifest themselves in a number of different ways. Some students are silent and sullen, some make lots of noise, some become the class clowns, some turn to violence, some get high on drugs, and some are just absent a lot. All of these are ways that they use to defend themselves against the feeling of not belonging. They also are all ways of failing.

Teacher efficacy can have a profound influence on instructional practice as well as student motivation. When teachers believe students are capable of only low levels of performance, this belief influences and in some ways predetermines the way they approach their teaching activities and their interactions with their students. Students who are felt to be more capable are often challenged more, taught with greater energy and vigor, involved in more dynamic lessons and activities, and receive a richer set of learning experiences than those who are not seen in this way. Teachers are encouraged to treat all students like the best students (Bottoms, 2007). By completing a rich and challenging program of study, all students are better prepared throughout their schooling experiences and to pursue their career goals beyond high school. While some argue that making schools, in particular high schools, more rigorous may prompt at-risk students to drop out before graduating, this is not the case. The High Schools That Work program reports that, as rigor and relevance are added to the curriculum, more students believe that their studies are worthwhile and linked to their future success (Bottoms, 2007). Students are more thoroughly prepared not just in academic and technical knowledge and skills, but also in such intangible assets as time-management skills, relationship-building skills, and the ability to work hard to achieve their goals. Table 2.8 presents an analysis of teachers' attitudes toward students and how teachers may communicate different expectations for different students.

Table 2.8
Teacher Communications and Differential Expectations

Characteristics	Students Believed to Be More Capable Have:	Students Believed to Be Less Capable Have:
Task environment (curriculum, procedures, task definition, pacing, quality of environment)	More opportunity to perform publicly on meaningful tasks. More opportunity to think.	Less opportunity to perform publicly, especially on meaningful tasks. Less opportunity to think.
Grouping practices	More assignments that deal with comprehension and understanding.	Less choice on curriculum assignments and more work on drill-like assignments.
Locus of responsibility for learning	More autonomy, more choice in assignments, fewer interruptions.	Less autonomy, frequent teacher monitoring of work, frequent interruptions.
Feedback and evaluation practices	More opportunity for self-evaluation.	Less opportunity for self-evaluation.
Motivational strategies	More honest/contingent feedback.	Less honest/more gratuitous/less contingent feedback.
Quality of teacher relationships	More respect for the student as an individual with unique interests and needs.	Less respect for the student as an individual with unique interests and needs.

Source: From Good, T., & Brophy, J. (2003). *Looking in classrooms* (9th ed.). New York: Pearson Education, Inc.

The following guidelines are offered for teachers to minimize the negative effects of teacher expectations (Jones & Jones, 2013).

1. **Use information from tests, cumulative folders, and other teachers very carefully**: some teachers avoid reading cumulative folders for several weeks at the beginning of the year; be critical and objective about reports from other teachers, especially "horror stories" told in the teachers' lounge.

2. **Be flexible in the use of grouping strategies**: review work of students in different groups often and experiment with new groupings; use different groupings for different subjects; use mixed-ability groups in cooperative exercises when all students can handle the same material.

3. **Make sure all students are challenged**: avoid saying, "This is easy, I know you can do it;" offer a wide range of problems and encourage all students to try a few of the harder ones for extra credit; try to find something positive about their attempts.

4. **Be especially careful about responding to low-achieving students during class discussions**: give them prompts, clues, and time to answer; give ample praise for good answers; call on low achievers as often as high achievers.

5. **Use materials that show a wide range of ethnic groups**: check readers and library books for ethnic diversity; ask the librarian to find multiethnic stories, video materials, etc.; if few materials are available, ask students to research and create their own, based on community or family resources.

6. **Be fair in evaluation and disciplinary procedures**: make sure equal offenses merit equal consequences; try to grade student work without knowing the identity of the student; ask another teacher to give a "second opinion" from time to time.

7. **Communicate to all students the belief that they can learn – and mean it**: return papers that do not meet standards with specific suggestions for improvement; if students do not have the answers immediately, wait, probe, and then help them think through an answer.

8. **Involve all students in learning tasks and privileges**: use some system for calling on or contacting students to make sure each student is given practice in reading, speaking, and answering questions; keep track of who gets to do what job and make sure that the tasks are distributed equally.

9. **Monitor nonverbal behavior**: do not lean away or stand farther away from some students; do some students get smiles

when they approach the desk while others get only frowns?; your tone of voice should not vary with different students.

Goals – Learning and Performance

The type of goals that teachers set influences the amount of motivation that students have to reach them. Goals that are moderately difficult, specific, and likely to be reached in the near future enhance motivation and persistence (Pintrich & Schunk, 2002). Specific goals provide a clear standard for judging performance and moderate difficulty provides a challenge, but not an unreasonable one. When goals are too complex, vague and/or confusing, too challenging, or perceived as having no importance, students are less likely to pursue them. Likewise, when goals are perceived as being too simplistic, they are not seen as being either interesting or important. While they may be achieved, the achievement has little meaning. Following are four important reasons why goal setting improves performance (Locke & Latham, 2002).

1. Goals direct attention to the task at hand and away from distractions.
2. Goals help to energize effort. The more challenging the goal, to a point, the greater the effort.
3. Goals help to increase persistence. When there is a clear goal, students are less likely to give up until they reach the goal.
4. Goals promote the development of new knowledge and strategies when old strategies fall short. If the goal is to make an A and the student doesn't reach that goal on the first attempt, the student might try a new study approach before the next attempt, such as explaining the key points to a friend.

Goals are often classified as to their orientation or type. Pintrich and Schunk (2002) identified four main goal orientations: *mastery (learning)*, *performance (looking good)*, *work-avoidance*, and *social.* Goal orientations are patterns of beliefs about goals related to achievement in school and include the reasons students pursue goals, or perhaps do not pursue goals, and the standards used to evaluate progress toward them.

What teachers establish as their desired goals for students has the potential to send an important message and have a significant effect on a student's level of motivation. Teachers communicate their values and what they want their students to value in many ways. One way they do this is in the selection of the goals that they would like for their students to pursue and attain. A **goal** is *that which an individual is striving to achieve or accomplish* (Locke & Latham, 1990). Teachers should remember that they frequently identify goals for their students that their students do not identify for themselves and that teacher goals are of limited value when students are not focused and dedicated to achieve them. Teachers can create higher levels of student motivation and achievement by being cognizant of their goal selections and emphasizing the use of mastery or learning goals as opposed to performance goals. This is especially true to the degree that students accept these goals as their own and see them as being achievable and of value.

Goals related to students and their academic achievement are often divided into two contrasting types: *performance (ability, ego) goals* and *learning (mastery, task) goals*. **Performance goals** are *goals that emphasize the demonstration of high ability and the avoidance of failure.* **Learning goals** are *goals that emphasize the challenge of learning and the mastery of a task.* The focus of a learning goal for the student is to improve and learn, no matter how many mistakes may be made. The focus of performance goals is on looking smart or informed and displaying accomplishments without failure. The teacher's primary responsibility, however, is, or should be, to get students to learn, not perform. When goals become too challenging, or perhaps in some way threatening, students may engage in self-handicapping behaviors such as not trying or cheat-

Table 2.9

Contrasting Goal Orientations: Characteristics of Learning and Performance Goals

Characteristics	Learning/Mastery	Performance/Ego
Value of learning	Has intrinsic value for learning in itself. The goal is to increase learning.	Learning is not an end in itself. The focus is on looking smart.
Ability/competence	Uses effort attributions. Increases with effort.	Is seen as one's capacity; attributions to ability are most frequent.
Error/failure	Learns from mistakes.	Doubts ability.
Feedback	Used to judge progress.	Used to compare performance with another.
Strategies	Cognitive and metacognitive.	Surface/rote.
Challenge	Seeks challenge.	Avoids risk taking and challenge.

Source: From Alderman, M. (2008). *Motivation for achievement: Possibilities for teaching and learning* (3rd ed.). New York: Routledge, p. 90.

ing when they are not sure they can be successful (Brophy, 2010). Table 2.9 provides an analysis of characteristics of performance and learning goal orientations toward academic tasks.

Goals that are specific, seen by students as being of at least moderate difficulty and having value, and which can be attained in a reasonable period of time, tend to enhance student motivation and persistence (Stipek, 2002). Specific goals provide greater clarity as to the teacher's expectations and standards for evaluating student performance. This quality, coupled with reasonableness of difficulty and time involved, contributes to increased levels of student motivation (Pintrich & Schunk, 2002). Students' beliefs about their abilities to be successful, i.e., self-efficacy, have impact on their engaging or not engaging in the teacher's learning tasks and their levels of persistence to stay with them once started. Because learning goals focus on mastery of information without great concern for or overemphasis on mistakes, these goals contribute to increased levels of student motivation. Performance goals, where the focus is on performing, looking good, and not being seen as failing, tend to lead to decreased levels of motivation. As related to established goals and student achievement, the classroom with a learning focus rather than a performing focus is recommended for its positive relationship to student motivation.

Table 2.10 offers another helpful comparison between the characteristics of learning and performance goals.

Table 2.10

Characteristics of Learning and Performance Goals

Characteristics	Learning Goals	Performance Goals
Definition of success	Improvement, progress, mastery, innovation, creativity	High grades, high performance compared to others, winning, recognition
Place(s) of value	Effort, persistence, attempting difficult tasks	Avoiding failure, succeeding with low effort
Reason for effort	Intrinsic and personal meaning of activity, learning, mastery	Demonstrating ability and one's own worth
Evaluation criteria	Absolute criteria (standard) evidence of progress	Norms, social comparisons, another individual
View(s) of errors	Part of the learning process, informational	Failure, evidence of lack of ability or worth
View(s) of competence	Increasing through effort, "incremental"	Inherited, fixed, and "entity"

Source: From Stipek, D. (2002). *Motivation to learn: Integrating theory and practice* (4th ed.). Boston: Allyn & Bacon, p. 162.

Anxiety

Who reading these pages has never had an anxious moment or felt worry or concern? Anxiousness too often characterizes students in school. **Anxiety** is *a feeling of apprehension, worry, tension, or nervousness* (Lefrancois, 2000) and *a general uneasiness with a sense of foreboding and feeling of tension* (Hansen, 1977). Though some feel that being anxious from time to time is not such a bad thing, research on the effects of anxiety on student achievement has consistently identified a negative relationship between anxiety and achievement (Covington & Omelich, 1987).

Anxiety has both cognitive and affective components. Cognitive components include worry and negative thoughts such as thinking about how bad it would be to fail and worrying that this is going to happen. Affective components include physiological and emotional reactions such as sweaty palms, upset stomach, racing heartbeat, or fear (Jain & Dowson, 2009; Schunk, Pintrich, & Meece, 2008). Anxiety can interfere with learning and test performance at three levels: (1) staying connected to the teacher's instruction (focusing attention), (2) understanding what is being taught (learning), and (3) showing or in some way demonstrating what is understood (test performance). Anxiety can be a reason for a student to lose focus, become irritable or act out, withdraw and not try, be physically ill, or perform poorly with the resulting poor performance serving to increase the student's anxiety. Anxiety can be both a cause and effect of school failure. Students do poorly because they are anxious, and their poor performance increases their anxiety. The relationship between anxiety, motivation, and achievement is curvilinear; that is, some anxiousness may be good while too much can be damaging (Cassady & Johnson, 2002).

The concept of equilibrium was introduced earlier with reference to the human desire to achieve balance in life. If not too extreme, mild or even moderate out-of-balance situations, i.e., situations of disequilibrium, can be situations that motivate students to do things in an effort to get back into balance. Some situations of anxiety, however, can be so great that students are not able to find the balance that they need and eventually withdraw from or never begin the process of seeking balance. A small amount of anxiety can help to improve performance by motivating students to positive action. This is referred to as **facilitating anxiety** or *anxiety in such a small amount that it actually helps to improve* *performance.* Too much anxiety can have the opposite effect of interfering with motivation and diminishing the student's performance. This anxiety is referred to as **debilitating anxiety** or *anxiety so extreme that it gets in the way of successful performance.*

It is important that teachers understand their students and their various learning and personal needs and characteristics. What may seem to create an anxious moment for one student may not for another student. Something that would be thought to not be anxiety producing to an internalizing student with a history of success might be quite debilitating to an externalizing student with a history of failure. Students frequently become anxious before taking a test that they perceive as being difficult or in giving a speech in front of others. This type of condition is referred to as **state anxiety** or *temporary feelings of anxiety brought about by certain situations.* Such anxiety in students is typically the result of a sense of fear, concern, or threat, especially when they feel that their performance will not be seen positively (Deci & Ryan, 1992).

Some students, however, appear to be anxious even where there is no particular cause to which their anxiety can be linked, such as in working on less complex assignments or assignments that do not appear as though they should bring about any reason for fear of failure. This is called trait anxiety. **Trait anxiety** is *when students are anxious in circumstances that should not be seen as threatening.* Students with trait anxiety are more difficult for teachers to motivate. Research suggests that students who report high anxiety in achievement situations perform poorly compared to students who report relatively low anxiety (Stipek, 2002). Anxious students have difficulty concentrating, and, because they worry about and even can expect failure, often misunderstand the information they are expected to learn and how to demonstrate their understanding of it when asked to do so.

Table 2.11 identifies seven common situations under which students may experience anxiety, even debilitating anxiety. Understanding and having the opportunity to prepare for these situations represents a chance for teachers to be proactive in working to decrease student anxiety and, therefore, increase student motivation.

Because high anxiety brought about by intense motivational situations can have a negative effect on student performance, moderate motivational situations are more desirable for increasing student success on learning complex tasks. Ideal motivation decreases in intensity with increasing task difficulty. As tasks become more challenging and com-

Table 2.11

Students and Anxiety-Producing Situations

Type of Situation	Definition
Physical Appearance	Students are often concerned about their appearance. They might see themselves as too thin, too heavy, too tall, or too short. Teachers should not take these concerns lightly as they can have significant impact on student motivation and performance.
New Situations	Students frequently experience uneasiness when encountering new individuals and situations such as teachers, peers, classes, and schools.
Judgment/Evaluation by Others	Most students experience worry over being judged by others. This includes being evaluated by teachers on assignments and activities as well as being accepted by classmates and friends.
Tests	Test anxiety is often not taken seriously enough by teachers. Comments such as "Just relax," "Don't worry," or "You will get it if you study harder next time," generally have little positive impact on students who are truly anxious or experiencing debilitating anxiety in testing situations.
Excessive Classroom Demands	What may not seem excessive to teachers may seem extremely excessive to some students, especially students with high levels of anxiety. Students normally feel anxious when confronted with expectations that they feel are beyond their ability to respond to successfully.
The Future	Though some current research suggests that young people have more positive than negative outlooks for the future, this does not mean all young people. Concern over the future, especially for students at the middle and secondary levels, can be significant and effect their motivation and performance in the classroom.
Situations Where Self Is Threatened	Fear of failure anywhere can be powerful and debilitating. Fear of failure in public can be especially so. Many students experience levels of anxiety that are virtually paralyzing in effecting their motivation and performance when the concern includes a dimension of public criticism.

Source: Adapted from Ormrod, J. (2011). *Educational psychology: Developing learners* (7th ed.). Upper Saddle River, NJ: Merrill Prentice-Hall, Inc.

plex, the level of student motivation, likely also driven by the student's level of confidence to be successful, tends to diminish. Increasing intensity improves performance, but only to a certain level. From that point where the performance is no longer improving, continued intensity results in a lessening of the level of motivation along with the quality of the performance. Having an understanding of the level of student confidence to complete a given task is important for the teacher as this ultimately will influence both motivation and performance.

Students use three kinds of coping strategies to lessen stress when faced with situations such as taking tests or performing in public: (1) problem-focused self-regulating, (2) emotional management, and (3) avoidance. **Problem-focused self-regulating strategies** include such activities as planning a study schedule, getting good notes from a friend, and finding a quiet place to study. **Emotion-focused strategies** are efforts to reduce anxious feelings and could include relaxation exercises or describing one's feelings to a friend. **Avoidance strategies** are simply ignoring the upcoming situation and engaging in something totally unrelated to the stressful situation (Woolfolk, 2013). In assisting students to reduce or cope with their anxiety, teachers should consider the following recommendations.

1. **Use competition carefully**: monitor activities to make sure no students are being put under undue pressure.

2. **Avoid situations where highly anxious students will have to perform in front of large groups**: ask anxious students questions that can be answered with a simple yes or no or some other brief reply.

3. **Make sure all instructions are clear as ambiguity can lead to anxiety**: write test instructions on the board or on the test itself instead of giving the instructions orally.

4. **Avoid unnecessary time pressures**: occasionally give take-home tests.

5. **Remove some of the pressures from major tests and exams**: avoid basing most of a report-card grade on one or only a few tests.

6. **Develop alternatives to written tests**: consider having students do projects, organize portfolios of their work, or make oral presentations to the teacher.

7. **Teach students self-regulation strategies**: encourage students to see the test as an important and challenging task that they have the opportunity to prepare for and do well on; help students to stay focused on the task of getting as much information as possible about the test; encourage students to be task focused in their testing and preparation.

Environment

Research supports that the creation of safe, supportive learning environments is a major factor that influences student motivation, achievement, and behavior (Jones & Jones, 2013). Abraham Maslow's Hierarchy of Needs, introduced earlier, offers an important perspective to the discussion of the impact of environment on student motivation. Environments where students feel safe, both physically and emotionally, where they feel desired and cared for, and where they feel as though they "fit in" or belong, contribute significantly to higher levels of motivation. Popular phrases found in educational literature today refer to the preferred classroom environment as being inviting, warm, student-centered, safe and secure, learner-oriented, nurturing, participatory, etc. While phrases such as these may only represent trendy language to some, they say a great deal with respect to student motivation. Perhaps the phrases might mean more if one were to think of a classroom environment that reflected the opposite of these characteristics.

The concept of *membership* is important when discussing motivation and the learning environment. When students are assigned to a teacher and a class, they become physical members of the class. But, do they also become psychological members? This is a critical question. **Psychological membership** is *the degree to which students feel personally accepted, respected, included, and supported in the classroom* (Goodenow, 1993). The greater the level to which this is achieved, the greater the level of student motivation. When students feel a sense of belonging in the classroom through a feeling of positive psychological membership, they are more likely to adopt the goals held to be valuable there. When students do not feel as though they belong or do not have positive psychological membership, goals will be perceived simply as the teacher's goals, not really applying or relevant to them and not be readily adopted by them. The social and psychological bonding that comes when students feel that they are true members of the classroom group influences the degree to which motivation will occur and academic engagement and learning will take place.

One widely researched theory of motivation is self-determination theory (Brophy, 2004; Pintrich & Schunk, 2002). Self-determination theory identifies a continuum that moves through stages of extrinsic motivation and ends in intrinsic motivation. While primarily a cognitive motivation theory, it also incorporates aspects of humanistic views of motivation. **Self-determination** is *the process of deciding how to act on one's environment.* In self-determination theory, having choices and making decisions are intrinsically motivating. People are not content if all of their needs are satisfied without their having had opportunities to make decisions. Self-determination theory identifies that individuals have three innate psychological needs: *competence, autonomy,* and *relatedness.* These three needs are linked to the student's adjustment, membership, and eventual success. They are defined as:

Competence: the ability to function effectively in the environment,

Autonomy: independence and the ability to alter the environment when necessary, and

Relatedness: the feeling of being connected to others in one's social environment and feeling worthy of love and respect.

Relatedness is comparable to Maslow's (1970) need for belonging, identified as the third level in the Hierarchy of Needs.

Higher levels of motivation are evident when student needs are met for belonging/social connectedness, autonomy/self-direction, and competence (Battistich, Solomon, Kim, Watson, & Schaps, 1995). A learning environment perceived by students as caring represents the type of classroom where higher levels of student motivation can be both achieved and maintained. Three characteristics considered essential for creating such an environment are: (1) a classroom structured for autonomy and responsibility, (2) social support through cooperative learning activities, and (3) teacher support (Alderman, 2008).

Just as teachers send many messages to students, schools and classrooms send messages as well. These messages come from the classroom context, i.e., the structure of the classroom, and influence whether a student is involved in more of a learning goal or performance goal teaching orientation. Classroom dimensions or cues that convey messages about the purpose of achievement include teacher expectations for learning, the type of evaluations used, how students are grouped, and the extent to which students have opportunities to make decisions. All of these factors influence how students see themselves in the classroom. Table 2.12 includes context factors for classrooms that contribute to a learning goal environment.

Student motivation is higher where students have a sense of freedom and responsibility, have opportunities to work with others in support of

Table 2.12

Classroom Context Factors and Student Motivation

Classroom Structure or Message	Example
Opportunities to develop an increased sense of competence	Students not only have a basic understanding of the content, but also develop competencies in other areas.
Opportunities for self-directed learning	Students evaluate their own work; transfer responsibility to students as they gain competence.
Emphasis on expectations and the intrinsic value of learning	The value of interest and application of what students are learning are emphasized, and all students are expected to learn.
Opportunities for cooperation and collaboration	Students are grouped with emphasis on working together effectively and on students helping each other.
Ability/effort messages	Progress is recognized and students are allowed to retake tests for improvement.

Source: From Alderman, M. (2008). *Motivation for achievement: Possibilities for teaching and learning* (3rd ed.). New York: Routledge, p. 92.

their own learning and the learning of others, and see their teachers as providing ongoing support. Even when they are not always successful, students in caring environments perceive their teachers as "being there for them" and this contributes to their ability to persevere and maintain their motivation.

CONCLUSION

Chapter 2 introduced the concept of motivation as it applies to student learning and the role of the classroom teacher. Three important theories of motivation, behaviorist, cognitive, and humanist, were introduced and discussed. Critical questions related to attribution, locus of control, teacher expectations, goals, anxiety, and environment as these affect student motivation were presented.

The need for teachers to be informed, reflective educators with respect to achieving student motivation cannot be overemphasized. Teachers in classrooms throughout the country can define the term motivation and even identify it when it occurs. Many of these same teachers, however, are not able to take what knowledge they have about motivation and apply it effectively to create motivating learning environments in their classrooms. It is often said that teachers should teach for transfer of learning in that they should assist their students to not only have the ability to "know and do" in the classroom but to be able to apply this knowledge and ability to novel situations. As with the students themselves, teachers need to be able to transfer and apply what they know about student motivation to their teaching to energize their instruction, engage their students in their learning activities, and increase student learning. Motivated students are happier, feel better about themselves, and learn more. Each of these three outcomes is desirable and attainable providing teachers understand and apply what is known about motivating students in today's classrooms.

QUESTIONS/ACTIVITIES FOR REFLECTION

1. Describe how you might motivate a student who has average ability but who does not regularly work up to his potential. The student comes from a home where neither parent is educated beyond the sixth grade and little English is spoken; Spanish is the dominant language spoken in the home. The student's parents, however, are very supportive and want their child to learn and do well in school.

2. What are some problems found in classrooms taught by teachers who lack high efficacy? How is it that some teachers come to a point where their efficacy is low?

3. Why might poor performance on a test motivate some students but not others to work hard in school? Is there any type of student that might be positively motivated by poor test results? Explain.

4. A father wanted his son to excel in baseball and practiced with him from the time he was five years old. He attended all youth league games and even served as a volunteer coach on his son's teams. Although the son progressed well and seemed to be headed toward high school stardom, he refused to play baseball when he reached high school. What do you think might be some possible explanations for this dramatic change in direction? How might this situation apply to the role of the teacher in the classroom?

5. If a student seems to be a victim of learned helplessness, how can the teacher address the student's need to be a successful learner and not lower his or her classroom standards at the same time? Is it possible to successfully address this problem in the traditional American education system today? Explain.

Chapter 3

CREATING A MANAGED ENVIRONMENT: MODELS AND THEORIES OF CLASSROOM MANAGEMENT

> During the past quarter century, it has become increasingly clear that theory as a guide for teaching has its limits. No single theory, indeed no combination of theories in the social sciences, can ever be adequate for dealing with the highly contextualized particularistic decisions that must be made by individual teachers in specific classrooms. (Eisner, 1998, pp. 207–208)

MANAGEMENT

The fundamental theme of this book is one that acknowledges the important relationship that exists between motivating students to learn and managing student behavior in the classroom. Effective classroom management, as well as motivation, is essential as it relates to the amount of time students spend meaningfully engaged in academic tasks. Researchers have found that classrooms where less time is spent managing behavior problems are environments where both teachers and students spend more time on learning activities (Baugous & Bendery, 2000; Ratcliff, Jones, Costner, Savage-Davis, Sheehan, & Hunt, 2010). Behavior problems attract the attention of everyone in the classroom, taking away from important instructional time, and, at the same time, making it more difficult to get students back on task (Clough, Smasal, & Clough, 1994). It is important to remember that behavior management issues get teachers off task as well as their students. As the research of Ratcliff, Jones, Costner, Savage-Davis, and Hunt (2010) indicates, teacher instructional interactions decrease as teacher behavior control interactions increase. If the goal is to create a classroom climate where teachers are teaching and students are actively involved in learning, teachers must develop plans that not only focus on how to address behavior problems when they occur, but, more importantly, these plans must focus on how to prevent behavior problems from happening in the first place. Such plans should include specific strategies for creating learning environments that motivate students and keep them on task as well as strategies for responding to student behavior issues that disrupt instruction and interfere with student learning. The major purpose of the current chapter is to provide the reader with the information needed to create such plans.

MANAGEMENT MODELS AND THEORIES

Ten models applicable to the management of student behavior in classroom environments are presented in the remaining pages of the chapter. The models focus on the implementation of strategies that address the most frequently asked questions related to classroom management. Some models rely less on the motivation of students in their learning than might be anticipated given the primary foundation of this text. While this may be the case, a lack of understanding of these basic models in terms of their underlying themes will limit readers as they endeavor to construct what will eventually be their own best models for classroom management for their own individual classrooms. To be effective, teachers must be well grounded in best practice information that relates to student motivation, classroom management, and instruction. A gap in knowledge in any of these three areas and a lack of understanding of the relationship that exists among them (motivation, classroom management, and instruction) will lessen the potential for optimum student learning in the classroom.

A central thread running through most of these models is the emphasis on creating environments that are conducive to *preventing* student misbehavior, not simply *reacting* to misbehavior once it occurs. However, even with the best prevention measures, the time will occur when students disobey their teachers or violate stated school and/or classroom rules. When this takes place, teachers must be able to respond effectively to such situations to maintain safe and productive learning environments. No other time is more critical to the mainte-nance of a positive learning environment than the moment after the teacher realizes a student has disobeyed the teacher or broken school rules (Jones & Jones, 2013; Ratcliff, Jones, Costner, Savage-Davis, Shee-han, & Hunt, 2010). As noted in Chapter 1, teachers must have a disci-pline plan and know how to use it when problems arise. Although it is important for the teacher to know how to respond to student misbe-havior so that the misconduct is ended, knowing how to establish a classroom environment that is preventive in nature is considered the more significant teaching skill (Good & Brophy, 2007; Marzano, Gad-dy, Foseid, & Marzano, 2009). Little learning is likely to occur in a class-room where teachers and students face constant distractions and inter-ruptions or where students feel unsafe (Borman & Levine, 1997; Jones & Jones, 2013; Rimm-Kaufman, La Paro, Downer, & Pianta, 2005).

An initial step in learning how to establish a well-managed classroom is to study and develop an understanding of models and approaches de-signed for this purpose. Following this study and gaining this under-standing, the next important step is to adopt a model, or perhaps fea-tures of one or more models, to a particular classroom situation. Be-cause it is unlikely that any one model will satisfy all circumstances, most teachers develop an eclectic, self-stylized approach to classroom management that borrows from the best ideas presented by one or more models or recommended behaviors. The approach that is then developed is one that is compatible with the teacher's own teaching style and philosophy of education.

Some management models are best used when the entire faculty and administration of a school participate in their implementation. Because many teachers discover theories and procedures they would like to im-plement in their own individual classrooms when other teachers and administrators in their schools may not be participating in their use, a personalized approach to management generally has greater appeal and can be more effective as opposed to an entire school approach. To help readers develop their own management plans, the major ideas found in ten different management models, and the theorists associat-ed with their development, are presented along with an emphasis on their most important characteristics as applied to best practice in the classroom. Figure 3.1 provides an overview of the ten models that will be considered and the theorists who are credited for their development.

Management Theorists and Management Models	
Theorists	**Focus of Management Models**
Jacob Kounin	The focus is on teachers learning behaviors that will allow them to become better leaders in the classroom.
Rudolf Dreikurs	The focus is on analyzing behavior problems to determine their source of origin and responding to them.
William Glasser	The focus is on empowering students to become better group members.
Haim Ginott	The focus is on improving communication to avoid alienating students inhumanely.
Fred Jones	The focus is on keeping students engaged in academically appropriate activities.
Thomas Gordon	The focus is on teachers using counseling techniques to improve communication with students.
Lee Canter	The focus is on teachers asserting their right to teach and their students' right to learn.
B. F. Skinner	The focus is on shaping student behavior with positive reinforcement.
David and Roger Johnson	The focus is on students resolving their own conflicts.
Alfie Kohn	The focus is on students becoming intrinsically motivated to value good behavior.

Figure 3.1. Management theorists and management models.

Jacob Kounin's Theories

Jacob Kounin's management theories have had great impact on the way many educators view the learning environment (Eggen & Kauchak, 2013). An interesting characteristic of Kounin's theories is that they tend to focus on constructs more often associated with a sociological study of small groups. Many of the other management theories that have been developed are grounded in what are more traditionally thought of as psychological rather than sociological constructs (Hunt, Wiseman, &Touzel, 2009). Central to the work of Kounin is the position that the classroom should be looked upon as a small community where interactions with any member of the community may affect the rest of its members. For the classroom community to function well and reach its goals (i.e., for high levels of academic progress to be realized), the teacher must be able to exhibit the characteristics of a successful group leader.

Five factors characterize the classrooms of teachers who adopt the ideas described by Kounin (1970).

1. Student boredom is avoided.
2. Transitions between tasks and momentum within tasks flow smoothly.
3. All students remain alert and focused.
4. Teachers are aware of what is taking place in all parts of the classroom.
5. Teachers understand that interaction with any one student may have an effect on the total group.

It is recommended that teachers use a variety of different methods and materials to maintain high levels of student interest and participation and to avoid student boredom. When students are aware that they are making progress toward their learning goals and are involved in a variety of interesting and meaningful activities, they are much less likely to become involved in misconduct behaviors and pose management problems for their teachers. It is also important that smooth transitions exist between learning activities and that *momentum* within lessons moves consistently toward closure. When instruction is characterized by positive momentum or *thrust*, the classroom group tends to function better and individual students are more likely to stay on task. Educational research suggests that there is a greater value in the teacher establishing a quicker paced as compared to a slower paced delivery of instruction (Hunt et al., 2009).

Keeping students alert and focused on assigned activities also lessens the probability of classroom disturbances. Most student misconduct occurs during "down times" or idle times when students are not on task, often because they either do not understand what they are supposed to do or how to do it. Kounin referred to keeping students alert and focused as maintaining **group focus** or *on-task behavior where all students in the classroom attend to the teacher or activities that the teacher has assigned at the same time.* Teachers who are able to create functional, effective learning environments have what Kounin called *withitness*. **Withitness** occurs *when a teacher displays the ability to have an ongoing awareness of events throughout the entire classroom, not just one area of the setting.* Sometimes referred to as having "eyes in the back of the head," this awareness allows teachers to pre-empt many disturbances and distractions before they become serious problems.

When teachers reinforce students or correct their misbehaviors, these interactions will have an effect on other students in the classroom creating what Kounin identified as the *ripple effect.* The **ripple effect** is *the effect on other students in the classroom when the teacher reinforces or corrects particular students for their behavior.* It is critical that teachers recognize the impact that their actions may have on all students in the classroom when they correct the behavior of only one or two. Kounin believed that there is a positive effect on all students in the class when one student's misconduct is handled firmly and fairly. The ripple effect can also have a positive impact when one student is praised or encouraged in front of classmates as the entire class has the opportunity to observe and learn which behaviors are desired and rewarded (Borman & Levine, 1997). Conversely, a negative ripple effect can result if the teacher handles a management problem inappropriately, thus sending the wrong or undesired message to students about unacceptable behavior.

Rudolf Dreikurs' Theories

Rudolf Dreikurs' theoretical position was founded on his experience with psychoanalytic psychology (Dreikurs, 1968; Dreikurs & Cassell, 1972). Dreikurs expanded on the concepts of Alfred Adler and provided a control methodology that allowed teachers to avoid the use of punishment, believing that students often misbehave because they desire recognition from the teacher and/or their classmates (Burden, 2006). Dreikurs believed that individual behavior can be understood using the following key premises (Levin & Nolan, 2010).

1. People are social beings who have a need to belong, to be recognized, and to be accepted.
2. Behavior is goal directed and has the purpose of gaining the recognition and acceptance that people want.
3. People can choose to behave or misbehave; their behavior is within their control.

It was also Dreikurs' belief that students develop certain defense mechanisms designed to protect their self-esteem. He theorized that student misbehavior is goal directed, perhaps to get recognition or to otherwise protect self-esteem. Goals that misdirect student behavior, listed from least to most severe, are: (1) *attention-seeking,* (2) *power-seeking,* (3) *revenge-seeking,* and (4) *overtly displaying inadequacy to receive special treatment.*

Attention-seeking is *a student behavior problem often exhibited by tattling and showing off, class-clowning, or in some other way drawing focus to one's self.* **Power-seeking** is *a student behavior problem where the student seeks to control the teacher instead of being directed by the teacher.* Students who seek revenge do things to hurt other students, either physically or emotionally. **Revenge-seeking** is *a student behavior problem where a student may do something to cause other students to be punished to "get back at them."* It was Dreikurs' belief that students who pretend that they lack the ability to do assigned work, *overtly displaying inadequacy in order to receive special treatment,* are exhibiting the most serious misconduct. Students may exhibit different behaviors to reach any of these four goals and teachers should create learning environments with distinct characteristics designed to prevent these problem situations before they occur. Some distinct characteristics of the desired learning environment are that:

1. students are not reinforced when they exhibit behaviors leading to undesirable goals,
2. when students exhibit undesirable behavior, they receive pre-announced logical consequences that will be unpleasant to them,
3. students should be involved in helping the teacher set logical consequences for misconduct,
4. teachers should not merely treat symptoms when dealing with misconduct but seek to determine the motivation behind the student's action(s),
5. students should feel a responsibility to influence their peers' conduct,
6. students must understand that, ultimately, they are responsible for their own behavior, and
7. students should be encouraged to develop self-respect while learning to respect others.

To fully utilize Dreikurs' theories in the classroom, teachers must be able to analyze their students' misbehaviors and focus on the cause(s) of the misbehaviors to determine the goals motivating the misconduct. They must also have the ability to develop and use the interpersonal guidance skills needed to help them understand and change their students' misdirected behaviors in the future (Hunt et al., 2009). The Cooperative Discipline model, introduced in Chapter 1, is basically an extension of the work of Adler and Dreikurs (Albert, 1996).

William Glasser's Theories

William Glasser's theoretical model for classroom management was known as Reality Therapy and has been widely used since the 1960s (Glasser, 1965; 1969). More recently referred to as Choice Theory (Glasser, 2001), the theories of Glasser have been a part of many classroom management studies and discussions for decades. Glasser refined his theories over the years and his work is widely endorsed by many educators today (Glasser, 1992; 1998; 2001). Glasser drew on the work of Dreikurs in developing his theories and believes that students often display misbehavior or apathy because they feel powerless in the adult world (Zabel & Zabel, 1996). Central to Glasser's concept of an effective learning environment is the belief that students must play an active role in the decision-making process. Glasser saw failure as the root of student misbehavior, noting that when students don't learn at the expected or anticipated rate, they get less positive attention and recognition from their teachers. In his system for bringing about desired student behavior, Glasser proposed that teachers direct students to appropriate behavior through the use of three questions. Known as Glasser's triplets, these questions are (1) *What are you doing?*, (2) *Is it against the rules?*, and (3) *What should you be doing?* Asked privately and not publicly, the questions are based on the teacher having already established clear rules for behavior in the classroom and recognizing that there is value in students acknowledging and accepting responsibility for their own behaviors (Glasser, 1969; 1992). To reduce the chance of an extended, negative confrontation ensuing from the use of Glasser's questions, it has been suggested that teachers use three statements instead of questions (Levin & Nolan, 2010). For example, the teacher might say, *Elizabeth, you are calling out during the instruction. Calling out is against the rules. You should raise your hand if you want to answer a question.*

Glasser identifies that people have five basic needs that drive all behavior: (1) survival, (2) love and belonging, (3) power, (4) freedom, and (5) fun or enjoyment. Student behavior in the classroom is directed toward satisfying these needs. There are times when meeting these needs can lead students to conduct themselves in ways that are in conflict with the teacher's rules for classroom behavior. An important tenet of Glasser's theory is that, when dealing with specific student misconduct, the teacher should help students become aware of and responsible for the consequences of their own behaviors. One way that this can be done is by developing individual student behavior contracts that result in the use of logical consequences, i.e., logical outcomes, when student misbehavior occurs. The behavior contract should be designed to clearly identify: (1) the expectations that the teacher has for the student, (2) the consequences that have been specified if the identified behavior is exhibited or if it is not exhibited, and (3) a system for recording or monitoring the student's behavior over time. In this approach, the teacher uses behavior modification techniques to reinforce positive behavior and end unwanted conduct. If the reinforcements through behavior modification do not bring about the desired results, the student is removed from the group through a series of steps beginning with simple isolation and moving to in-school suspension (ISS), out-of-school suspension (OSS), and, finally, expulsion (Bennett, 1997). Research indicates that positive effects can be expected when Glasser's theories are applied correctly (Good & Brophy, 1986).

Glasser's approach to management also includes the use of a formal strategy of holding **class meetings** as *a process to involve students in establishing guidelines for acceptable behavior and a forum for collaborative problem solving.* When rules and regulations must be adjusted or unique situations arise, the class meets to discuss and make decisions about the situation. Class meetings are regularly recurring events used to enable students to be an ongoing part of the decision making process in the classroom and to help prevent possible behavior problems, not just react to unwanted behavior problem occurrences. When students believe their interests and ideas are considered important and valued, they become stakeholders in the group. They then are more likely to assume needed responsibility and ownership for their behaviors (Zabel & Zabel, 1996).

Glasser notes that the learning environment should include at least five distinct characteristics. These are that:

1. the teacher functions as a democratic leader,
2. students take part in the decision making process,
3. students have an opportunity for cooperative or team activities,
4. students being part of the group is seen as a privilege and source of satisfaction and enjoyment, and
5. the classroom is a place where guidelines are established and problems are solved through collaborative *class meetings.*

Glasser has long been recognized as a leader in the field of classroom management and student motivation. Like Dreikurs, Glasser recognizes that students taking responsibility for their own behavior and helping in the establishment of guidelines for acceptable classroom conduct are critical elements in establishing and maintaining a well-managed learning environment. Glasser has more recently moved to a position that identifies that, in many instances, school managers are responsible for creating many of the management problems that take place in schools today. Schools too often accept low standards for student work which leads to many management problems that could and should have otherwise been avoided (Glasser, 2000).

Haim Ginott's Theories

Haim Ginott (1965; 1969; 1972) was a very popular child psychologist whose books, weekly syndicated newspaper column, and television appearances (he was a regular guest on the Today Show) influenced many parents and teachers in terms of how they interacted with children and teenagers. Ginott stressed the importance of what he called *sane messages*. **Sane messages** are *messages that focus on the undesired behavior of a student, not on the student as a person.* The messages never represent an attack on a student on a personal level. When teachers use sane messages, they lessen the chance of alienating students while, at the same time, provide an important model for the type of behavior students themselves should demonstrate. Since positive modeling should be an important aspect of any teacher's approach to classroom management, Ginott stressed that teachers need to maintain self-discipline, thus serving as models of disciplined individuals for their students. Ginott's communication model of management relies almost exclusively on one-to-one conferencing between teacher and student, something that is at times difficult to achieve in a classroom of 25 to 30 students.

Ginott felt that a system of effective management evolved over time through what he called "a series of little victories." To achieve these "little victories," teachers should:

1. avoid labeling students,
2. avoid using sarcasm,
3. avoid praising personalities instead of behaviors,
4. send *sane messages*,
5. model desired behaviors,

6. accept student apologies, and
7. help students build their self-esteem.

Ginott encouraged teachers to create learning environments where students can realize a genuine feeling of satisfaction and believed that students are much more satisfied in classrooms where teachers use team or cooperative learning activities. Teachers should make a conscious effort to encourage or invite this type of cooperation, thus giving students an opportunity to make choices and behave independently. Rather than try to boss and force students to comply through positions of power, teachers need to give students the opportunity to decide on their own which alternatives to take. For example, saying *Do we want to work together quietly on the floor or do we want to get back in our desks? It is up to you*, is a better way for teachers to address students than by saying something like, *Be quiet or I will make you get in your desks*. When teachers avoid ordering, bossing, and commanding, students are much more willing to cooperate and less likely to become negative and hostile.

Ginott recommended that teachers speak to the situation, not the person. In so doing, while a teacher might label a student's behavior as bad or undesirable, the teacher would not label the student as bad or undesirable. Ginott (1972) and later Jones (1980) identified the following guidelines for sending messages to students about their behavior (Levin & Nolan, 2010).

1. Deal with the here and now. Don't dwell on past problems and situations.
2. Make eye contact and use congruent nonverbal behaviors. Avoiding eye contact when confronting a student about misbehavior gives the student the impression that you are uncomfortable or perhaps uncertain about the confrontation.
3. Make statements rather than ask questions. Asking questions is appropriate for eliciting information, but, when the teacher has specific information or behaviors to discuss, the teacher should state specifically what is on his or her mind.
4. Use "I" – take responsibility for your feelings. Teachers have a right to express their own feelings. Students need to know that teachers have their own legitimate feelings and that their feelings need to be considered in determining the effects of the student's behavior on others.
5. Be brief. Get to the point quickly.

6. Talk directly to the student, not about him or her. Even if other people are present, talk to the student rather than to parents or counselors.

7. Give directions to help the student correct the problem. Don't stop at identifying the problem behavior; be specific about what behaviors must be replaced.

8. Check student understanding of the message. Once you have communicated clearly what the problem is and what steps are suggested for solving it, ask a question to be sure the student has received the message correctly.

Ginott believed that teachers should be compassionate, understanding role models who communicate to students in such a way as to confirm positive expectations. A teacher who demonstrates polite, respectful behavior toward students creates an atmosphere where students learn to communicate their own feelings in a similarly acceptable fashion. This is accomplished when it is clear that teachers are aware of students' feelings and communicate with them through the use of sane messages.

Fred Jones' Theories

Fred Jones (2000) supported the management theory of Positive Discipline which is grounded in the belief that most classroom management problems occur because students are not on task. It is Jones' position that the majority of classroom management problems take place when students are not focused and not using their time constructively. Students often exhibit unwanted behaviors simply because they are allowed to be idle or waste time, not because they are naturally unruly, defiant, or aggressive. If teachers can control the learning environment so that "down time" is minimized, management problems will be greatly reduced (Borman & Levine, 1997; Burden, 2006). The teacher's ability to plan and develop a positive and motivating learning environment is the key to effective management (Manning & Bucher, 2013). To provide an environment where time is not wasted and where students are productive, teachers must:

1. learn to send messages to students through clear nonverbal communication,

2. develop reward systems for students who are on task,

3. arrange the physical environment to facilitate communication, and
4. use teaching methods that keep all students focused and on task.

When the teacher does not have to interrupt the lesson to address unwanted behavior problems, the flow of the lesson is maintained and instructional time is not wasted. Facial expressions, gestures, and movement toward students (an element of what is sometimes called proximity control) can many times stop unwanted behavior problems without interrupting the teacher's lesson. Teachers should avoid the overuse of corrective verbiage. Rather, students whose behavior is task-oriented should be rewarded, and this reward should then become an incentive for all students in the class. A student who finishes his or her work appropriately and in a timely manner, for example, might be allowed to spend extra time on favorite activities.

To facilitate a student's time on task and avoid idle time, the physical environment of the classroom should be arranged in such a way that the teacher can quickly and efficiently help students who are having difficulty. Students should not be seated in seating arrangements that make it difficult for teachers to easily get to them or near them without interrupting the flow of instruction. Desks arranged in semi-circles, for example, may be preferable to desks arranged in straight rows.

In addition to possible seating arrangement problems, students often waste time because they:

1. cannot do what has been assigned to them,
2. do not understand what is expected of an assignment,
3. finish their work and have nothing else to do, and
4. see the task assigned as boring, too difficult, or unchallenging.

To maintain a positive and motivating flow of instruction, teachers need to provide activities for their students that are interesting, challenging, and that keep them moving toward a desired and meaningful goal. Jones recommends that teachers use models, charts, examples, and illustrations to provide clear directions to students. He further emphasizes that the majority of the students in the class should not be kept waiting for extended periods of time while the teacher is explaining or re-explaining something to one or only a few individuals. This type of situation creates unnecessary idle time for the majority of the class. Jones' theory stresses the importance of the teacher's role in managing the classroom in such a way to prevent student behavior problems from occurring. The environment that is structured to foster consistent student time on task behavior limits wasted time and minimizes student misconduct. The use of effective teaching practices is clearly a key part of Jones' model.

Thomas Gordon's Theories

Thomas Gordon (1974) developed the highly popular Teacher Effectiveness Training (TET) model for classroom management that is based on a Gestalt psychology point of view similar to the position taken by Carl Rogers (Rogers & Freiberg, 1994). Gordon emphasizes the necessity of effective communication between teacher and student if productive relationships are to exist and does not support the use of rewards and punishment as management tools (Manning & Bucher, 2013). Through the use of TET, the teacher is encouraged to utilize certain counseling behaviors to create an effective, well-managed learning environment. In this approach:

1. teachers should diagnose problems to determine problem ownership,
2. teachers should avoid sending accusatory messages when correcting student behavior,
3. teachers should practice active listening when communicating with students, and
4. students are encouraged to resolve their own conflicts through a no-lose process.

Diagnosis of problem ownership is an important aspect of the successful functioning of TET. When unacceptable student behavior occurs, teachers should first determine if the problem that is being experienced is actually theirs or their students. Student-owned problems may be associated with fears or anxiety. Teacher-owned problems often involve student misconduct that frustrates the teacher because it interrupts the flow of instruction. In TET, the owner of the problem needs to be the one who initially talks or moves ahead to solve the problem. If the problem belongs to the student, the teacher needs to use appropriate questioning and listening techniques to counsel the student through the problem or otherwise guide the student to a positive resolution. If the problem belongs to the teacher, a clear, nonaccusatory message should be sent by the teacher to the student creating the problem letting the student know the impact that his or her behavior is having on what the teacher is trying to accomplish in the classroom.

When the teacher owns the problem, in pursuing this interaction, Gordon recommends that the teacher send what he calls an *I message* to the student. The teacher's *I message* (as opposed to a *You message*) explains how a specific student behavior affects the teacher without making an accusatory assault on the student or students who exhibited the unwanted behavior. The **I message** is *a three-part communication that:* (1) *delineates the undesired behavior,* (2) *describes the effect the behavior has on the teacher,* and (3) *lets the student know how the teacher feels when the behavior occurs.* I messages focus on behaviors, not students. For example, the teacher might say to a misbehaving student, *When you talk out loud when I am teaching I am unable to finish the activity that I have underway. This frustrates me and makes it difficult for me to complete the lesson that I had planned.* This approach does not criticize the student personally, but makes it clear that the student's behavior, talking out loud during the lesson, creates problems for the teacher as well as the learning of the other students. A *You message,* on the other hand, such as, *You are really creating problems for me today with your constant talking and I am tired of it,* comes across as being directed at the student personally and not to the student's behavior. The **You message** is seen *as a statement to the student interpreted as a personal attack or put down of the student.* Such a message or statement is counterproductive in terms of helping to develop the desired positive atmosphere in the classroom and relationship between the teacher and student(s).

Active listening, an important aspect of TET, is *a specific approach to listening where the teacher gives full attention to both the emotional as well as intellectual content of what the student is saying* (Sokolove, Garrett, Sadker, & Sadker, 1990). Active listening is especially important when the student owns the problem and needs to talk about emotions and feelings. The teacher's aim in using active listening is to show students that he or she takes their problems seriously, wants to hear what they have to say, and is willing to help them arrive at their own solutions. Through this process, teachers are encouraged to:

1. maintain eye contact with the student who is talking,
2. paraphrase what was said by the student back to the student to give assurance that the message is both understood and important to the teacher, and

3. project an open, nonjudgmental demeanor communicating to the student that what is being said by the student is genuinely important.

Gordon encourages students, where possible, to resolve their own conflicts through a process he calls the *no-lose approach*. The **no-lose approach** is *an approach to help students resolve their own conflicts or problems in such a way that all students involved feel positive about the resolution and no one is considered a loser.* In using this approach, the student first defines the problem and then suggests a possible solution. The concerned parties then work together to establish an acceptable solution through consensus building that is satisfactory to all involved. Following this, the solution is then implemented on a trial basis. If the solution is found to be unsatisfactory, another solution is similarly developed and tried. This process, recommended as following the steps of the Model for Reflection and Inquiry introduced in Chapter 1, is designed to teach students how to solve their own conflicts in a logical and reasoned way without the need for teacher intervention. Gordon's model is based and relies on effective communication among students and teachers. When students believe their teachers listen to them when they share their feelings, they are more likely to trust their teachers and respond openly to them. While recognized as a well-established system for managing the classroom, some feel that Gordon's theory is less effective with serious problems that call for immediate responses (Manning & Bucher, 2013).

Lee Canter's Theories

Lee and Marlene Canter developed the popular model for classroom management known as *Assertive Discipline* in the 1970s. **Assertive Discipline** is *a management model based upon the fundamental position that teachers have the right to teach while students have the right to learn, and no one has the right to disrupt the learning environment* (Canter, 2010; Canter & Canter, 1976). Assertive Discipline encourages teachers to make their expectations clear to their students and to follow through systematically with established consequences for those students who choose to break established rules. Canter (2010) identifies that it is essential for teachers to hold high expectations, both for their students as well as themselves. Included in this consideration of high expectations are the following principles.

1. **Expect 100% compliance with your directions 100% of the time**. Teachers with high expectations basically follow one primary rule of effective classroom management. Teachers shall not give a direction to students if they are not prepared to follow through with a disciplinary consequence if the students choose not to comply.

2. **Allow no excuses for disruptive behavior**. Effective teachers know that one of the most important gifts they can give their students is to let them know that, despite their problems, they can behave and be successful in the classroom.

3. **Always sweat the small stuff**. Teachers with high expectations will not let minor things slide by in their classrooms. Such teachers know that the more they let students know they are going to firmly deal with even the small matters, the more quickly students learn that the teachers have high standards in their classrooms.

4. **Never back down**. Even with a good management plan, there are times that students will make the choice to defy a teacher's authority and disrupt the learning of their classmates. Effective teachers know that if they are to clearly demonstrate their high expectations for student success in their classrooms, they cannot lose such power struggles with a strong-willed, defiant student.

5. **Let students know you are not going away**. Many teachers get frustrated when students don't respond to their classroom management efforts and continue to test the limits. Some teachers simply seem to give up their leadership positions in such circumstances and retreat from the situation. However, effective teachers don't retreat. Through their words and actions, they communicate that they are going to stay the course and ensure that they are the leaders in charge of their classrooms.

6. **Avoid excessive praise**. Praise has the potential to be one of the most significant strategies teachers have to motivate their students. However, praise must be used appropriately, be justified and "fit" the circumstance of the student's behavior. The teacher is not doing anything positive in using praise when students are simply doing what is expected. Some research suggests that students interpret frequent praise as a sign that they are doing poorly and need extra encouragement from their teachers (Dweck, 2007).

Clarity and consistency are critical if the teacher's use of Assertive Discipline is to be successful. Important features of Assertive Discipline are that:

1. students must face the consequences for their own misconduct,
2. teachers are neither hostile nor passive when dealing with misconduct,
3. teachers do not debate or argue about the fairness of rules with students, and
4. teachers rely heavily on the use of proper nonverbal communication and behavior monitoring strategies when managing specific student misconduct.

In a well-managed classroom, students understand what their teachers expect of them and the consequences of not fulfilling these expectations. Canter stresses that teachers need to communicate their expectations to students firmly and clearly and then consistently follow these communications with appropriate actions responding in ways that increase student compliance.

Effective teachers are firm but not hostile to students and always avoid making attacks on a student's character. Such teacher comments as, *You are acting immaturely!* or *You should be ashamed of yourself!* are ineffective, alienating, and should not be used. Comments such as, *You might get away with that when you are home, but you will not do it at school in my classroom!* actually can be seen as attacking the character of the student's parents and also should be avoided. The passive teacher ignores student misbehavior and fails to assert needed leadership in the classroom while the hostile teacher alienates students with a "me against you" attitude. Effective teachers appropriately assert themselves and become firm managers of student behavior. This firm approach to management, however, must never conflict with the best interests of the students for whom they are responsible.

Assertive Discipline stresses the importance of avoiding arguments with students, especially arguments in public. Because everyone should know and be clear about the rules of the classroom, teachers must not nag, fuss, lecture, and debate the rules with a misbehaving student. The overuse of such verbiage is a waste of valuable instructional time and only lessens the teacher's stature in the eyes of the students and, in turn, weakens the teacher's classroom leadership position.

To avoid superfluous talking while correcting student misbehaviors, teachers are advised to learn to use appropriate nonverbal communications. Eye contact, gestures, touches, and proximity are all effective means to help teachers assert that they are serious and in charge. Gestures, as Canter instructs, can give added impact to verbal messages along with factors such as tone of voice and facial expression. Such nonverbal communication will help the total communication of the teacher be clearer to the student and minimize the necessity for the teacher to repeat directions and use longer, and, at times, protracted verbal interactions. The use of appropriate nonverbal communication and a specific recordkeeping system that monitors the frequency of a student's misbehavior that leads to increased levels of consequences are keys to the success of Assertive Discipline.

The public's concern, along with the fact that many teachers fail in the profession as a result of not being able to manage the behavior of their students, has led advocates of Assertive Discipline to believe that effective teaching is dependent upon the teacher's ability to exhibit the firmness needed to control behavior in the learning environment. Some educators, however, have questioned the use of Assertive Discipline, identifying that there is little research supporting the effectiveness of Assertive Discipline conducted by researchers other than Canter and his associates (Render, Padilla, & Krank, 1989). While there is evidence that Assertive Discipline may work in severe cases with highly disruptive students, there is no evidence to recommend or support the approach for schoolwide or district wide adoption. Curwin and Mendler (1988) and Covaleski (1992) voiced concerns that go beyond whether or not Assertive Discipline does or does not work to control student behavior. These educators have noted that management models like Assertive Discipline do little to teach students self-control or bolster their self-worth or value systems. Canter and his associates have answered their critics with arguments related to the research base for Assertive Discipline (McCormack, 1989) and the issues surrounding the model's impact on students (Canter, 1988). While there are those who have been critical of Assertive Discipline, thousands of teachers have tried it and found that it works for them (Manning & Bucher, 2013). It is clear that teachers should thoroughly examine as many theories and models of management as possible, including Assertive Discipline, to determine what will be best for them to use in their own individual classrooms to bring about the greatest benefit to their students and themselves.

B. F. Skinner's Theories

B. F. Skinner's theories have been widely applied to behavior management and his work goes beyond what one might consider as representing only theories of behavior management in the classroom. The application of operant conditioning principles in everyday settings (i.e., not laboratory) has been common practice since the late 1950s (Kauffman, 1989). **Operant conditioning** is *a form of learning where an observable response changes in frequency or duration as a result of a consequence; the response increases in frequency as a result of its being followed by reinforcement.* Originally called Behavior Modification, the techniques were commonly used with the severely retarded, the autistic, and the emotionally disturbed. As positive outcomes were documented, the techniques began to be used more broadly with nondisabled populations (Zirpoli, 2007). Since the late 1980s, the term Behavior Modification has been replaced by Applied Behavior Analysis because, to many, the term Behavior Modification has taken on a negative connotation (Alberto & Troutman, 2012).

Early in the twentieth century, E. L. Thorndike (1905; 1911) established that people repeat behaviors that bring pleasant feelings and that the more a behavior is repeated the better one's performance in the behavior becomes. These findings lay the foundation for today's Applied Behavior Analysis. **Applied Behavior Analysis** is *an approach to management that focuses on the positive, rewarding appropriate behaviors, as opposed to concentrating on the negative, punishing unwanted or inappropriate behaviors* (McCaslin & Good, 1992).

Teachers who manage their classrooms using Applied Behavior Analysis exhibit characteristics derived from behaviorist principles. Examples of these principles are:

1. students receive positive reinforcements after exhibiting desired behaviors,
2. teachers do not punish students who exhibit unwanted behaviors, and
3. teachers shape students' behaviors to become more desirable over time.

The concept is simple. Students are reinforced (i.e., given a positive reinforcement or reward) when they behave in a manner the teacher desires. Based on behaviorist theory, the student who receives a reward will repeat the desired behavior because the reward brings pleasure or some type of positive feeling. If the teacher wants a student to stay seated, for example, the student will be rewarded in some way for being seated. Applied Behavior Analysis has been referred to as a remunerative strategy because students receive a type of payoff or remuneration for doing what the teacher wants done.

Not only does the model emphasize reinforcing or rewarding good behavior, teachers practicing Applied Behavior Analysis are advised to avoid the use of punishments. The positive aspect of this approach is that teachers focus on the students who are behaving in an acceptable manner, not the ones who are not. Teachers are encouraged to spend more time rewarding and praising their students, not punishing or giving them verbal retributions for misdeeds. Some behaviorists, however, have warned against a "praise good behavior while ignoring bad behavior" philosophy (Pfiffner, Rosen, & O'Leary, 1985). In some cases, especially those of a more serious nature, disruptive behavior will persist and may even escalate if ignored. Teachers are advised to channel students to positive behavior and then reinforce this conduct. While it may be that no teacher can be positive and complimentary all of the time, in general, it is strongly recommended that emphasis be placed on what students are doing correctly as opposed to what they may be doing incorrectly.

Shaping behavior is an important aspect of Applied Behavior Analysis. **Shaping** refers to *the practice of gradually changing a student's unwanted actions to more acceptable behavior over time through the use of reinforcements.* There are several ways that shaping can take place, varying from an informal approach where the teacher simply waits for a student to exhibit desired behavior and then rewards it, to a more structured system where the teacher elicits desired behavior through the use of tangible rewards. To shape an individual student's behavior, the teacher must first carefully measure the degree to which the behavior occurs (i.e., establish baseline data) and then analyze the environment to determine what precedes the behavior and what may be reinforcing the behavior after it occurs. Following this careful analysis, a schedule can be developed by the teacher to intervene by offering appropriate reinforcers when desired behaviors occur to change the unwanted behavior to more acceptable conduct. Finally, the changed behavior also must be measured to determine if the new behavior is greatly different from the previous, baseline behavior.

The unwanted behavior of a student could be something like the student's failing to complete any of the teacher's assigned homework. In using Applied Behavior Analysis in such a situation, the teacher would first observe the student for some period of time (e.g., one week) to determine the degree to which the student failed to complete the work that had been assigned. Following the completion of the observation, the teacher then would institute a reward system to motivate the student to complete the homework assignments (e.g., some tangible reinforcer could be given each time the student satisfactorily completed a set amount of work). After a period of time (perhaps two-to-three weeks), the teacher would then measure the student's level of homework completion again to determine the degree of progress that has been made. The teacher should maintain an assessment of the student's progress over time and make modifications as needed in the reinforcement schedule.

The use of behaviorist principles to shape student behavior is not universally accepted and, for many, is controversial (Kohn, 1993). Although supported by many (Alberto & Troutman, 2012; Zirpoli, 2007), questions have been raised about its use (Travers, 1977). It has been noted that ethical questions may be involved regarding its use in that some students may be reinforced for some actions that might be viewed as negative when exhibited by others. The question has also been raised as to whether or not the wrong message is being sent when some students receive rewards for doing what they are normally expected to do anyway, while other students exhibit the same behavior without being rewarded. Though evidence suggests that behavior can be changed through the use of Applied Behavior Analysis, questions remain concerning which students benefit most from such techniques and the impact the techniques have on the entire class (Hunt et al., 2009). As with many highly systematic classroom management models, Applied Behavior Analysis techniques can only be used successfully with maximum benefit after professional training has been received.

David and Roger Johnson's Theories

David and Roger Johnson and their associates developed the *Conflict Resolution* model for student behavior management where students receive formal training to prepare them to be able to deal with their own problems and the problems of their classmates (Johnson & Johnson,

2005; Johnson & Johnson, 2009; Stevahn, Johnson, Johnson, Green, & Laginski, 1997). **Conflict Resolution** is *a management model used in school settings where students are trained to use creative problem solving in such a way as to increase the probability that students involved in a conflict can get what they want in terms of a problem solution.* This is not unlike Thomas Gordon's no-lose approach to management. To use Conflict Resolution, students complete a designed training program where they learn how to engage in peer mediation with their classmates when conflicts arise. The goal of Conflict Resolution is to involve students in the decision-making process to develop a workable solution to a problem that will allow all parties involved in the conflict to feel satisfied about the problem's ultimate resolution. The program is most commonly used on a schoolwide basis where students take part in specialized training before using the approach to ensure that their negotiations and problem-solving actions can be successful and are conducted in a consistent and appropriate manner. The traditional role of the teacher is somewhat minimized in Conflict Resolution in that the model emphasizes the role of students in the management of their own conflicts.

Many claims have been made supporting this integrative approach to mediation of conflicts as a model which helps decrease management problems in schools (Tolson, McDonald, & Moriarty, 1992). It is clear that more research needs to be done on the impact of the process (Johnson & Johnson, 2005). For example, it has been argued that the model requires specialized training that takes place in ways that are not cost effective and that take students away from their academic studies (Webster, 1993). Johnson and Johnson (2004), however, report that, in schools where students were trained in conflict resolution and peer mediation, there were fewer management problems in classrooms and on school grounds and students continued to use their conflict resolution strategies at home as well as at school. Given its perceived positive impact, the approach is believed to be cost effective and can provide positive results when students receive proper training.

Conflicts among students today have become all too common in schools across the country. Some of these conflicts have been manifested in violent acts where students and teachers have experienced serious injury or loss of life for little or no understandable reason. Although these extreme acts of violence account for a very small percentage of the total number of student conflicts that take place in schools, they are extensively covered by the media and are widely publicized. Many school conflicts result in arguments and verbal taunting and some even culminate in physical fights; too many end when one or more students has been seriously injured. As a result of the serious and frequent nature of these problems, many educators suggest that students themselves need to be involved in and learn how to find solutions to their own conflicts in a constructive manner. Conflict Resolution has promise as a model that can be used to ease management problems on a schoolwide basis. Further research, especially in middle and high schools, is needed to determine how it can be instituted most effectively.

Alfie Kohn's Theories

Unlike some of the other theorists that have been presented, Alphie Kohn has discussed and written on a wide variety of topics in education. Many who are familiar with his work may not associate him with issues of behavior or classroom management as with other current areas of interest in the profession. For example, Kohn is considered one of the leading opponents of the national movement toward a greater emphasis on test scores; his *The Case Against Standardized Testing* (Kohn, 2000) is a short but powerful argument that the testing movement is hurting, not helping education. His *No Contest: The Case Against Competition* (Kohn, 1992) is seen as an important critique of the impact of competition on American life. Kohn's work is broad-based and has implications for many aspects of the profession. In *Ten Obvious Truths that We Shouldn't Be Ignoring* (Kohn, 2011), Kohn reinforces how many aspects of education are closely intertwined and impact each other. In considering the ten *Truths* and issues of student motivation and management, this is particularly clear in items 3, 4, 6, 7, 9, and 10.

1. Much of the material students are required to memorize is soon forgotten.
2. Just knowing a lot of facts doesn't mean you're smart.
3. Students are more likely to learn what they find interesting.
4. Students are less interested in whatever they're forced to do and more enthusiastic when they have some say.
5. Just because doing *x* raises standardized test scores doesn't mean *x* should be done.
6. Students are more likely to succeed in a place where they feel known and cared about.

7. We want children to develop in many ways, not just academically.
8. Just because a lesson (or book, or class, or test) is harder doesn't mean it's better.
9. Kids aren't just short adults.
10. Substance matters more than labels.

Kohn (1993) takes the position that rewards and punishments represent "opposite sides of the same coin" and both should be avoided as teacher tools used to motivate and manage students. Kohn describes himself as a person who has long been an opponent of the principles of behaviorism, which he believes are flawed and contribute to many educational problems that directly affect the way teachers motivate and manage students. His position is that rewards (often referred to by Kohn as "bribes") and punishments can change behaviors, but that the change will be short in duration because rewards and punishments function only to change specific behaviors in specific situations. Rewards and punishments do not function to change value systems and individual character. While they may be used to produce temporary compliance, they tend not to help bring about long-term, worthwhile goals such as increased student self-reliance, creative thinking, or self-confidence. The essence of Kohn's theory is that, for long-term positive change to occur, students need to internalize prosocial values and become a part of a caring community. Based on these prosocial values, students must exhibit prosocial behavior for the desired caring community to be the end result. **Prosocial behavior** is *behavior directed toward promoting the well-being of someone else.* This is opposed to **antisocial behavior**, or *behavior directed toward bringing about a negative consequence for someone or something.* Rewards and punishments merely train students in much the same way animals are trained. As opposed to being trained like animals, students need to become a part of the culture of a learning community where they can think about and act on basic human values such as kindness, fairness, and personal responsibility. Central to the functioning of this type of community are the teachers' abilities to communicate with students while allowing students to communicate with them and each other (Powell, McLaughlin, Savage, & Zehm, 2001). Prosocial behavior is represented by positive actions that benefit others, prompted by empathy, moral values, and a sense of personal responsibility rather than a desire for personal gain (Kidron & Fleischman, 2007). Research suggests that the following schoolwide approaches can promote prosocial behavior in schools: (1) train teachers to integrate values instruction into classroom management, (2) foster a caring community throughout the school, and (3) use positive discipline practices.

When one sets out to not only change observable behavior, but to transform a student's core being, the task seems almost Herculean in nature. Kohn (1993) has provided a set of guidelines for teachers to follow that can serve as a framework for developing what he sees as the proper learning environment in schools and classrooms. The following eight elements are included in the formation of this framework.

1. Collaboration
2. Choice
3. Caring
4. Modeling
5. Explaining
6. Attributing Positive Motives
7. Offering Opportunities to Care
8. Emphasizing Perspective Taking

Collaboration: As children mature, they should be brought into the decision-making process more and more and be allowed input into deciding what is and is not acceptable. Mutual problem solving is at the heart of this type of collaboration. Teacher and student should plan together how a problem can be faced and prevented in the future. Kohn suggests that students will often make restitution and avoid future problems when they do not fear punishment for their mistakes.

Choice: Children should be given the opportunity to participate in meaningful decision making concerning what will happen to them as a result of their exhibiting unacceptable behavior. Students need to have real autonomy to make choices after giving their input.

Caring: Children will care for other people more if they feel other people care for them. A caring, supportive environment is at the heart of Kohn's theory.

Modeling: Adults teach by example. If students are to be intrinsically motivated to do good deeds and care for one another, they need to have well respected teachers to model desired conduct (e.g., listen respectfully, care for students, and treat all students honestly and fairly).

Explaining: It is not enough just to model desired traits. Explanations of what is desired and why certain things should or should not be done must be given in language that is understood by the students. Such clear explaining behavior leads to reasoning with students instead of demanding simple obedience. Explanations are not lectures but are explorations of why things should be done in certain ways.

Attributing Positive Motives: A basic belief that children are born good and not bad and a desire to accept a reasonable excuse for undesired activity are at the core of providing the type of learning environment that students need. Teachers who believe that students are basically good, and attribute to them the best possible motive for behavior consistent with the facts, are more likely to help students develop good values.

Offering Opportunities to Care: Teachers who want their students to be caring individuals need to provide them with opportunities to demonstrate caring behaviors. Students who tutor other students, care for pets, and help classmates solve problems, for example, will more readily become caring individuals themselves.

Emphasizing Perspective Taking: If a goal is to produce students who perform good deeds from a desire to do good and to help others, as opposed to receiving rewards, teachers must help students view the world from the eyes of those who are less fortunate or in some way weaker. Students must empathize and perform what is called "perspective taking." Questions such as, *How does it feel to be called names?*, *How does it feel to be bullied?*, and *How does it feel to be laughed at by others?* can advance this perspective taking. These are questions students might reflect on to appreciate the effect negative behavior can have on others. Failure to take on or at least understand other people's points of view accounts for much of the behavior seen as troublesome in schools today.

Beyond this framework for developing the proper learning environment which focuses on the teacher as a stimulus for creating a positive classroom atmosphere, entire schools can be organized to help students develop prosocial behavior (Kohn, 1993). For this to take place, activities should be adopted across the entire school that will assist educators in developing the type of caring environment that children need and deserve. Certain elements are important to establishing this type of environment. These include the use of: (1) class meetings, (2) unity-building activities, (3) schoolwide programs, and (4) prosocial literature.

1. **Class Meetings**: Kohn believes that students at all ages benefit from opportunities to take time to plan together, make deci-

sions, solve problems, and reflect on the happenings of the day. These types of activities have the potential to create a feeling of community in the school and classroom and provide an opportunity to take on the perspectives of other students. This approach is consistent with the theories of other educators such as William Glasser.

2. **Unity-building Activities**: Activities designed to build a feeling of community and belonging to the group or team are important. Such activities help students communicate better and develop understanding and empathy for one another. Some groups or teams create logos, develop newsletters, put on plays, participate in intramural activities, and arrange for many other unity-building activities that strengthen the ability of students to communicate with and understand their fellow students.

3. **Schoolwide Programs**: Schoolwide community service programs can help to develop a feeling of community within and among students. Programs that foster older students mentoring or tutoring younger students, for example, have great value when trying to develop feelings of caring.

4. **Prosocial Literature**: The stories teachers use in their classrooms serve a similar function as modeling. A schoolwide literature program, as an example, can stress the use of materials that emphasize desired values such as fairness, kindness, tolerance, and honesty.

Kohn's theory of behavior management or behavior development emphasizes the education of students to value goodness and respect for others. Students must want and desire to be good. It is not enough to just avoid negative behavior or to act acceptably. Students do not look for rewards or seek to avoid punishment, but, learn to become good human beings. While it is hard to argue with this theory, an important question is one of utility. Can teachers show the patience that is needed for such a long, slow process of personal development to take place? Kohn and his supporters would ask if teachers can afford not to show such patience.

SELECTING MANAGEMENT MODELS

The information presented in the first part of this chapter provided an overview of key theories and models for managing students in school and classroom settings. Teachers are advised to analyze this information to determine which model, collection of models, or parts of models would be best suited to their individual personalities and classrooms. Before making the decision to adopt any management model, it is suggested that teachers undertake more in-depth study to include, when possible, visits to classrooms or schools where the model is being successfully utilized.

A list of helpful questions to ask to guide teachers in their study of theories and models of classroom management is provided in Figure 3.2. A brief analysis of each theory and model presented in the first part of the chapter is offered as related to each question.

Guidelines to Assist Teachers in Selecting Management Models

1. What happens to students who break rules? Punishments or consequences?
2. Is it realistically possible to reinforce the program consistently?
3. What do students learn as a result of the program?
4. Are the principles of behavior as visible and as important as the rules?
5. Do students have a say in what happens to them?
6. Do teachers have discretion in implementing consequences?
7. Is adequate time given for professional development of teachers and administrators? Is the training completed in only a day or two? Is there continuous follow-up and administrative support?
8. Does the plan account for the special relationship between teaching and discipline style, or does it focus exclusively on student behavior? Does it encourage teachers to examine their own potential contributions to discipline problems?
9. Is the dignity of the students preserved? Are students protected from embarrassment?
10. Is the program consistent with the stated goals of the school?

Figure 3.2. Guidelines to Assist Teachers in Selecting Management Models. Source: From Curwin, R., & Mendler, A. (1988). Packaged discipline programs: Let the buyer beware. *Educational Leadership, 46*(2), 68–71.

1. What happens to students who break rules? Punishments or consequences?

Kounin: The teacher handles the misconduct firmly to positively impact the entire class.

Dreikurs: Students receive logical consequences that they perceive as being unpleasant.

Glasser: Behavior contracts are used and make students aware of and responsible for the consequences of their misconduct. If a student's behavior cannot be modified, the student is removed from the group.

Ginott: Students are given the choice of conducting themselves correctly or losing certain freedoms. The teacher's focus is on the behavior, not the person.

Jones: Emphasis is placed on keeping students on task to prevent misconduct.

Gordon: The teacher sends an *I message* to the student that identifies the misconduct, why it is unacceptable, and how it impacts the teacher's work or makes the teacher feel.

Canter: Students are given consequences when rules are broken.

Skinner: The focus is placed on channeling students in the correct direction so that positive reinforcements can be given for good conduct. As a result, the misdirected student is shaped into a student behaving acceptably. Serious misconduct is not ignored.

Johnson and Johnson: Emphasis is directed toward student-to-student conflict. Students should resolve these conflicts in ways that all parties see as acceptable.

Kohn: The teacher talks to the student about the misbehavior and tries to induce the student to reflect on ways to improve the situation. The teacher seeks input from the student concerning what should happen while avoiding the use of rewards and punishments.

2. Is it realistically possible to reinforce the program consistently?

Kounin: The model focuses on individual teacher behavior in the classroom. When the suggested behaviors become part of the teacher's everyday conduct, consistency should be maintained.

Dreikurs: Yes. The model focuses on individual teacher behavior. Consistency will come as teachers master the behavior.

Glasser: Yes. However, consistency becomes a bit more difficult; with In-School Suspension (ISS), for example, teachers and administrators must work with all teachers. High levels of coordination are needed to maintain consistency.

Ginott: Yes. The model focuses on the interaction between a teacher and student or a group of students. There will be the challenge to make certain that *sane messages* are provided equitably to all students.

Jones: Yes. Nonverbal communication, reward systems, and time on task are emphasized. The challenge is to maintain the same level of effectiveness with students of varying ability and motivation.

Gordon: Yes. Like Ginott's theory, Teacher Effectiveness Training (TET) is based on interaction between teacher and student. As students increase in number and diversity, consistency will become a greater challenge and concern.

Canter: Yes. When teachers learn the procedures involved, they will be able to consistently reinforce the program.

Skinner: The behaviorist principles guiding Applied Behavior Analysis are designed to provide consistency in the reinforcement of the program.

Johnson and Johnson: The model relies on the support of trainers, counselors, administrators, and teachers to produce the desired results and focuses on the peer mediation skills of individual students. Consistently reinforcing such a program is a challenge. Further evidence is needed to answer this question.

Kohn: Yes. As was true with Ginott and Gordon, effectiveness of this model is based on the teacher's ability to communicate with students. Some students are more likely to respond to this type of reasoning than others.

3. What do students learn as a result of the program?

Kounin: Students learn to stay on task and remain focused. An emphasis on reducing student boredom may lead to learning to enjoy school more.

Dreikurs: Students learn to feel responsible for their own behavior as well as the behaviors of classmates. Students develop more self-respect and more respect for others.

Glasser: Students learn to feel more empowered to make decisions, control their own environment and improve their ability to work and communicate in groups.

Ginott: Through cooperative activities students learn self-respect, self-esteem, and to develop greater satisfaction with themselves.

Jones: Students learn the importance of staying on task and making academic progress.

Gordon: Students learn to communicate their own feelings, relate to the feelings of others, and resolve problems.

Canter: Students learn that there are consequences for interfering with the rights of others and that it is not necessary for teachers to debate and defend their positions of authority.

Skinner: This is an important point for debate. Critics of behaviorist principles often maintain that students learn to think they should be rewarded for doing what they should be doing as a matter of fact. Behaviorists feel students learn whatever adults want them to learn by shaping the students' behaviors. Some critics are concerned that student creativity is hampered.

Johnson and Johnson: Students learn to resolve conflicts in mutually satisfying ways that are fair to all concerned parties.

Kohn: Students learn to develop and use their critical thinking skills when they reflect on their own behaviors as they relate to specific situations. Perhaps most importantly, students learn to be caring, responsible, empathetic human beings who value good conduct.

4. Are the principles of behavior as visible and as important as the rules?

Kounin: Yes. The principles of good leadership by the teacher and appropriate conduct by students are not lost to any rigid set of rules and procedures.

Dreikurs: Yes, as in the case of Kounin's theories.

Glasser: The principles of behavior are explained clearly and the rules of conduct and consequences for misconduct are evident; if the teacher understands Glasser's theory, the principles for behavior and the theory's foundation should not be lost.

Ginott: Although Ginott dedicated much time to explaining the rules (i.e., the *do's* and *don'ts*) for teacher and student behavior, he also carefully explained the principles guiding these rules.

Jones: The basic principle guiding this theory is that most problems occur because students are allowed to waste time. This principle does not get lost in the discussion of rules and procedures.

Gordon: Although TET was developed on the principles of Gestaltist psychology similar to those of Carl Rogers, teacher techniques and student rules often seem to dominate when educators discuss the model.

Canter: Teachers often focus on the rules for behavior and techniques of administering Assertive Discipline instead of the principles upon which it is based.

Skinner: The principles of operant conditioning go hand in hand with techniques and rules for behavior. The principles upon which the system is based are not lost.

Johnson and Johnson: The principle that students should learn to resolve their own conflicts in an amiable fashion is reinforced in the process.

Kohn: The principle that students should become caring, empathetic people is central to the theory. There is no reliance on a long list of rules.

5. Do students have a say in what happens to them?

Kounin: The emphasis is on teacher behaviors. Concern about student input is not paramount.

Dreikurs: Yes. Dreikurs suggests that students should take part in setting logical consequences for their misconduct.

Glasser: The teacher utilizes *class meetings* to ensure student input concerning the setting of logical consequences. Students are encouraged to develop their own plans for correcting behavior throughout the process.

Ginott: An emphasis is placed on students making choices, not on forced compliance. The teacher is asked to remain sensitive to students' feelings.

Jones: The emphasis is on the prevention of problems. Student input into what will happen when rules are broken is not a major concern.

Gordon: Much emphasis is placed on student input as teachers are encouraged to use *active listening* techniques.

Canter: The theory is based on the need for students to comply with established, non-debatable rules.

Skinner: Students have little control over what happens to them as their behavior is shaped. This has been an issue with the critics of behaviorism.

Johnson and Johnson: Conflict Resolution stresses the importance of training students so that they determine what happens to them when conflicts arise.

Kohn: For the theory to be actualized, students must always be involved in deciding what happens to them.

6. Do teachers have discretion in implementing consequences?

Kounin: Yes. Teachers are encouraged to be leaders and decision-makers.

Dreikurs: Yes. Teachers provide logical consequences to students who exhibit misconduct. However, teachers use their own discretion in determining, along with students, the actual consequences.

Glasser: Teachers can use their discretion to a point. When student misconduct reaches a level where isolation is necessary, consequences are prescribed.

Ginott: Teachers are asked not to order, boss, or force students to comply. Teachers are given guidelines by these directions and do not lose their freedom in making judgments concerning the implementation of consequences for student misbehavior.

Jones: Teachers should limit verbal corrections while using nonverbal expressions and gestures to communicate with students. The emphasis is on avoiding problems by keeping students active and engaged. Consequences for misbehavior are not a central issue. Teachers have freedom to make judgments as needed.

Gordon: TET is a structured, systematic program emphasizing clear communication between teacher and student. The structure does limit teacher discretion in the use of consequences.

Canter: Teachers have discretion to set consequences for misconduct. After the consequences are set, teachers are expected to consistently adhere to the system.

Skinner: Although consequences are sometimes used, especially when misbehavior is severe, the model specifically emphasizes rewarding good behaviors. Teachers have freedom to set rewards and consequences as judged appropriate.

Johnson and Johnson: Conflict Resolution does not focus on teachers setting consequences for misconduct. Students resolve problems without teacher intervention.

Kohn: Teachers have discretion since the emphasis is on individual problem solving and growth, not on consequences. Punishments (consequences) and rewards are to be replaced by reasoning, reflection, and support.

7. Is adequate time given for professional development of teachers and administrators? Is the training completed in only a day or two? Is there continuous follow-up and administrative support?

These questions must be answered in the context of a specific school environment. The successful use of any model requires adequate training and administrative support over an extended period of time if maximum results are to be achieved. Some models, for example TET, Reality Therapy or Choice Theory, Conflict Resolution, and Applied Behavior Analysis, require extensive and long-term specialized training and support.

8. Does the plan account for the special relationship between teaching and discipline style, or does it focus exclusively on student behavior? Does it encourage teachers to examine their own potential contributions to discipline problems?

Kounin: The relationship between teaching style and management style is apparent in the discussion of concepts such as *withitness*, *thrust*, and *ripple effect*.

Dreikurs: The plan allows teachers to make their personal contribution to solving problems as they analyze student behavior and react accordingly. The relationship between teaching style and discipline style is not as obvious.

Glasser: The group and cooperative activities link the management and teaching styles of teachers. Teachers have a great potential to contribute in leading class meetings.

Ginott: Sending *sane messages*, modeling desired behaviors, and eliminating sarcasm toward and labeling of students are all avenues to link teaching and discipline styles.

Jones: The theory is built upon the relationship between teaching and discipline styles. Methods of instruction used to diminish discipline problems by keeping students on task are emphasized.

Gordon: While *active listening* techniques can be used in management and instruction, the focus is more on management styles. Teachers using TET should feel they are making an important contribution to the solution of problems.

Canter: Management of student behavior is the main focus. The model is also designed to empower teachers to help them realize their potential to contribute to the successful management of discipline problems.

Skinner: The behaviorist principles of Applied Behavior Analysis can be used for instructional practices in a method similar to the ones used to manage behavior; however, there is a definite focus on isolated behaviors as opposed to an interaction of management and instructional style.

Johnson and Johnson: Conflict Resolution focuses on student behavior, not the relationship between teaching and discipline styles. The potential contribution that teachers make is limited.

Kohn: The theory focuses on the special relationship between teaching style and discipline style. In the tradition of the early Progressive Educators, reflection in a democratic classroom permeates Kohn's ideal for managing and teaching students.

9. Is the dignity of the students preserved? Are students protected from embarrassment?

Kounin: Yes. The importance of maintaining student interest and participation is stressed. Any incident that embarrasses a student would have a definite negative *ripple effect* on the entire class.

Dreikurs: Students must develop self-respect to adjust to the environment of the classroom. Any action that negatively impacts the student's self-image is inappropriate.

Glasser: The teacher is a democratic leader who involves students in group discussion and decision making processes. The type of relationship encouraged between teacher and student could not exist if students were not treated with dignity.

Ginott: Central to the theory is the position that teachers avoid sarcasm and labeling when interacting with students. Teachers should treat students with dignity to foster growth in their self-esteem.

Jones: Yes. Students are rewarded for productivity. There is nothing to suggest that students should be treated in an undignified manner.

Gordon: Teachers are encouraged to avoid being accusatory and to treat students with dignity.

Canter: Yes. It is important to remember that, although teachers should avoid passive behaviors, Assertive Discipline opposes teacher hostility. When being assertive, teachers must guard against crossing the line that would result in students being treated in an embarrassing, undignified manner.

Skinner: The behaviorist focus is on rewarding desired behavior; the purpose is to encourage students to behave well so that they can be rewarded. Although Behaviorism is often discussed vis-à-vis Humanism, this in no way implies that behaviorists lack concern in their treatment of students.

Johnson and Johnson: Yes. Conflict Resolution is designed to empower students to solve their own problems in ways that are fair to all parties concerned.

Kohn: Fundamental to this model is the belief that no student's self-worth should ever be compromised. The teacher models a caring, empathetic attitude so students will learn to treat each other with dignity.

10. Is the program consistent with the stated goals of the school?

This question can only be answered in the context of a specific school environment. It can be said, however, that it is important to match the school's goals and philosophy with any management model to be used by the faculty to ensure maximum consistency and support from administrators and parents. For example, if the school has the goal of increasing time spent on academic activities, Kounin's and Jones' theories may be more of a match with the school's needs than would be the theories of Johnson and Johnson and Kohn.

CONCLUSION

Chapter 3 has provided an overview of ten popular theories and models for classroom management and identified the theorists associated with their development. An extensive amount of material (e.g., books, journal articles, tapes, training kits, etc.) can be found on each of the models and theories that have been discussed. Teachers should review this information, find ideas that appeal to their personal style and philosophy, and do further research prior to making a final decision about what would work best for them. It is recognized that other theories and models exist and that new theories and models will evolve as the knowledge base in this area continues to grow and as societal changes take place.

Questions developed to assist teachers in the selection of management models were used as a way to systematically analyze and examine the models and guide decision making about their use in particular settings. Preliminary answers were provided for each question from the perspective of each of the models presented. Teachers are encouraged to answer these questions themselves in greater detail based on further analysis of the models and a comparison to their own educational settings.

Without a theoretical basis to guide their actions, teachers run the risk of becoming inconsistent in their behaviors and making managerial decisions without understanding the full ramifications and implications for the students involved. The information presented in this chapter can serve as a starting point to the development of this important and needed theoretical foundation.

QUESTIONS/ACTIVITIES FOR REFLECTION

1. Why should a teacher be aware of such a large number of models or theories for management when he or she is not likely to use most of them? What are important points to consider in adopting any model or part of a model for classroom use?

2. Take the side of a teacher who does not agree with the principles upon which Applied Behavior Analysis are based and develop an argument against its use. Now, take the opposite point of view and argue in support of the use of Applied Behavior Analysis.

3. Create a scenario illustrating how a teacher might apply Alphie Kohn's principles of management to a classroom management problem dealing with student cheating.

4. Of all of the models discussed in this chapter, which one do you think is the most sound? Explain why you chose this one. Which one do you think is the least sound? Why?

5. In what way or ways is the theory of William Glasser (Reality Therapy/Choice Theory and the use of *class meetings*) more or less applicable to teachers who teach in the upper grades (grades 7-12) as opposed to the lower grades (grades PreK-6)?

Chapter 4

BEST PRACTICE IN TEACHING FOR BEST PRACTICE IN STUDENT MOTIVATION AND CLASSROOM MANAGEMENT

> The best learning activities and assignments are built around powerful ideas. Students will not necessarily learn anything important from merely carrying out the processes of an activity (i.e., spending "time on task"). The key to the effectiveness of good activities is their cognitive engagement potential – the degree to which they get students actively thinking about and applying key ideas, preferably with conscious awareness of their learning goals and control of their learning strategies. The most valuable activities are not merely hands-on, but minds-on. (Brophy, 2004, p. 35)

No study of motivation and management in the classroom would be complete without addressing the topic of best practice in teaching. The relationship between best teaching practice and best practice in motivation and management is well documented. Where motivation and management problems arise, problems in teaching practice generally will also be found. Educational research reinforces the fact that higher levels of student motivation and fewer instances of student management problems are evident where teachers use effective teaching practices. One recommended strategy for improving low student performance begins with seeking answers to three basic questions: (1) *Who are our students?* (2) *What do we want them to learn?* (3) *What do we want them to do differently when they are not learning?* A straightforward approach to answering these questions reinforces the need for the continued, deliberate and combined study of motivation, management, and instructional practice (Lieberman, 2007).

Regardless of the classroom management or student motivation technique used, no approach will be effective for long if the teacher does not also use effective teaching practices (Tauber, 1999). Classroom management models and the accompanying theories and recommended strategies that go with them cannot serve as substitutes for good teaching. In many ways, effective teaching itself represents a preventive measure in that, when teaching is effective, students are interested and engaged in their learning to the degree that they are not inclined to cause problems (Glasser, 1990). As identified here, however, merely understanding effective teaching is not sufficient. It is the teacher's ability to understand and implement sound teaching practices, along with sound practices in student motivation and classroom management that aligns the entire learning experience together. This alignment makes the most optimum levels of learning possible for students and comparable levels of teaching possible for teachers.

It is easy to sometimes underestimate the ongoing challenges found in today's typical classroom and not fully comprehend the power of the impact of these challenges on both teachers and students. In 1907, William Chandler Bagley of the University of Illinois wrote:

> Absolute fearlessness is the first essential for the teacher on whom rests the responsibility for governing an elementary or secondary school. This fearlessness is not alone or chiefly the expression of physical courage, although this must not be lacking. It is rather an expression of moral courage . . . standing firm in one's convictions even though the community may not approve . . . it is this sort of courage that is the rarest and, at the same time, the most essential. (Curwin, Mendler, & Mendler, 2008, p. 9)

Courage will always be an important part of the learning process and, for many, the greatest challenge is in the courage to establish, manage, and teach in the type of classroom environment that produces the best learning for all students involved. The following statement of a high school senior represents the significance of this environment:

Silent Defiance

I'm the one who watched,
as you laughed;
I'm the one who listened patiently,
while you talked unceasingly;
I'm the one who sat silent,

as your shouts grew louder;
I'm the one who always came,
while your chair sat empty;
I'm the one whose dreams were hidden,
as yours were fulfilled;
I'm the one who cared,
while you butchered knowledge;
I'm the one who reasoned,
as you discussed;
I'm the one who will remember
when all of you will forget.

(by Heather Osborn, high school senior, from
Curwin, Mendler, & Mendler, 2008, p. 9)

Recognizing that effective student motivation and classroom management rest on a solid foundation of effective teaching, an overview of best teaching practices that have been identified through educational research is presented in this chapter. The relationship between quality teaching, quality student motivation, and quality classroom management will be evident in this analysis.

In establishing the overall framework for this text, Chapter 1 introduced the Model for Reflection and Inquiry and it was identified that, to be effective, teachers must be good reflective practitioners. Three case studies of beginning teachers who had experienced problems of motivation and management in their classrooms were included in the presentation of the Model. Of the three teachers featured in these case studies, Tameka (in the case study *Tameka's Planning and Analysis*) was the only teacher of the three who actually embraced and dealt directly as a reflective practitioner with the problems that she encountered in her classroom. Unlike the other two teachers, she systematically reflected on the events of her difficult day and how they contributed to her problems in student motivation and classroom management. With her reflection being offered as an example of the use of the Model for Reflection and Inquiry, Tameka's behaviors were consistent with those of a reflective educator. She reviewed and clarified the problems that she had encountered, reviewed specific events of the day related to them, analyzed the events with respect to their impact on her classroom management and ability to motivate her students, and, based on this information, made decisions as to how she should move forward in making adjustments in her classroom practice. Tameka was engaged in guided problem solving and reflective thinking. Of special importance, she accepted the responsibility for her student motivation and classroom management difficulties and did not lay blame for the problems she encountered on the "type" of students she was working with, their parents, her administrative support, or anything else. While her problems involved others, the problems were hers to solve.

Tameka's situation and the process of reflection that she went through needs to be considered as both the situation and the process relate to the information on best practice in teaching that is developed throughout the remainder of this chapter. A formal model such as the Model for Reflection and Inquiry can be used to bring logical reasoning to problems associated with student behavior and help combat what is often the emotionally charged environment that accompanies challenges of student motivation and dealing with student behavior problems. It can also guide the development of well-grounded decision making with respect to identifying solutions to these problems. Such an approach will systematically lead to higher quality in instruction, motivation, and management in the classroom.

The search for best practice in teaching, and, therefore, in student motivation and classroom management, must always be continuous and may at times seem to be an intellectually exhausting endeavor. A mistake made by some teachers occurs when they believe that they already know what they need to know about best teaching practices. Full understanding of best teaching practices will never be reached as the knowledge base related to effective teaching continues to develop and expand. For example, a group of cognitive and educational psychologists recently did a detailed review of the evidence on ten popular study techniques to answer the question, *What are the most effective study techniques students can use to help increase their learning?* (Dunlosky, Rawson, Marsh, Nathan, & Willingham, (2013). The two most effective study techniques across a range of learning conditions were reported to be practice testing and distributed practice. The application of this and other knowledge from educational research should always be situational in its use with respect to not only knowing "what works" in teaching but also knowing when, where, and with whom it works best. Regarding reflective practice and best practice in teaching, Henson and Eller noted:

> Effective teachers are always looking for better ways to teach . . . are willing to explore different approaches. . . . This is why curiosity, ex-

perimentation, and risk-taking are so important to teachers. Throughout their careers, successful teachers improve their ability to reflect on
their behavior and use their reflective judgment to improve their
teaching. (Henson & Eller, 1999, p. 10)

Educational research has identified and continues to reinforce certain
teacher characteristics related to effective teaching that, when evident,
result in higher student achievement. These characteristics are often referred to as best practices in teaching.

ESTABLISHING A FOUNDATION
FOR BEST TEACHING PRACTICE

Much of what is known about best practice in teaching is related to
the areas of instructional planning and classroom organization, goal setting and communication, teacher instructional strategies, time management, teacher-to-student interactions, relationships with students, and
classroom management rules and procedures. For example, the following teacher characteristics and behaviors are well documented in the
research on effective teaching practice (Armstrong, Henson, & Savage,
1997). Effective teachers:

1. **play a central, dominant role in the classroom but involve
   students in planning and organization**: Effective teachers accept their important responsibility in classroom leadership, but
   also that students who are personally invested in their own
   learning will develop a greater sense of ownership for their
   learning and achieve at higher levels.
2. **set high goals and communicate these goals to their students**: It is important that teacher expectations be high though
   realistic; it is critical that teachers make their goals for their students clear, not only in terms of the learning experiences that
   will be undertaken, but also in terms of how students will be
   evaluated.
3. **work mostly with the entire class and less often with small
   groups, sometimes providing independent work for students**: Teachers who are able to coordinate the learning of all
   students at the same time through large group instructional experiences will develop a greater sense of community in the

classroom and allow students to more clearly understand their own progress, but also the work and activities of others at the same time.

4. **maintain a brisk lesson pace, requiring public and overt student participation**: Lessons that are felt by students to be moving too slow, essentially only dragging along, allow for greater opportunities for students to drift away and become disengaged; students who move forward with the lesson at a quicker pace, and who are overtly involved in the teacher's instruction, typically learn at higher levels and enjoy their learning more.

5. **use little criticism, shape student responses so that they are correct, hold students responsible for their work, and attend to students equitably**: Treating students fairly, providing uplifting rather than negative comments, and letting students know that they have responsibilities as learners, just as the teacher has responsibilities as a teacher, result in a more wholesome and positive learning environment; students who feel safe in the classroom, and who are meaningfully involved in it, are more successful in their work.

6. **set and maintain clear rules for students' academic and social behavior**: Though perhaps not thought to be the case by some, students do desire and need clear boundaries in the classroom; students work better in environments that are well-defined in terms of the *do's* and *don'ts* and the *right's* and *wrong's* than they do in settings where there is ambiguity and inconsistency as to what is acceptable and unacceptable behavior.

Five additional teacher characteristics that consistently appear in the teacher effectiveness research are organized into the broad categories of: (1) lesson clarity, (2) instructional variety, (3) teacher task orientation, (4) engagement in the learning process, and (5) student success rate (Borich, 2011).

Lesson Clarity

Lesson clarity refers to how well students understand their teachers' lessons. While it is important that teachers recognize the importance of clear communication and believe that they are clear, it is more important that their students truly understand them. Teachers that are vague, who use vocabulary that students do not understand, or who are generally not well organized in their work, are not considered to be clear in their teaching. When students do not understand the various communications of their teachers, there is little reason to think that they will be able to perform at the highest levels of their potentials. Students need to understand what their teachers are saying and expect of them to benefit the most from their learning experiences. Table 4.1 provides an overview of clarity indicators and strategies that a teacher might use for lesson clarity to be achieved.

Table 4.1
Teaching Behaviors to Achieve Lesson Clarity

Teacher Behaviors to Achieve Lesson Clarity	*Examples of Teaching Strategies to Achieve Lesson Clarity*
1. Inform students of the lesson objective, e.g., describe what behaviors will be tested or required on future assignments as a result of the lesson.	Prepare a behavioral objective for the lesson at the desired level of complexity and indicate to the students at the start of the lesson in what way(s) the behavior will be used in the future.
2. Provide students with an advance organizer, such as using something that puts the lesson in the perspective of past and/or future lessons.	Prepare a unit plan to determine what relevant prior learning is required for the lesson and what prior learning the current lesson represents for future lessons.
3. Check for relevant prior learning at the beginning of the lesson to determine the level of understanding of prerequisite facts and reteach prior information if needed.	Ask questions of students at the beginning of a lesson or check assignments regularly to determine if they have relevant prior knowledge.

Source: From Borich, G. (2011). *Effective teaching methods: Research-based practice* (7th ed.). Boston: Pearson, p. 9.

Instructional Variety

Instructional variety refers to the overall teaching repertoire of the teacher. For example, *Does the teacher use a number of different teaching strategies or only a very few?*, or, *Does the teacher utilize many different resources in his or her teaching or use the same resources over and over?* Having variety in instruction contributes to the perceived energy of the teacher and offers students different stimuli during lesson activities to which they may respond. Using different instructional approaches makes the teacher appear more interesting and exciting to students, piques students' natural curiosity to learn, and varies the stimuli in the classroom.

Most students learn best through encounters with a variety of different stimuli. The teacher with variety in the use of instructional techniques is able to offer students a greater number of connecting points to the subject matter as lessons are delivered. Consequently, the teacher who is skilled in using a number of different types of strategies is more effective than the teacher who is limited to only a few approaches.

Teacher Task Orientation

Time on task is a powerful concept when analyzing the teaching-learning process. When one considers that there are only a limited number of hours in the day in which students are in school, and that a good portion of the typical school day is given over to noninstructional activities (e.g., moving from class to class, recess in the lower grades, lunch, traveling to and from the restroom), the question of time available for learning becomes especially critical. Having a high level of meaningful and successful time on task communicates to students that the teacher is well prepared and "in charge" of what is taking place in the classroom. It also communicates where the teacher's instruction is headed and what students will be expected to know or be able to do when the end of the instructional period is reached. Students who are on task are less likely to present behavioral problems for their teachers.

Engagement in the Learning Process

Effective teachers use their time wisely and ensure that their students are active, not passive in the learning process. Jones' theory of management was presented in Chapter 3 identifying that problems of student management are frequently brought about by poor or inappropriate use of time in the classroom. Wasted or idle time leads to problems in management that should and could be avoided. Time in schools and classrooms is often broken down into the following four dimensions.

1. **Allocated Time**: the amount of time a particular teacher or school designates to an identified course, topic, or activity.
2. **Instructional Time**: the portion of Allocated Time that is actually devoted to learning activities.
3. **Engaged Time**: sometimes referred to as time-on-task, Engaged Time is the portion of Instructional Time that students ac-

tually spend directly involved in learning activities.

4. **Academic Learning Time**: Academic Learning Time takes all other forms of time into account and is characterized by students not only paying attention during instructional activities, but also interacting successfully with the content that is being taught; it is that portion of classroom time where students are successfully engaged in meaningful learning experiences.

Teachers who have greater levels of **Academic Learning Time**, *time when students are actively and successfully involved in the lesson's activities*, have students who learn at higher levels.

Given the multifaceted nature of any school, many events take place on a regular basis that compete for time which otherwise could be available for instruction. Instructional time is lost through different disruptions, interruptions, late starts, and less than smooth transitions. Out of a typical school year only 30% to 40% of the time is given over to quality Academic Learning Time (Karweit, 1989; Weinstein, Romano, & Mignano, 2011). Research supports that, the greater the amount of Academic Learning Time in the classroom, the greater the level of student achievement. The best use of time in the classroom is determined, to a large extent, by the degree to which the teacher is fully planned for instruction. The better planned the teacher is for instruction that is relevant to the interests and needs of the students in the classroom, and responsive to their learning styles and abilities, the greater will be the levels of student achievement that are reached.

Student Success Rate

Not only is wise use of time an important characteristic of effective teachers, effective teachers also have higher rates of student success in their teaching. **Student success rate** is defined as *the rate at which students understand and correctly complete their work*. Students should not be involved in just "doing things" in the classroom. What they do should be meaningful, learning-related as to what the teacher has planned for instruction, and result in successful achievement and productivity. Teachers need to know the abilities and interests of their students and plan their instruction accordingly based on this knowledge. Student success is directly related to the level of difficulty of the content being taught. Level of difficulty may be measured by the rate at which students understand and correctly answer questions asked of them and complete their assignments (Borich, 2011). Three levels of difficulty and related success levels are identified as follows:

- **High Success**:   The student understands the subject matter taught and makes only occasional careless errors.
- **Moderate Success**: The student has a partial understanding of the subject matter but makes some substantive errors.
- **Low Success**:   The student has little or no understanding of the subject matter.

Instruction in which few students can be successful falls far short of what needs to be accomplished in the classroom. This type of situation serves no one well. Success breeds success, and students who are successful one day will be more likely to see themselves as being successful on another day (see the discussion of Attribution Theory, Locus of Control, and Teacher Expectations in Chapter 2 as related to reasons given for student success). Likewise, students who experience little or no success have much greater difficulty seeing themselves as being successful and, in the end, actually being successful. If teachers desire for their students to be successful in their learning, they must plan, teach, and evaluate in ways that ensure success for them. Student engagement, i.e., the time students are actively engaged with, thinking about, and working with the content being taught, is closely tied to student success rate (Good & Brophy, 2007; Marzano, Pickering, & Pollock, 2004). Indicators of student success in learning and strategies that a teacher might use to achieve increased levels of student success are presented in Table 4.2.

A problematic characteristic of the American society today is one that focuses on identifying quick solutions or quick fixes to problems. The United States has even been referred to as a "fast food" or "microwave" society. It is no wonder that many teachers take this same outlook into their classrooms expecting to find quick solutions for many of the problems that they find there. The fact is, there are no quick solutions or quick fixes to difficult and complex problems of student learning, motivation and classroom management, and the solutions that work best will be found in the research related to best practice in these areas. It is for this reason that teachers need to not only be informed as to what is in this research but also have the ability to in-

Table 4.2

Teaching Behaviors to Increase Student Success Rates

Teacher Behaviors to Increase Student Success Rates	*Examples of Teaching Strategies to Increase Student Success Rates*
1. Establish unit and lesson content that represents prior learning such as planning lesson sequences that take into consideration relevant prior information.	Create a top-down unit plan where all the lesson outcomes at the bottom of the hierarchy needed to achieve unit outcomes at the top of the hierarchy are identified. Arrange lessons in the order most logical for achieving unit outcomes.
2. Divide instructional stimuli into small chunks, i.e., parts, such as using discrete, focused lessons that can be easily understood by students at their current level.	Plan interdisciplinary thematic units to emphasize the relationships and connections that are easily remembered.
3. Vary the pace at which instructional stimuli are presented and continually build toward a significant ending or key event	Use review, feedback, and testing sessions to create intervals of increasing and decreasing intensity and expectation.

Source: From Borich, G. (2011). *Effective teaching methods: Research-based practice* (7th ed.). Boston: Pearson, p. 15.

vestigate further on their own for satisfactory solutions to problems where such solutions may not be immediately apparent.

EARLY RESEARCH ON BEST TEACHING PRACTICE

As motivation relates to management and management relates to motivation, so does best practice in teaching relate to both of these concepts together. One of the most significant and thorough reviews of research on teacher effectiveness was conducted over forty years ago and is still considered important reading in the field today (Rosenshine & Furst, 1971). Although considerable research has been conducted more recently, the early work of Rosenshine and Furst serves as a sound beginning for the study of effective teaching behaviors related to student achievement. The characteristics of effective teaching identified by Armstrong et al. (1997) and Borich (2011) may be looked upon to some degree as an elaboration and refinement of many of the factors identified in this earlier research.

Of particular importance to the work of Rosenshine and Furst is the understanding given to the meaning of effective teaching. While teachers are expected to accomplish many things in their work, perhaps the most important accomplishment is guiding students to achieve at higher levels. Defining effective teaching as teaching that results in higher levels of student achievement is not to discount the importance of students developing positive feelings about themselves and the world around them and toward learning itself. It does recognize, though, that the primary purpose of the teacher is to guide and advance students in their learning. Rosenshine and Furst identified eleven teacher behaviors or variables (i.e., teaching characteristics or practices) related to student achievement; they are presented here in the order of the degree to which they are so related.

1. Clarity
2. Variability
3. Enthusiasm
4. Task-Oriented and/or Business-Like Behavior
5. Student Opportunity to Learn Criterion Material
6. Use of Student Ideas and General Indirectness
7. Criticism
8. Use of Structuring Comments
9. Types of Questions
10. Probing Behaviors
11. Level of Difficulty of Instruction

Clarity

Teachers who have the ability to explain concepts clearly and who are able to answer student questions so that their students understand the answers that they give are characterized by having clarity in their instruction. When teachers are clear in their communications, their students feel more secure in their learning. They are able to comprehend what is expected of them and, as a result, perform at higher achievement levels.

Variability

Also referred to as instructional variety, variability is represented by the teacher's diversity of information-sending techniques or strategies used during the presentation of lessons. Teachers who have variability in their teaching utilize multiple strategies to get the main ideas of their lessons across to their students. As determined by the purpose of the lesson, effective teachers have the ability to utilize expository lesson delivery as well as organize students for cooperative learning activities. They are capable of exhibiting many different strategies in teaching and do so regularly. Through this variety, especially when strategies are matched to student learning styles, students remain more interested in the learning activities that their teachers have planned for them and learn more as a result.

Enthusiasm

Enthusiasm has been identified as the estimation of the amount of vigor and power displayed by the teacher. It also has been associated with the teacher's level of excitement, energy, involvement, and interest regarding both the subject matter and teaching itself. Although an abstract concept, students definitely have their own ideas about the enthusiasm of their teachers. Students feel they know when their teachers enjoy their work and are excited about being in the classroom and when they are not. Students draw from the enthusiasm shown by their teachers, or at least from what they perceive as their teachers' enthusiasm, and respond accordingly. Teacher enthusiasm is related to the concept of *teacher efficacy* discussed earlier in Chapter 2 as a part of the teacher's attitude toward teaching and student learning. Teachers who exhibit enthusiasm communicate that they are confident in what they are doing, not only in their own abilities, but also in the abilities of their students.

Task-Oriented and/or Business-Like Behavior

Task-oriented teachers project that they know what they expect in student performance and the lessons that they teach and how to attain the student performance that they desire. They are seen by their students as being in charge, knowing what they are doing, organized, and focused on what needs to be accomplished. Being task-oriented and business-like does not mean that the teacher is impersonal, aloof, or distant when working with students. It does communicate that the teacher knows that something important needs to be accomplished and that the teacher and students together will be successful in completing the task that is to be undertaken.

Student Opportunity to Learn Criterion Material

Teachers who are criterion-focused in their teaching communicate to students their expected instructional outcomes prior to beginning their teaching and then teach specifically to the students' successful attainment of these desired outcomes. What is desired is not kept secret; there is no mystery. Students know what is expected of them and how they will be evaluated (i.e., the criteria used) as to their level of success in achieving the identified learning outcomes. This security of direction and understanding of the evaluation process is important to students as they engage in the teacher's planned learning activities. This understanding also is important to the teacher in that it offers the teacher additional focus and direction in addressing stated learning objectives.

Use of Student Ideas and General Indirectness

The use of student ideas by teachers during instruction and, in so doing, communicating to students that their ideas and input are important enhances student achievement. The use of student ideas is a good way to personalize the instruction and is an important part of *indirect teaching*. Students have higher levels of meaningful participation and interest in their learning when their ideas are regularly incorporated into the learning process and they have greater academic success as they perceive their teachers as valuing both them as individuals as well as their ideas.

Criticism

A negative relationship exists between the use of teacher criticism and student achievement. This point was identified earlier by Armstrong et al. (1997). Teachers who are characterized by using criticism in their teaching, often seen by students as an attempt to justify their authority, typically have students who achieve less in most subject areas. Teachers who use frequent criticism are often perceived by their students as being less prepared for their work and less sure of themselves. The use of criticism can create a threatening environment for students, push students away, and detract from the learning process resulting in lower student achievement.

Use of Structuring Comments

The teacher's use of structuring comments in communicating with students, i.e., alerting students to the more important instructional events or important points which are to follow in the lesson, is highly recommended and supported by educational research. The use of structuring comments is appropriate at the start of lessons and at the start of different sections of lessons. Such comments help students focus on and attend to what will take place during the instruction that is to follow. Using structuring comments also projects to students that the teacher is well planned and has a clear understanding of where the learning activity is headed.

Types of Questions

Effective teachers are skilled at asking both higher and lower level questions of cognition; the use of both types is related to student achievement. The classic system of question categorization identified by Gallagher and Aschner (1963) is helpful in understanding levels and types of questions. This system places questions into four categories: *cognitive memory, convergent, divergent,* and *evaluative.* It can serve as a guide for teachers to the different cognitive levels of questions that they may use in their teaching and the intellectual processing on the part of students that they invoke. The use of different types of questions helps to stimulate student thinking, maintain student interest, and projects greater variability in teaching. Researchers have found that many teachers ask a small proportion of high level questions; this has been found to be true even when teaching high ability students (Ratcliff, Jones, Costner, Knight, Disney, Savage-Davis, Sheehan, & Hunt, 2012). The following elaborations in Table 4.3 of the basic characteristics of the questions used in this system will help in the analysis of this teacher behavior.

Table 4.3

Types of Questions and Question Examples by Cognitive Level

Types of Questions	*Examples of Questions*
Cognitive Memory Questions: questions that ask students to recall previously learned and memorized information; single-word answers are often used; answers tend to sound alike and are predictable; even though answers could be lengthy, they do not require creative thought and are classified as being clearly right or wrong; behaviors such as recalling, recognizing, and reporting are common responses to such questions.	Examples of **Cognitive Memory Questions**: 1. Who painted the Mona Lisa? 2. What is the city with the largest population in Indiana? 3. In what year was the Declaration of Independence signed?
Convergent Questions: questions that ask students to put facts or concepts together to obtain the single correct answer; answers to convergent questions are more complex than answers to cognitive memory questions but are still classified as either right or wrong; questions may require students to make comparisons, explain facts or concepts, state or describe relationships, or solve problems using learned procedures.	Examples of **Convergent Questions**: 1. What is the relationship between crude oil and plastic? 2. How are amphibians and reptiles alike? 3. How are present methods of communication different from those used in the 1800s?
Divergent Questions: questions that ask students to engage in divergence of thought and produce responses that are original; student thinking is more creative at this level of questioning; questions may require students to predict, hypothesize, or infer; expressions such as "what if" are common to questions in this category.	Examples of **Divergent Questions**: 1. What do you think our society will be like in terms of technology in one hundred years? 2. If you were in charge of our town, what is the first thing you would do? 3. What might happen to our voting system if all voting was done electronically?
Evaluative Questions: questions that ask students to make judgments or evaluations based on logically derived evidence; evidence is derived from the use of the levels of thought identified in the previous three question categories; students also must defend or explain their judgments based on criteria that they designate or which have been established by others.	Examples of **Evaluative Questions**: 1. Do you believe that people are more inquisitive today than in the past? Why do you think this? 2. Who do you think is the best candidate in the presidential election? Why? 3. Where do you think would be the most exciting place to go on a winter vacation? Why?

Source: From Hunt, G., Wiseman, D., & Touzel, T. (2009). *Effective teaching: Preparation and implementation*. Springfield, IL: Charles C Thomas.

Probing Behaviors

Probing behaviors occur when the teacher asks students to go deeper into their thinking or to elaborate on comments made or positions taken. The use of probing behaviors, typically through the use of probing questions, communicates to students that the teacher is interested in knowing more about their ideas. Such behaviors cause students to review their ideas and explore them more deeply. They also help the teacher in creating a classroom atmosphere that includes student ideas and general indirectness that was described earlier. Since by its very purpose probing for student ideas does not involve looking at what students say as being right or wrong, probing behaviors offer excellent opportunities for teachers to praise students for their thinking. To be effective, probing behaviors need to be carried out in a way that is seen by students as being authentic, nonthreatening, and nonjudgmental.

Level of Difficulty of Instruction

Teachers who have created learning environments where students feel appropriately challenged, but not overchallenged, have established environments where students achieve at higher levels. Teachers should offer instruction that is neither too hard nor too easy for students. Much has been said in recent years about the importance of increasing academic rigor in schools and holding students to higher standards. While important, this should not be done at the expense of students who are simply unable to reach the higher standards that have been established. If students perceive that the teacher's level of difficulty of instruction is beyond their ability, they may either withdraw from the instruction or act out against it. Knowing the abilities and interests of their students, it is important for teachers to establish levels of instruction which are out of the immediate reach of their students (therefore not too easy), but which are reachable with effort and teacher assistance (therefore appropriately challenging). In terms of fully knowing their students and utilizing this knowledge in planning and delivering their instruction, it is helpful for teachers to apply the concept of the *zone of proximal development* to their teaching. The **zone of proximal development** is defined as *a range of tasks that a student cannot yet do alone but can accomplish when assisted by a more skilled partner* (Eggen & Kauchak, 2013). To continually challenge students in appropriate ways, it is important for learning tasks to be presented at the outer reaches of this zone. Presenting tasks that are simply too complex and thought to be unreasonable by students will cause student interest in the tasks to diminish as they will see the tasks as being too difficult for them to be successful. Working toward them will appear to be not worth their effort for this reason and whatever interest they may have will wane. Likewise, if the teacher too regularly presents tasks at the lower end of this zone, students will lose interest because the tasks will be viewed as being not challenging enough, too simplistic, and unimportant.

MORE CURRENT RESEARCH ON BEST TEACHING PRACTICE

Additional research on best teaching practices has been conducted since the work of Rosenshine and Furst in the early 1970s. Such factors as teacher knowledge, clarity and organization, and warmth and enthusiasm have each been consistently identified over the years as characteristics of effective teachers (Woolfolk, 2013). Although more current research has expanded the knowledge base related to best teaching practice, it has not contradicted earlier findings. The essential teaching characteristics or skills in Table 4.4 are correlated with student achievement.

Teacher Beliefs and Behaviors

The consideration of teacher beliefs and behaviors goes beyond seeing the teacher as merely exhibiting "good" or "bad" beliefs and behaviors. Were it this simple, the influence of teacher beliefs and behaviors on student learning would have been much more completely understood long before now. Teachers have studied these characteristics, researchers have studied these characteristics, and students have responded to the beliefs and behaviors of their teachers since the beginning of formal education. Teachers have responsibility for their beliefs and behaviors and those of their students, both positive and negative. Where students have negative beliefs and behaviors regarding themselves or their learning, teachers need to identify the causes of these beliefs and behaviors so that they may help them become more positive for their learning to advance. An important aspect of this process re-

Table 4.4

Essential Teaching Skills and Cognitive Theory Applications

Teaching Skills	Teaching Skill Components	Application to Cognitive Learning Theory
Teacher Beliefs and Behaviors	✓ Personal teaching efficacy ✓ High positive expectations ✓ Modeling and enthusiasm ✓ Caring	Models desired behaviors, increases self-efficacy and helps students meet their need for relatedness.
Organization	✓ Starting instruction on time ✓ Having materials ready ✓ Creating well-established routines	Reduces the cognitive load on teachers' and students' working memories and helps establish and maintain students' equilibrium.
Review	✓ Beginning-of-lesson review ✓ Interim reviews	Activates prior knowledge retrieved from long-term memory, to which new knowledge is attached.
Focus	✓ Capture attention ✓ Maintain attention	Attracts students' attention and provides a conceptual umbrella for the lesson.
Questioning	✓ Questioning frequency ✓ Equitable distribution ✓ Prompting ✓ Wait-time	Encourages students to become cognitively active. Provides scaffolding.
Feedback	✓ Immediate ✓ Specific ✓ Corrective information ✓ Positive emotional tone	Provides students with information they use to determine whether the knowledge they've constructed is valid.
Closure	✓ End-of-lesson summary	Contributes to schema construction and meaningful encoding.
Communication	✓ Precise terms ✓ Connected discourse ✓ Transition signals ✓ Emphasis	Makes information understandable and meaningful. Maintains learner attention.

Source: From Eggen, P., & Kauchak, D. (2013). *Educational psychology: Windows on classrooms* (9th ed.). Boston: Pearson, p. 445.

lates to teachers themselves and the degree to which they understand their own beliefs and behaviors.

As presented earlier, teachers who hold the belief that they and their schools can have a positive effect on their students and their learning are said to have high *teacher efficacy* (Bruning, Schraw, & Ronning, 1995). A teacher's sense of efficacy is one of the few personal characteristic of teachers that predicts student achievement (Tschannen-Moran & Woolfolk Hoy, 2001; Tschannen-Moran, Woolfolk Hoy, & Hoy, 1998; Woolfolk Hoy, Hoy, and Davis, 2009). Classrooms with such teachers have increased student achievement. Teachers with high efficacy work well with low achieving students and use praise rather than criticism to motivate and reward them. Such teachers use their time effectively and are more accepting of the unique, individual qualities of their students. High efficacy teachers do not give up on students and readily change their strategies and adopt and adapt instructional materials as needed to meet their students' needs (Poole, Okeafor, & Sloan, 1989). Low efficacy teachers are more critical of their students and persevere less when seeking solutions to their students' learning and motivational problems. Such teachers do not hold strong beliefs that they really can make a difference in the lives of their students (Kagan, 1992). Teachers with low efficacy tend to stratify their classes more by student ability, or what they perceive to be student ability, while giving more effort, attention, and affection to those students felt to have higher ability (Ashton & Webb, 1986). Low efficacy teachers also perceive their students' behaviors, particularly those of low-achieving students, in terms of potential threats to the orderliness of their classrooms. Teachers with high efficacy are not as likely to feel threatened by the misbehavior or potential misbehavior of their students. They are less likely to experience burnout and to be more satisfied with their jobs.

Organization

Being well organized does not mean being overly restrictive. Students can tell if a teacher is organized or not. Teachers who are organized, or at least perceived by their students as being organized, have higher achieving students than those who do not have or do not project this quality.

Organization involves management of the classroom in terms of its physical elements and rules and procedures as well as academic concerns with respect to the teaching process. **Management organization** refers to *the general organizational structure and procedures that the teacher has developed to keep the classroom running smoothly.* Organized teachers have their teaching materials ready when it is time to begin their lessons, start on time, have established learning routines (e.g., certain ways of taking roll and collecting papers to minimize the time these activities take and making transitions from one activity to another quickly and smoothly), and engage their students throughout the entire instructional period. Established routines in the classroom enable teachers and their students to know what to anticipate as the teacher's instruction moves forward. Effective management organization allows for classroom time to be used productively. Although the ability to be spontaneous as the situation dictates is important, teachers who have well-established routines and procedures bring a positive predictability to their teaching giving their students a greater sense of order, balance, and direction. This order and balance, i.e., equilibrium, and the direction that results from it, contribute to higher levels of student learning. **Academic organization** is seen as *the teacher's means of ordering and arranging information for instruction so that students will be able to understand the information communicated.* Effective teachers have specific organization schemes to assist students in ordering and arranging information. Being well organized academically does not mean teachers lack spontaneity or the ability to teach to the moment. Rather, academic organization refers to the teacher being well prepared to carry out instruction in a way that assists the students as they learn and remember what is being taught. The use of diagrams, outlines, hierarchies, schematics, and technology can be significant instructional resources in not only helping teachers in presenting organized lessons, but also in assisting students in making better organization of and use of the information being presented. The teacher's ability to be clear in communications with students discussed earlier is related to the teacher's ability to be academically organized. Good teacher organization is founded upon the routines, procedures, and rules the teacher has developed for both student motivation and classroom management that effectively organize and use time wisely, thus enabling the classroom to run in an efficient and effective manner.

Review

Clear *review* consistently serves as an aid to learning and enhancing academic achievement. **Review** is *when the teacher summarizes important points from previous work in helping students to link what has been learned to what will be taught in the future; review can occur at different points of the lesson, either close to the beginning, midpoint during the body of the lesson, or at the end.* Review at the end of the lesson is also referred to as closure. The knowledge that students construct depends on what they already know. Beginning reviews help students activate their prior knowledge needed to construct their new understanding. When review is used effectively, teachers are able to guide students beyond a focus on only the specific information presented in the lesson into more substantive conceptual understandings (Dempster, 1991). Review provides the teacher with valuable information to identify the most important place, or perhaps way, to begin the next lesson or part of the lesson.

Focus

Focus is an important aspect of the teacher's ability to communicate and attend to ideas in the classroom. An important part of focus is bringing student attention to the lesson at the very beginning of the instructional experience and then maintaining this attention throughout the remainder of the lesson. This has been identified as establishing an *anticipatory set* (Hunter, 1984). **Anticipatory set** is *the mental or attitudinal foundation established by the teacher for the students at the beginning of the instructional experience that helps students understand what they may anticipate in the instruction which will follow.* This has also been described as using a "hook" to gain students' attention and interest and then to maintain both during the lesson (Lemov, 2010). When students are focused at the beginning of the lesson, they are better connected to the body of the lesson that follows. Teachers who have good introductory focus more easily gain and maintain student attention and provide a stronger connection for the students with the material being taught as the lesson progresses. Focus motivates students, increases their curiosity, and makes the lesson more interesting. Teachers often can gain student attention successfully through the use of certain visual or auditory sensory techniques such as pictures, models, songs, concrete objects, riddles, whiteboard, Internet, PowerPoint, and other computer technology. The importance of using such aids, classically referred to as **advance organizers**, or *the use of introductory statements or activities to frame new content as a part of the lesson focus,* was developed in detail by Ausubel (1978). The use of focus techniques brings students more into the overall mainstream of the lesson than into any specific part of it. This helps students avoid difficulties in understanding the main intent of the teacher's instruction and assists them in attending to the important individual components that make it up.

Questioning

Research on teacher questioning has increased considerably over the last twenty years. Questioning is considered by many to be the most important tool that teachers have for helping students build understanding. While it is important that teachers have well-developed questioning skills, such skills do not develop naturally. The development of such skills comes only through specific question-asking applications that are consistently analyzed in terms of whether or not the questions, and the way they were asked, elicited the desired outcomes (Eggen & Kauchak, 2012; Kauchak & Eggen, 2012). Research continues to reinforce the relationship between the quality of teachers' questioning and student achievement.

Though some might think that certain questions are preferred over others, such as high cognitive over low cognitive or vice versa, this is not the case. Different types of questions serve different learning and teaching purposes. The teacher should select questions as they relate to the learning outcomes desired. If the objective of the lesson is to focus on the development of certain basic skills or remembered information, low cognitive questions are of greater value. If the lesson's purpose is to place students in situations where they will be expected to analyze or evaluate information, or share their personal ideas, high cognitive questions are more appropriate (Bloom, Englehart, Furst, Hill, & Krathwohl, 1956; Good & Brophy, 2000). Both high and low cognitive questions correlate positively with student achievement. *Frequency, equitable distribution, prompting,* and *wait-time* are considered to be characteristics of effective questioning strategies (Eggen & Kauchak, 2013; O'Flahavan, Hartman, & Pearson, 1988; Tobin, 1987).

1. **Frequency**: generally, the more questions the better; greater numbers of questions allow for more students to be involved in the dynamics of a lesson and more opportunities for the teacher to monitor the students' and the lesson's progress; questioning increases the opportunity for student involvement and contributes to improved achievement.
2. **Equitable Distribution**: teachers should strive for a pattern of questioning where all students are called on as equally as possible; more questioning with equal distribution across the class increases the opportunity for giving students more feedback and helps students stay motivated and connected to the lesson; this

reduces the likelihood that students will drift away from the instruction and become involved in misconduct behaviors.

3. **Prompting**: prompting helps students respond to questions by
   providing cues after an incorrect or incomplete answer or silence; an additional question or statement the teacher uses to
   elicit an appropriate student response after a student answers incorrectly is considered prompting; prompting is not appropriate
   if the question calls for remembering specific factual information
   but is of value when studying conceptual, procedural knowledge
   and when using cognitive processes beyond remembering (Anderson & Krathwohl, 2001).

4. **Wait-time**: wait-time is the period of silence before or after a
   student is asked a question and when the teacher speaks again;
   the use of wait-time increases student learning by giving students time to think; in most classrooms, regardless of grade or
   ability level, wait-times are very short, frequently less than one
   second (Rowe, 1986); research suggests that increasing wait-time
   to at least three seconds will positively impact classroom climate
   and student learning (Kastens & Liben, 2007); wait-time should
   be implemented strategically; for example, if students are practicing basic skills such as multiplication facts, quicker answers
   are desirable and wait-times should be short, and, if a student
   appears to be uneasy, the teacher may wish to intervene earlier.

Feedback

Few individuals function well in environments characterized by ambiguity and uncertainty; students certainly do not learn in environments characterized by confusion that brings about stress and pressure.
Teachers who regularly provide feedback to their students regarding
the accuracy or appropriateness of their responses and their work have
higher achieving students (Hattie & Timperley, 2007). The most effective feedback provides constructive information, praise, and encouragement as appropriate and is immediate and specific. Individual feedback that is aimed at constructively correcting errors made during
learning positively affects student performance and attitude (Elawar &
Corno, 1985). Such feedback not only results in increased motivation,
but also in increased achievement (Brophy, 2010). It contributes to a
greater sense of balance and self-regulation as students are able to mon-

itor their own progress and helps students create associations that result in more meaningful learning and advancement toward stated goals.

Teacher feedback to students generally comes in one of two forms: written or oral. Providing written feedback poses a challenge for some teachers as it is more time consuming. Because providing constructive written feedback can take more time, many teachers often provide only sketchy written feedback for their students or information that is not terribly helpful. Although it may take more time, written feedback that is specific to the nature of the students' performance is an important part of effective teaching and is positively related to student achievement. Specific written feedback helps students focus on their weaknesses and correct them through their own efforts. The time spent in giving more detailed feedback should result in savings in instructional time. It should also result in improvements in student attitudes that will have a positive impact on classroom climate. It is suggested that teachers regularly ask themselves the following four questions when they review their students' work: (1) *What is the key error if there is one?* (2) *What is the probable reason for the error?* (3) *How can I guide the student to avoid the error in the future?* (4) *What did the student do well that could be noted?* Using questions such as these as guides in responding to student work in written form will result in benefits to student learning and to the learning environment as a whole (Elawar & Corno, 1985). As teachers use more and more electronic instruction, the ability to use written feedback will be especially important. Oral feedback is more easily given as it can be used in ongoing discussions and question-and-answer periods. The constructive value of oral feedback is also important to enhancing student achievement. Quick, one-word responses, or responses that merely inform the student that he or she is correct or not correct, are not as helpful as more elaborate responses. More elaborate or extended responses not only let the student know that he or she was correct or incorrect but why this was the case.

Praise

Praise is one of the most common and adaptable forms of teacher feedback. Some interesting and not especially positive patterns in teacher use of praise have been identified through educational research (Good & Brophy, 2007).

- Praise is not used nearly as often as most teachers believe, being used less than five times per class.
- Praise for good behavior is actually quite rare and occurs only once every two or more hours in the elementary grades and less than that as students get older.
- Praise is influenced by the type of student as much as by the quality of the responses that students give. High-achieving, well-behaved, and attentive students receive greater amounts of praise than do low achieving and inattentive students.
- Praise is often given by teachers based on the responses that they expect to receive as much as it is on the answers that the students actually give.

Table 4.5 provides a helpful analysis of the difference between the effective and ineffective use of praise.

Considering the potential for positive impact from the use of praise in the classroom, in particular in the areas of student motivation, management, and learning, it is recommended that teachers praise:

1. genuinely,
2. immediately,
3. accomplishments that students may not be aware of,
4. strategically with different types of students,
5. the effort as well as the answer,
6. specifically, and
7. judiciously.

Understanding the characteristics of the effective use of praise is important as they impact the student's motivation to stay on task or become involved in the teacher's lesson. Teachers are advised to use variety as well as frequency in their approaches to praising their students. Some teachers fall into a routine pattern of using the same praise words over and over again, such as "good" or "well done." In that praise is a very special type of reinforcer, its potency is enhanced when it avoids being too routine. To add variety to their approaches used to praise, and keep themselves and their praise exciting and more interesting, it is recommended that teachers utilize as much variety as possible in their praising vocabulary. For example, words and phrases such as "terrific," "very good job," "outstanding," "excellent," "awesome," and "wonderful" will make the teachers' praise efforts more interesting and positively received by their students. In the end, the teacher's praise

Table 4.5

Characteristics of Effective and Ineffective Use of Praise

Effective Praise	*Ineffective Praise*
Is delivered contingently	Is delivered randomly or unsystematically
Specifies the particulars of the accomplishment	Is restricted to global, positive reactions
Shows spontaneity, variety, and other signs of credibility; suggests clear attention to the student's accomplishment	Shows a bland uniformity which suggests a conditioned response made with minimal attention
Rewards attainment of specified performance criteria (that can include effort criteria)	Rewards mere participation without consideration of performance processes or outcomes
Provides information to students about their competence or the value of their accomplishments	Provides no information at all or gives students no information about their status
Orients students toward better appreciation of their own task-related behavior and thinking about problem solving	Orients students toward comparing themselves with others and thinking about competing
Uses students' own prior accomplishments as the context for describing present accomplishments	Uses the accomplishments of peers as the context for describing students' present accomplishments
Is given in recognition of noteworthy effort or success at difficult (for this student) tasks	Is given without regard to the effort expended or with meaning of the accomplishment (for this student)
Attributes success to effort and ability, implying that similar successes can be expected in the future	Attributes success to ability alone or to external factors such as luck or easy task
Fosters endogenous attributions (students believe that they expend effort on the task because they enjoy the task and/or want to develop task-relevant skills)	Foster exogenous attributions (students believe that they expend effort on the task for external reasons such as to please the teacher, win a competition or reward, etc.)
Focuses students' attention on their own task-relevant behavior	Focuses students' attention on the teacher as an external authority figure who is manipulating them
Fosters appreciation of and desirable attributions about task-relevant behavior after the process is completed	Intrudes into the ongoing process, distracting attention from task-relevant behavior

Source: From Alderman, M. (2008). *Motivation for achievement: Possibilities for teaching and learning* (3rd ed.). New York: Routledge, p. 259.

will be more motivational as it will be seen as being more dynamic and individualized by the students.

Closure

Closure is *a type of summary review that occurs at the end of the instructional period that enables the student to end the lesson with a better understanding of the topic and a place to build on in the future.* This can be accomplished through a number of techniques such as the use of questions, short written assignments, or classroom discussion. The use of closure normally provides the teacher with valuable information related to identifying the most important place, or perhaps way, to begin the next lesson. An effective use of closure is to ask students to state in their own words important points of information covered in the lesson. This enables students to end the lesson with a better understanding of the lesson's content. It also serves to inform the teacher. If teachers are uncertain as to what level of understanding their students have at the end of one lesson, they will not be well prepared to begin the next lesson that follows. They may know what they taught, but this does not mean that they know what their students have learned and understand.

Communication

As previously discussed, there is a positive correlation between language clarity and student achievement, reinforcing the importance of teachers being precise and clear in the use of their verbal communication (Cruickshank, 1985: Snyder, Bushur, Hoeksema, Olson, Clark, & Snyder, 1991). Four aspects of language clarity have been identified related to best teaching practice:

1. **Precise Terminology**: the teacher eliminates or restricts the use of vague and ambiguous words and phrases, e.g., perhaps, maybe, usually, might, and so on, from explanations and responses to students' questions, presentations, and interactions with students.

2. **Connected Discourse**: the teacher's presentation is thematically well connected and leads to a goal, going point by point; the absence of this type of discourse is communication that may seem rambling to the student, being disjointed and not appropriately linked; if the lesson isn't clear, is presented in a poor or confusing order of events, or if incidental information is included without indicating how it relates to the topic, classroom discourse becomes disconnected.

3. **Transition Signals**: transition signals assist in blending one topic area with the next that follows; without such signals, the teacher may be seen as merely, and abruptly, moving or jumping from topic to topic or point to point; transition signals are verbal statements indicating that one idea is ending and another is beginning; since all students are not at the same place cognitively, transition signals alert the students that the lesson is making a conceptual shift, i.e., moving to a new topic, and allows them to prepare for it.

4. **Emphasis**: emphasis denotes the teacher specifically identifying information that is to be remembered; phrases such as, "This is important," and "Be sure to remember this," are examples of the use of emphasis; if something is of special importance, tell the students; emphasis consists of verbal and vocal cues that help students focus on important information; repeating a point or asking a question about a point previously introduced can also be an effective form of emphasis.

Students cannot be expected to learn at their maximum potentials when their teachers are not clear. Though a teacher may comment that a particular student does not pay attention and does not understand something, this is really more the teacher's problem than the student's. It is the teacher who must be expert in communication and reaching students with the language used in the classroom. Teacher clarity was first on the list of teacher behaviors or characteristics identified in the early research on effective teaching related to student achievement (Rosenshine & Furst, 1971).

Having in-depth skills and knowledge of instructional strategies will produce only limited results if the teacher does not also know when as well as how to use them. Knowing and understanding skills may be considered the science of teaching where knowing when to use certain skills, and with whom, may be considered the art. Marzano (2007) suggested a comprehensive model, i.e., framework, for ensuring quality teaching that balances the need for research-based information with the importance of understanding the strengths and weaknesses of individual students. The model is presented in the form of the following 10 teaching and instructional design questions.

1. What will I do to establish and communicate learning goals, track student progress, and celebrate success?

2. What will I do to help students effectively interact with new knowledge?
3. What will I do to help students practice and deepen their understanding of new knowledge?
4. What will I do to help students generate and test hypotheses about new knowledge?
5. What will I do to engage students?
6. What will I do to establish or maintain classroom rules and procedures?
7. What will I do to recognize and acknowledge adherence and lack of adherence to classroom rules and procedures?
8. What will I do to establish and maintain effective relationships with students?
9. What will I do to communicate high expectations for all students?
10. What will I do to develop effective lessons organized into a cohesive unit?

In addition to the work already cited, Rosenshine and his colleagues identified six specific teaching functions or basic teaching skills and processes building on the research on effective teaching (Rosenshine, 1988; Rosenshine & Stevens, 1986; Woolfolk, 2013). These include:

1. **Review and check the previous day's work**. Reteach if students do not have an acceptable grasp of the material.
2. **Present new material**. Make the purpose of the lesson clear, teaching in incremental steps, and provide examples and nonexamples.
3. **Provide guided practice**. Give practice problems, question students, and listen for misunderstandings. Reteach as needed.
4. **Give feedback and correctives**. This needs to be regularly done and based on the answers that students give. Reteach as needed.
5. **Provide independent practice**. Give students the opportunity to apply the new learning on their own in various settings such as homework, seatwork, and cooperative groups. The success rate during independent practice should be about 95%. Based on prior teaching, students should practice until the skills become over-learned and automatic and where they are confident with their understanding.

6. **Review weekly and monthly**. This will help consolidate learning and should be done regularly; this can be done through reviews of homework and tests. Reteach as needed.

The six teaching functions identified here are not considered as being necessarily sequential, i.e., to be followed in a particular order. However, they are recognized as elements of effective teaching practice and should be used as needed and appropriate to organize lessons and content, present material, check for understanding, and guide new teaching and reteaching as these activities are used to enhance student learning.

The last fifteen to twenty years has seen special attention given to teaching practices related to student learning styles, brain research, and teaching and learning standards. The teaching practices that have been identified can be important to teachers when paired with the best research linked to their implementation. These practices reinforce earlier educational research and are based on research findings from field settings along with actual classroom experiences of teachers. Most teachers today are especially interested in information that is as real-world oriented and as practical as it can be. The following ten teaching practices are believed to meet these criteria (Tiletson, 2005). They incorporate current brain research and learning styles information to provide a framework for classroom instruction.

1. Create an enriched and emotionally supportive learning environment.
2. Differentiate instruction using a variety of teaching strategies that address different learning styles.
3. Select and use strategies that help students make connections from prior learning and experiences to new learning and across disciplines.
4. Teach for long-term memory as a primary goal.
5. Guide students to construct knowledge through higher-level thinking skills.
6. Use collaborative learning as an integral part of the classroom.
7. Bridge the gap between all students, regardless of race, socioeconomic status, sex, or creed.
8. Evaluate student learning through the use of a variety of authentic assessments.
9. Teach for in-depth understanding that leads to real-world prac-

tices; promote real-world applications of learning.

10. Teach in ways that provide a seamless integration of technology for high-quality instruction.

When examining effective teachers and building on the research reported, teacher characteristics felt to be the most essential may be placed into the three organizing categories: *knowledge, skills,* and *dispositions* (Burden & Byrd, 2013).

Knowledge: Although subject matter knowledge in and of itself is not sufficient to ensure effective teaching, teachers must know the subjects that they teach to be effective. In addition to knowledge of subject matter, teachers also need to have three other types of knowledge.

1. **Professional Knowledge**: knowledge about teaching in general; this includes knowledge about the historical, economic, sociological, philosophical, and psychological understanding of schooling and education. It also includes knowledge about learning, diversity, technology, professional ethics, legal and policy issues, pedagogy, and the roles and responsibilities of the profession of teaching.

2. **Pedagogical Knowledge**: knowledge that includes the general concepts, theories, methods, and research about effective teaching, no matter the content area. This knowledge includes general teaching methods.

3. **Pedagogical Content Knowledge**: knowledge of teaching methods and approaches specific to the particular subject, or the application of certain strategies in a special way. This includes a level of understanding of the content to be able to teach it in a variety of ways, drawing on the cultural backgrounds and prior knowledge and experiences of the students.

To be effective, teachers must have: (1) knowledge about their particular subject matter content, (2) foundational knowledge about teaching and learning, (3) knowledge about teaching methods in general, and (4) knowledge about teaching strategies and methods unique to their particular subjects.

Skills: Teachers must have the necessary skills to use their knowledge effectively in making decisions about basic teaching functions such as planning for, implementing, and assessing instruction to ensure that all students are learning.

Dispositions: Teachers must have appropriate dispositions, i.e., values, commitments, and professional ethics, that influence their behaviors to promote learning for all students. Dispositions are guided by beliefs and attitudes related to values such as caring, fairness, honesty, responsibility, and social justice. While affective concepts, and in the minds of teachers, dispositions may be seen in teacher behaviors.

One important way to illustrate the connectedness between motivation, management, and instructional practice is to look at the potential for the teacher to be proactive in avoiding student misbehavior problems through his or her teaching practice. This approach to preventing problems typically pays great dividends in terms of the reduction of management problems and the improvement of the quality of the teacher's instruction at the same time. Table 4.6 offers a review of principles to follow for working with students in a way that establishes a positive and productive classroom where students learn and have a satisfying educational experience.

ANALYZING CLASSROOMS
FOR BEST PRACTICE IN TEACHING

While it is critical that teachers have a solid knowledge base of information related to student motivation, classroom management, and best practice in teaching, as discussed, having this knowledge base alone is not sufficient for teachers to consistently establish and maintain well-managed classrooms where motivated students achieve at high levels. Given the availability of so much information related to effective teaching, if this were the case, many teachers would be experiencing far fewer student motivation and classroom management problems than they presently do. And, students would be learning at much higher levels than they presently are. It is clear that merely having information on best practice in teaching does not guarantee the appropriate application of this information to the teacher's behavior in the classroom.

Teachers must take charge of their own individual classrooms and act in informed and deliberate ways for those classrooms to reflect the best practice that they desire (Cangelosi, 2000). The role of the teacher in instruction is integral to the teacher's role in student motivation and classroom management. The Teaching Process Model is recommended as a system for approaching classroom instruction in such a way that

Table 4.6

Considerations for Preventing Misbehavior Through Classroom Practice

Principle for Practice	Explanation of Principle
Maintain focus on your major tasks in teaching.	Maintain a focus on the major tasks at hand. These tasks are to help students be successful in achieving educational objects, to promote student learning, and to help students develop the knowledge and skills to be successful in the classroom and beyond.
Understand your students' needs and how to meet them.	Know what the student' like and dislike, what motivates them, their needs and desires, and what influences their lives. Use this information to create an appropriate learning environment.
Understand and respect ethnic/cultural differences.	Teachers will be more prepared to facilitate learning and guide behavior with an understanding of the ethnic or cultural background of their students.
Know what causes misbehavior and how to deal with those causes.	Take steps to reduce or remove the causes of misbehavior.
Provide clear rules and procedures to guide student conduct.	Rules and procedures need to be clearly identified and taught so students understand the behavioral expectations of the classroom.
Have a specific plan for responding to misbehavior with a hierarchy of interventions.	Have a specific set of strategies to stop the misbehavior, keep students positively on track, and preserve good relations.
Reduce the use of punitive methods of control.	Coercive or punitive environments may promote antisocial behavior. Other techniques that involve the students in creating a positive learning environment are more desirable.
Take actions to establish a cooperative, responsible classroom.	Use techniques to maintain attention and involvement, reinforce desired behaviors, promote student accountability and responsibility, and create a positive learning community.
Involve students meaningfully in making decisions.	Decisions can involve things such as the selection of classroom rules and procedures, instructional activities and assessments, and curriculum materials. Student involvement generates commitment to the learning process and to the classroom environment.
Teach critical social skills.	Many students lack the social skills necessary to relate positively to peers and to do well academically. Teachers who help students develop these social skills help promote learning and successful classroom discipline.
Involve families to a reasonable degree.	Communicate with families regularly about what is taking place in the classroom and about the progress of their children. Make it clear that their support is needed and desired.

Source: From Burden, P., & Byrd, D. (2013). *Methods for effective teaching: Meeting the needs of all students* (6th ed.). Boston: Pearson, pp. 227–228.

the instruction will be systematically responsive to issues of motivation and management. The Model is comprised of the following six procedural steps.

1. Determine needs of students.
2. Determine learning goal.
3. Design learning activities.
4. Prepare for the learning activities.
5. Conduct the learning activities.
6. Determine how well students have achieved the learning goal.

The Teaching Process Model provides an advance organizer for systematically and effectively teaching organized, well-thought-out lessons and to, if needed, teach students to replace uncooperative behaviors or misbehaviors with cooperative, positive ones. Through the teacher's instruction, in particular through the first step in understanding student needs, followed by clearly identifying learning goals and activities, the teacher will be able to proactively approach the teaching process in a way that will lessen the occurrence of unwanted student behaviors.

It is the ability of the teacher to reflect on and use this information that makes the greatest difference between a teacher who is a poor manager and motivator and one who is skilled in these areas. Recall Tameka's case study (*Tameka's Planning and Analysis*) presented in Chapter 1. Tameka reflected on her problems and made direct plans to deal with them. The Model for Reflection and Inquiry introduced earlier is recommended to guide this reflection.

Reflection in and of itself, though, may produce little positive change. The key to the most effective reflection includes the appropriate use of relevant information. The third step of the Model for Reflection and Inquiry is Collection of Relevant Data. It is in this step, where relevant information is deliberately sought, that teachers perform a key step in the inquiry process. The knowledge that teachers have about student motivation, classroom management, and best teaching practice greatly influences the benefits that will come from this step. The depth of information collected and the appropriate use made of it will determine the level of the quality of the teacher's problem solving.

A variety of helpful approaches are available for the systematic review of one's teaching practice. While they have the potential to be evaluative, virtually all approaches are grounded in the purpose of assisting teachers in improving their instructional practice.

Table 4.7

Rating Scale for Teaching Effectiveness

Effectiveness Concept/Behavior	*Rating 1*	*Rating 3*	*Rating 5*
Lesson scope	No learning objective is apparent. The focus and scope of the lesson are uncertain.	The learning objective is unclear. The lesson covers too much or too little content.	A clear learning objective is apparent. The scope of the lesson is effective for reaching the objective.
Organization	Materials are not prepared and ready prior to the lesson. Routines are not apparent. Instructional time is wasted.	Some materials are prepared in advance, and some routines are apparent. Instructional time is used reasonably well.	Instructional time is maximized with materials prepared in advance and well-established routines are apparent.
Quality of examples and nonexamples	Examples and nonexamples are not used.	Examples and nonexamples are used but are inadequate to accurately represent the topic	A variety of high-quality examples in context are used to represent the topic.
Review	No review of previous work is conducted.	A brief and superficial review of previous work is present.	A thorough review of ideas necessary to understand the present topic is conducted.
Questioning frequency	The teacher lectured. Few questions were asked.	Some questions were asked. Much of the content was delivered through lecture.	The lesson was developed with questioning throughout.
Equitable distribution of questions	Questions were not directed to specific students.	Some questions were directed to individual students. Volunteers were called on most frequently.	All students in the class were called on as equally as possible, and questions were directed to students by name.
Wait-time and prompting	Little wait-time was given. Unanswered questions were directed to other students.	Intermittent assistance was provided as well as adequate wait-time in some cases.	Students were consistently given wait-time and were prompted when they were unable to answer correctly.
Closure	The lesson lacked closure.	The teacher offered a summary and closure of the lesson.	The teacher guided students as they stated the main ideas of the lesson.
Instructional alignment	Learning objectives, learning activities, and assessment are out of alignment.	Objectives, learning activities, and assessment are partially aligned.	Learning objectives, learning activities, and assessment are clearly aligned.

Source: From "Rating Scale for Teaching Effectiveness" adapted from an *Examination of the Relationships Between Elementary Teachers' Understanding of Education Psychology and Their Pedagogical Practice*, paper presented at the annual meeting of the American Education Research Association, Chicago, April 2007, in Eggen, P., & Kauchak, D. (2013). *Educational psychology: Windows on classrooms* (9th ed.). Boston: Pearson, p. 498.

Rating Scale for Teaching Effectiveness

Table 4.7 provides an overview of one approach to renew teaching practice using a rubric created to guide ratings made on nine teacher effectiveness behaviors, e.g., lesson scope, organization, quality of examples and nonexamples, etc. In using the scale, raters are asked to rate each behavior following an observed lesson giving each behavior a 1, 3, or 5 rating as guided by accompanying explanations of the meaning of each rating. A rating of 5 is the highest rating possible.

The *System for the Analysis of Teaching Practices* that follows represents another approach for the systematic review of classroom practice and has been developed to assist teachers as they review and reflect on their teaching behaviors. The *System* is built on the knowledge base of best practice in teaching and can serve as a helpful tool for teachers for self-review and in making decisions to strengthen the instructional process. This approach does not use a rubric as was the case in the scale presented in Table 4.7 but is designed for ratings to be given on a 1 through 5 scale with the rater responding to how frequently the identified behavior, as defined in the *System*, is present in the teacher's practice. The *System* may be used to provide feedback on an individual lesson or summary feedback following the observation of a number of lessons. Return to the *Seth's Confidence, Susan's Problem Ownership*, or *Tameka's Planning and Analysis* case study from Chapter 1 and use the instrument as though you were one of the three teachers in the case studies.

System for the Analysis of Teaching Practices

Circle the appropriate number on the scale provided as you reflect on your teaching with respect to each teacher behavior. Before making your selection, consider the accompanying statement(s) associated with each item as to how well the statement consistently describes your professional behavior.

	Seldom				*Always*
1. Clarity	1	2	3	4	5

My students understand the words that I use in my teaching; I get my ideas across clearly without needing to repeat myself.

2. Variability   1 2 3 4 5

My teaching reflects the regular use of many
different teaching strategies and resources
rather than only a few.

3. Enthusiasm   1 2 3 4 5

I am energetic and my teaching reflects this
energy; my enthusiasm shows in my teaching,
my preparation, and the classroom
environment that I establish.

4. Task-oriented   1 2 3 4 5

I conduct my classroom in a positive yet
business-like manner. Students know where they
are headed in their learning activities; my
teaching is focused on the desired learning
outcomes at all times.

5. Students Learning Criterion Material   1 2 3 4 5

My students know in advance of the learning
activities what is important to be learned and
how they will be evaluated. My assessments do
not include "extras" that my students were not
aware of.

6. Use of Student Ideas   1 2 3 4 5

My teaching is characterized by a heavy
involvement of student ideas. Students know
from the way I teach that their ideas are
important.

7. Structuring Comments   1 2 3 4 5

I use structuring comments at the beginning of
my lessons and as I move through my lessons
to help my students stay focused on my
objectives and know what is expected of them.

8. Level of Difficulty   1 2 3 4 5

My expectations are challenging but not
beyond the reach of my students. Students are

not "left behind" in my teaching; they know
that they can be successful.

9. **Success Rates**   1 2 3 4 5

My students are consistently successful; no
student considers himself or herself a failure
as my approach to teaching ensures success
for all.

10. **Attitude**   1 2 3 4 5

I know that if I plan my lessons thoroughly and
select learning activities appropriately that all of
my students can succeed. It may take extra
effort, but I can make a positive difference with
all of my students.

11. **Use of Time**   1 2 3 4 5

Students do not have idle time in my classroom
but stay actively and successfully engaged in
meaningful experiences.

12. **Organization**   1 2 3 4 5

My classroom and teaching are organized, and
my students recognize this. I am well prepared
and my teaching transitions are smooth and
controlled.

13. **Communication**   1 2 3 4 5

I communicate clearly to my students. This
includes both verbal as well as nonverbal
messages. I seldom need to repeat myself.

14. **Focus**   1 2 3 4 5

Students understand the purpose of my lessons,
and my lessons stay focused. Spontaneous
events do take place, but my students know
where my lessons are headed and the outcomes
that are desired.

15. Feedback   1 2 3 4 5

Students receive ample feedback related to
their progress during my lessons and through
my assessments. They regularly receive oral
and written feedback that explains their
progress to them.

16. Questioning   1 2 3 4 5

I routinely use both higher and lower order
questioning. Students are asked many questions
to develop their thinking and so I can know
what they understand.

17. Probing Behaviors   1 2 3 4 5

My teaching includes probing students so that
they may go deeper into and expand on their
ideas, especially as their ideas relate to what I
am teaching.

18. Pacing   1 2 3 4 5

My lesson pace is normally quicker as opposed
to slower.

19. Review and Closure   1 2 3 4 5

I review at the beginning of my lessons what
has just been previously taught. I review again
through closure at the end of each lesson.

20. Criticism   1 2 3 4 5

My classroom environment is positive, open,
and inviting. I seldom use criticism with my
students.

Scoring Your Analysis

Twenty items make up the *System for the Analysis of Teaching Practices*
with a maximum possible rating of 5 on each item. The instrument is
not intended for evaluation purposes but as a guide for reflection and
determining future instructional directions. It offers a way to analyze in-

dividual teacher behaviors as well as a teacher's performance in its entirety by combining individual ratings. Each behavior is treated as having the same level of importance.

The following scoring scheme may be used when seeking a combined rating of all items.

Points	Self-Rating
93–100	Excellent
86–92	Above Average
79–85	Average
70–78	Below Average
Below 70	Unsatisfactory

CONCLUSION

Chapter 4 has included a detailed review of educational research related to what is popularly referred to as best practice in teaching. The information provided reinforces two important points. First, for teachers to be effective, they need to have a strong knowledge base of information about best teaching practice, student motivation, and classroom management. The body of knowledge in these areas has continued to grow steadily since early studies were conducted and will continue to expand in the future. Second, teachers need to be able to use what they know about best practice in teaching, motivation, and management to make sound decisions and to deliver more dynamic and effective instruction. Knowing important information and not being able to use it leaves the teacher at a less than optimal level with respect to the effectiveness of his or her teaching and students at a level where they are not learning at their greatest potentials.

The Rating Scale for Teaching Effectiveness and the *System for the Analysis of Teaching Practices* were introduced as ways to help teachers systematically analyze their teaching in behavior areas supported by educational research as being linked to best teaching practice. The *System* and the rating scale are built on the best teaching practices introduced throughout the chapter and are research-based in their designs. Teachers and those who desire to be teachers are encouraged to study and then use these instruments in real or hypothetical situations as they represent the most current thinking on characteristics and behaviors of effective teachers as related to student achievement.

It is also important to recognize that the knowledge base related to best practice in teaching, student motivation, and classroom management will never be complete as those who are engaged in educational research, and those who are classroom practitioners, continue to search for instructional strategies and teacher and student behaviors that will enhance student learning. This is a critically important characteristic of the teaching profession. Just as students have expectations placed upon them for what they need to know, so too do their teachers. Teachers cannot afford to be complacent regarding their own need to be active learners themselves. This learning must include the knowledge of effective practice in teaching, motivation, and management, and the skills in how to apply this knowledge.

QUESTIONS/ACTIVITIES FOR REFLECTION

1. Evaluate Susan's teaching in the case study *Susan's Problem Ownership* as completely as you can with the Rating Scale for Teaching Effectiveness or the *System for the Analysis of Teaching Practices*. Rate each item of the Rating Scale or the *System* and then total the score. Discuss your ratings with another student in the class.
2. What are some strategies that a teacher might use to improve his or her questioning technique? Explain what it means to match questioning practices to the purpose of a lesson.
3. What can a teacher do to maintain high efficacy when working with students who are working below grade level?
4. All of the items on the instrument *System for the Analysis of Teaching Practices* are given equal value. If it is the case that they all are not equal, which do you consider to be the five most important of the twenty items included in the instrument? Why have you selected these five?
5. While teachers strive for higher levels of Engaged Time in their teaching, this is different from Academic Learning Time. What are the main differences between Engaged Time and Academic Learning Time and what can a teacher do to increase the amount of Academic Learning Time in the classroom?

Chapter 5

CREATING AND MAINTAINING SAFE LEARNING ENVIRONMENTS

Instruction is, after all, an effort to assist or to shape growth. In devising instruction for the young, one would be ill advised indeed to ignore what is known about growth, its constraints and opportunities. A theory of instruction . . . is in effect a theory of how growth and development are assisted by diverse means. (Bruner, 1971, p. 1)

No topic has received more attention in national media outlets in recent months than has school safety. On April 20, 1999, 12 students and one teacher were gunned to death by two high school seniors at a high school in Columbine, Colorado. This tragic event stimulated a long and at times heated debate in the United States concerning gun control laws, availability of firearms, and gun violence involving youth. After photographs of the tragic shootings and subsequent funerals stopped being shown and reported by the news media, time passed and the debate lost much of its initial motivation. Other similar events have taken place since then that have caused a peeking of discussion which, over time, lessened in intensity. However, as your authors worked on the current edition of this textbook, a new tragedy took place that shook our nation to a degree never reached during other school-based disasters. On December 14, 2012, in Newtown, Connecticut, a twenty-year-old gunman with known psychological issues entered Sandy Hook Elementary School and shot to death 20 first-grade students and six adults. Only time will tell if the degree of horror associated with the killing of so many young, helpless children and the adults who tried to protect them will also fade away as in the past. It is our belief that, because of this tragedy, actions will be taken by legal bodies and Boards of Education across the country to ensure that schools will be safer environments for both students and their teachers. This chapter will focus on strategies teachers and administrators can use to make the learning environments of specific classrooms and entire schools safe for students and the adults who work there.

An issue that many researchers have had in the field of school safety is the lack of what may be referred to as a coherent conceptual structure concerning school safety to act as a guide to their research on this important topic (Mayer & Furlong, 2010). For example, much attention is drawn to major violent events such as shootings that actually are somewhat rare when one considers the total number of schools that exist across the nation. Some would argue that the horrific events such as those in Columbine, Colorado, and Newtown, Connecticut, do not tell the entire story about school violence because there are other less newsworthy events such as bullying and intimidation which can lead to long lasting psychological problems that should also be included in school violence discussions. To truly understand school violence, it is suggested that research is needed that describes the real-life experiences of students and teachers as opposed to only studying school safety from statistical reports based primarily on survey data. Real-life experiences clearly indicate that the quality of students' lives and their ability to learn can be negatively impacted when they are victims of school violence. National survey data indicate that, in the 2002–2003 school year, 242,000 teachers reported being threatened with a weapon while 120,000 reported that they had been physically attacked by a student. In 2005, 6% of high school students indicated that they had avoided school activities or certain locations due to fear of attack or physical harm (Dinkes, Cataldi, & Lin-Kelly, 2007). This type of fear, which is typically associated with bullying and other concerns associated with personal safety, consistently distracts both students and teachers from instruction (Hanish & Guerra, 2002). Students who feel the threat of violence frequently have problems associated with depression, anxiety attacks, lack of attention, and social withdrawal; all of these factors can lead to avoidance of school and a lack of motivation to learn (Buhs, Ladd, & Herald, 2006; Flannery, Webster, & Singer, 2004; Nishina, Juvonen, & Witkow, 2005; Schwartz, Gorman, Nakamoto, & Tobin, 2005).

ADDRESSING SCHOOL VIOLENCE

Shooting deaths of students and teachers have served as stark reminders that school violence still occurs and that cause for concern still remains. For example, the number of weapons confiscated in and around Boston's public schools rose 42% in the last five years, mirroring a citywide rise in youth violence (Tracy, 2006). School police found 577 weapons, mostly knives, in the 2005–2006 school year compared with 407 just four years earlier in 2001–2002. Violent crimes, mostly assaults and robberies, increased 14% during the same period with 902 occurrences in the 2005–2006 school year. These crimes included assaults against teachers, other school staff, and students. The United States has been reported as having the highest rates of childhood homicides, suicides, and firearm-related deaths of any of the world's 26 wealthiest nations (Aspy, Oman, Vesely, McLeroy, Rodine, & Marshall, 2004). Events and statistics such as these frighten parents as well as students and have elicited serious questions about school safety across the nation. Concern for discipline in schools and school safety were well documented in Chapter 1.

Lasting solutions to problems of school violence lie in effective measures of problem prevention and in being proactive, not in dealing with problems once they have occurred. Students who are at the point where they are ready to commit violent acts against their classmates or teachers are not likely to be thwarted by discipline threats or zero tolerance policies. More systemic solutions (i.e., well-planned preventive solutions) must be developed and implemented which involve the school, the family, and other support agencies found in the community.

In reacting to the reasons why two students shot and killed a number of their classmates at Columbine High School in Columbine, Colorado, it has been asserted that a problem exists in society in general when high status and recognition are granted to some students, e.g., athletes and members of certain clubs, while those who excel in less glamorous activities such as band or drama, by comparison, are ignored (Wallace, 2000). Students who do not excel in high-profile activities often feel alienated, especially if they lack popularity with those who do excel. Schools must make every effort possible to address the needs of all students including the gifted, the introverted, and those interested in non-mainstream activities. It is important that those students who enjoy high status in school do not malign those who do not and who are seen as nonconformist.

Early identification of students who are at risk of committing violent acts in the future is critical (Sprague & Walker, 2000). Several models exist that can be used that are felt to predict future violent behavior that focus on pathology within the student, ecological factors, and past behaviors. Youth who have shown a number of antisocial behaviors in multiple settings, for example, are more prone to be violent in the future than students who have not displayed these behaviors. Such factors as living in poverty, living with adults who abuse drugs and alcohol, and being a victim of child abuse are among the factors that can interact with other characteristics to predict a greater likelihood of future dysfunctional behaviors. One recommended model for the prevention of violent behavior has three distinct tiers (Sprague & Walker, 2000).

1. All students in the school are given instruction in such fundamental skills as conflict resolution and violence prevention in an effort to create a positive learning environment throughout the school.
2. Students who exhibit a pattern of factors that indicate that they are apt to be involved in future violent behavior are identified and provided with a specialized intervention program designed to lessen the impact of their risk factors.
3. Students who are already engaged in dysfunctional, antisocial behavior are identified and provided with specialized, professional help designed to change their attitudes and behavior patterns.

Although most classroom problems are minor and easily resolved, during behavior escalation, where both the teacher and student become engaged in a confrontation, classroom instruction predictably comes to a standstill and other students become anxious or curious spectators (Shukla-Mehta & Albin, 2003). Table 5.1 includes twelve practical strategies that have been identified as effective in preventing behavioral escalation.

The importance of being well informed and proactive cannot be overstated. The following behaviors represent early warning signs of potential violent behavior in students. Teachers and students alike are advised to not ignore known warning signs but to be observant for

Table 5.1

Strategies to Prevent Behavioral Escalation

Strategy	*Strategy Explanation*
1. Reinforce calm and on-task behaviors.	Because most behavior is maintained by virtue of some kind of reinforcement, e.g., teacher attention, peer approval, teachers should immediately reinforce students when they display target behaviors like working calmly and being on task.
2. Know the triggers.	Most student behavior is set off by something; anything that prompts an action from others is a trigger. Teachers need to learn these triggers.
3. Pay attention to anything unusual about the student's behavior.	When the student arrives at school each day, note if the student appears distraught, anxious, or preoccupied.
4. Do not escalate along with the student.	Teachers are models for socially appropriate behavior and should maintain that stature. If teachers lose self-control, both student and teacher will escalate together and act inappropriately.
5. Offer students opportunities to display responsible behavior.	Most behavior is a matter of choice. Students choose to display a given behavior on the basis of their past experience with using the behavior to obtain specific outcomes.
6. Intervene early in the sequence.	By intervening when less severe problem behaviors occur, teachers can avoid potentially more serious incidents.
7. Understand how such behavioral incidents ended in the past.	Whether an incident is minor or major, how it ends will determine the likelihood of future occurrences. Teachers should evaluate the effectiveness of their strategies on the basis of the effect they have had on a student's prior behavior.
8. Know the function of problem behaviors.	Most students use problem behavior to either get access to something they find pleasant or to avoid or escape something they find unpleasant.
9. Use good judgment about which behaviors to punish.	It is important to make sure that the consequence matches the severity of the problem behavior. Do not use severe punishment for mildly disruptive behavior problems or the same consequence for all types of problem behaviors.
10. Use extinction procedures wisely.	Extinction is the withdrawal of the consequent stimulus that previously maintained the problem behavior. It is better to use extinction in combination with differential reinforcement of alternative responses that are more socially acceptable.
11. Teach students socially appropriate behavior to replace problem behavior.	Teachers should use their knowledge of the main reasons for the occurrence of behavioral problems and teach alternative social and communication skills that will succeed in producing the same effect the problem behavior does for the student.
12. Teach academic survival skills and set students up for success.	Academic failure is positively correlated to behavioral problems. Teachers should teach academic survival skills to students and promote their active engagement so they are less likely to be challenged with disruptive behavior.

Source: From Shukla-Mehta, S., & Albin, R. (2003). Twelve practical strategies to prevent behavioral escalation in classroom settings. *The Clearing House, 77*(2), 50–56.

these behaviors and respond accordingly:

1. social withdrawal,
2. excessive feelings of isolation and being alone,
3. excessive feelings of rejection,
4. feelings of being picked on and persecuted,
5. low school interest and poor academic performance,
6. uncontrolled anger,
7. patterns of impulsive and chronic hitting, intimidating, and bullying behaviors,
8. history of discipline problems,
9. intolerance for differences and prejudicial attitudes,
10. drug use and alcohol use,
11. affiliation with gangs,
12. inappropriate access to, possession of, and use of firearms,
13. serious threats of violence,
14. being a victim of violence,
15. expression of violence in writings and drawings, and
16. past history of violent and aggressive behavior.

One major concern related to violence in schools is the existence of organized gangs. Dowling-Sendor (1998a), an appellate defender from North Carolina, provided important advice for school administrators and teachers when reacting to the existence of gangs within their schools. First, all school policies must be comprehensive, serve to prohibit gang activity, and work to motivate students to not engage in such activity. Second, policies must recognize that a student's First and Fourteenth Amendment rights cannot be violated when dealing with the prohibition of certain types of dress or symbols. Third, a student should be allowed the opportunity to deny any accusation that an item of clothing or symbol has any gang significance. Educators need to seek help from students, parents, law enforcement, and community agencies to provide students with alternatives to gang activities (Dowling-Sendor, 1998b). Parent involvement at the time gang behavior is suspected is especially important. If administrators and teachers have started to build a positive relationship with parents before a problem begins, parental contacts concerning problems are more likely to result in greater parental cooperation than if such a relationship has not been established (Levin & Nolan, 2010). Three factors may be identified that influence positive parent involvement. These are:

1. the belief about and acceptance of the role of parents as it relates to providing home support for the school,
2. parents' sense of efficacy concerning their ability to help, and
3. the perception given to the invitation for parental involvement in the school.

School principals should appeal to parents for their assistance in finding immediate resolutions if problems are identified. Parents need to be told that the school will not tolerate gang activities and that the principal is prepared to take action, including contacting any authorities and agencies as necessary, to maintain a safe school environment. After parents have had an opportunity to react and propose solutions to identified problems, students should join the dialogue to hear their parents say that the problems will come to an end, that violent behavior is not acceptable, and that it will not be tolerated.

Personality factors and peer relations clearly impact school violence; however, the overall impact of the school's culture also has a significant influence on violent behavior. Bryner (2007) and Reis, Trockel, and Mulhall (2007) pointed out that certain characteristics of middle schools can be predictors of aggressive behavior in students. Reis and her associates found three cultural features of schools that lead to a reduction in school violence; they are:

- teaching that emphasizes understanding, not memorization,
- student participation in making school rules, and
- education about cultural diversity.

Violence in schools is a problem that parents, educators, and students alike agree cannot be allowed to occur. Though school violence is not a new phenomenon, the tragic events of recent years have aroused parents, educators, and school boards to take what are sometimes felt to be dramatic actions to prevent further violence from taking place in their communities. While popular with some, stringent school rules for behavior and zero tolerance policies do not ensure the prevention of radical, dysfunctional behavior. Educators have come to recognize that dealing with crime and violence in schools requires a total community effort (Rossman & Morley, 1996). Many schools have formed effective alliances with other agencies in their communities, e.g., law enforcement and mental health, to combat crime and violence in a more cohesive and comprehensive way. Because school violence is something that must be prevented and not just dealt with after the fact, it is in a school district's best interest, and the best interest of all involved, to have a sound prevention plan in place. Any comprehensive strategy to curb school violence needs to deal with both school safety programs and access to guns (Dealing With School Violence, 2006). These two issues go hand in hand, in addition to the financial resources that must be invested in problem solutions from the federal, state, as well as local levels.

Bullying: A Frequent Cause of Violence

Bullying among students is a very old and well-known phenomenon (Olweus, 2003). Although many educators are acquainted with the problem, researchers only began to study bullying systematically in the 1970s. **Bullying** is *a negative behavior which is intentionally designed to cause real, or threatening injury or discomfort to another individual that may reflect physical harm, psychological harm, or both* (Olweus, 1993). In the wake of school shootings and lawsuits brought against individuals, schools and school districts, numerous state governments mandated that schools take active steps to reduce bullying (Cooper & Snell, 2003). South Carolina, for example, passed the Safe Schools Climate Act in 2006 (Safe Schools Climate Act, 2006). The Act calls for school districts to establish policies that include a statement prohibiting harassment, intimidation, or bullying of a student. Harassment, intimidation, or bullying is defined as a gesture, an electronic communication, or a written communication that:

1. harms a student physically or emotionally or damages a student's property, or places a student in reasonable fear of personal harm or property damage; or
2. insults or demeans a student or group of students causing substantial disruption in, or substantial interference with, the orderly operation of the school.

"School" refers to in a classroom, on school premises, on a school bus or other school-related vehicle, at an official school bus stop, at a school-sponsored activity or event whether or not it is held on school premises, or at another program or function where the school is responsible for the child.

Although specific mandated actions vary by state, many schools recognize that the most effective approach to bullying prevention is one that is inclusive of school staff, parents, students, and community. The amount of literature addressing the topic of bullying in schools has increased significantly in recent years. Many experts emphasize that bullying behavior occurs during repeated or successive encounters. Such acts can be carried out through physical blows but can also take the form of verbal attacks through insults, name calling, and the use of other psychologically damaging words. Boys bully other students more often than girls do, and a relatively large percentage of girls, about 50%, report that they are bullied mainly by boys (Olweus, 2003).

Bullies are people who take advantage of weaker people. While weakness is often thought to be related to physical strength, this is not always the case. The imbalance between the bully and the victim might be related to more subtle differences such as social skills or language facility. Bullying is a type of aggression aimed at a weaker (physically, socially, emotionally, or cognitively) individual designed to give the victim feelings of oppression. This oppression frequently builds up because bullying, by its very nature, happens repeatedly over time, beginning with a desire to hurt and followed by a hurtful action as a result of a power imbalance (Rigby, 2007). This unjust use of power is typically used over and over for the enjoyment of the aggressor and the oppression of the victim. Bullying is a very complex behavior and is not apt to be controlled merely by telling the aggressor that his or her behavior is not nice, unacceptable, or hurtful. Moreover, imbalances in power may be very difficult to detect and analyze; bullying may be taking place when the observer cannot believe the victim could possibly be bullied by the perpetrator.

The National Council of Urban Boards of Education reported that many students commonly witness other children being bullied, physically or psychologically intimidated, or belittled (Croft, 2006). From a nationwide survey of 32,000 students, two particularly worrisome findings were that more than half of the students surveyed said that they had seen children being bullied at least once a month, and that almost 40% said teachers and schools could not stop the bullying. Manning and Bucher (2013, pp. 21–22) reported the following observations regarding bullying or peer victimization:

- 32% of adolescents have been bullied at school with 18% the subject of rumors; 11% pushed, tripped, shoved, or spit on; 6% threatened with harm; and 5% excluded from activities;

- victims of bullying are often victims of other crimes at school; and
- studies have found connections between being bullied and thinking of suicide, especially adolescents who may be at a heightened risk for depression and anxiety.

Dillon (2012, p. 14) noted the following points concerning the status of bullying in today's schools:

- adults are aware of only about 4–5% of the bullying that occurs in schools, i.e., 95% of the bullying that occurs in schools goes undetected by school staff;
- adults think that they are aware of over 70% of the bullying that occurs in schools and that they intervene all the time;
- only 35% of students who are bullied tell an adult about it; this percentage decreases as students get older;
- about 60% of the students who witness bullying think that sometimes the bullied student deserves to be bullied. And, many of the students who are bullied think they have brought it on themselves;
- bullying is observed by over 85% of the students;
- 27% of the bullied students report that the bullying happens in the classroom with the teacher present; and
- many students who bully are well liked by others, including the staff.

The reported figures related to bullying and school violence may be lower than the actual number of incidents themselves because of the overreliance on self-reporting data often used by school districts across the country (Swearer, Espelage, Vaillancourt, & Hymel, 2010; Stollsteimer, 2010). In any given day, over 50,000 young people will be absent from school because they are being bullied; this is one-third of all truancies (Bindel, 2006). One estimate is that 160,000 children miss school each day because of fear (Newman-Carlson & Horne, 2004). Research has identified an irrefutable link between bullying and truancy and persistent truancy and a young person's opportunities in later life. Reasons given by students for bullying-related truancy include the desire to be somewhere safe where no one can bring harm to them and to be removed from environments where there are feelings of being worthless and hated. The link between poor behavior, truancy, and bullying is also evident with respect to affective and cognitive development.

A unique and growing type of bullying is cyberbullying or web bullying. While school officials have begun to address the student rumor mill and notes left in bathrooms, the Internet has become a major forum for bullying as well (Schreirer, 2006). Online threats are real and powerful. One poll identified that one in three teenagers and one in six preteens have received threats or verbal abuse online. For the teens, this means receiving mean, threatening, or embarrassing messages, mostly through instant messaging, email, or a website posting. About 60% of the messages focus on a student's crush or friendship with a classmate; 38% said the messages were about physical appearance, such as weight or clothes. Other incidents involved race, religion, or sexuality. About 20% of adolescents have been a victim of cyberbullying with 20% admitting to actually having been a cyberbully. Females are more likely than males to be victims of bullies and cyberbullies (Manning & Bucher, 2013). The Pew Internet & America Life Project reported that about one-third of all teenagers who use the Internet say they have been targets of menacing behavior online (Joyce, 2007). These behaviors include receiving threatening messages; having their private emails or text messages forwarded without consent; seeing an embarrassing picture posted without permission; or having rumors about them spread online. The most common form of cyberbullying is reported as taking information once thought to be private and placing it across the Internet. The Project also indicated that girls are more likely than boys to be targets and teens who share their identities and thoughts online are more likely to be targets than are those who lead less active online lives.

The typical bully used to torment victims out in the open, in school hallways, or playgrounds, calling out insults and disparaging remarks for anyone to hear and see. Bullying has now gone high-tech and anonymous (Tseng, 2006). The Internet and cell phone text messages are the new mediums for cyberbullies who post nasty pictures or messages about others in blogs and on websites, or exploit another person's online user name to spread rumors. Some school districts have introduced cyberbullying policies that prohibit this behavior on school computers. Parents must sign a form confirming they have read the policy and discussed it with their children. Punishment could range from a phone call home to an out-of-school suspension, depending on the offense. While not directed specifically and only to cyberbullying, through the direction of former governor Corzine, the state of New Jersey initiated a program in all New Jersey schools to train teachers and administrators in Internet safety (Corzine: Train Teachers to Help, 2007). Teachers and administrators are expected to use their training to instruct students, parents, and community groups on the potential dangers that can be found on the Internet.

Bullying today is actually an international problem. For example, it has been reported that more than 150,000 students in the United Kingdom have been targeted by school bullies because they are gay (Ross, 2007). Two-thirds of lesbian and gay students surveyed indicated that they had experienced homophobic bullying ranging from verbal abuse to violence and even death threats. About half of the teachers did not intervene when students used homophobic language like "dyke," or "queer," or "rug muncher." The study conducted indicated that 41% of gay and lesbian students had experienced physical abuse, 17% had received death threats, and 12% had been sexually assaulted. Some students reported that their teachers joined in with the abuse.

A relationship also has been drawn between bullying and suicide. In recent years, a series of bullying-related suicides in the United States and other countries have drawn attention to the connection between bullying and suicide. Although many adults still see bullying as just a part of growing up, it is a serious problem that leads to many negative effects for victims. The statistics on bullying and suicide are significant (Bullying and Suicide – Bullying Statistics, 2013).

- According to the Centers for Disease Control, suicide is the third leading cause of death among young people resulting in about 4,400 deaths per year;
- For every suicide among young people, there are at least 100 suicide attempts;
- Over 14% of high school students have considered suicide and almost 7% have attempted it;
- Bully victims are between 2 to 9 times more likely to consider suicide than non-victims;
- A study in Britain found that at least half of suicides among young people are related to bullying; and
- According to statistics reported by ABC News, nearly 30% of students are either bullies or victims of bullying.

In recent months, bullying-related suicides have been reported in the United States in California, New York, Indiana, and Michigan as well as in Canada (Giammona, 2013; New York Police Probe, 2013; Angel Green; 2013; Josh Pacheco, 2013; Audrie Pott, Rehtaeh Parsons, 2013). At least six students being bullied in Japan were so desperate to stop the torment that the only way they could find to end their suffering was through suicide (Bullying Is Behind Teen Suicide, 2006). Numerous victims overloaded a hotline service wanting to tell someone how they were bullied at school because they could not tell their families. In one week, Childline Japan received over 27,500 calls but could only answer 2,890 of them due to a shortage of lines. The Japanese government acted on schoolyard bullying with the Education Rebuilding Council calling for clearer standards for punishing student bullies, recommending that teachers who turn a blind eye to bullying be disciplined, and that students who want to change schools because of bullying be allowed to do so (Doi, 2006). Japanese law barred primary and middle schools from expelling students who bully or tease schoolmates; even school suspensions were rare. Of the 464 suspensions at middle schools in the past decade, only 24 cases involved bullying. One recent report from Japan identified that a thirteen-year-old boy in southern Japan committed suicide after classmates systemically bullied him, even making him practice suicide while teachers ignored the abuse, or laughed (Kids and Laughing Teachers, 2012). Experts say that concealment of bullying is part of a crisis in the educational system, leaving school administrators trying to save face.

Although bullying has been an issue in schools for a number of years, many educators are only now becoming aware of how harmful the practice can be to the development and learning of the victims and the overall environment of the school. The cost to society of ignoring bullying is higher than it would be to develop anti-bullying strategies. It has been observed that it is not normal to act like a bully and, in anonymous surveys of several large middle schools, the vast majority of students reported that they had not hit, teased, threatened, excluded, or gossiped maliciously about classmates in the past thirty days from when the survey was conducted (Teicher, 2006). However, a majority of the students were convinced that their own nonbully status was an exception to the norm. One observation of these data is that much of the bullying, violence, or substance abuse continues because the people engaged in it think that everyone else is doing it. Social norms intervention is applicable when dealing with this phenomenon. In this intervention approach students are presented with credible bullying data from their own school, not just state or national average information, and come to realize that the behavior is not a behavior in which everyone is engaged. Through social norm intervention students understand that bullying is not the norm.

Family-level intervention with bullies and victims can also be critical to reducing the level of bullying found in schools with the aim of the intervention program being to help change the maladaptive family processes that contribute to children's bully-victim problems (Curtner-Smith, Smith, & Porter, 2011). Table 5.2 identifies characteristics and processes that have been found to be typical of families of children who bully and of children who are victims.

Table 5.2
Profile of Typical Families of Children Who Bully and Who Are Victims

Family Profile of Children who Bully

1. Angry, hostile parent-child interactions
2. Low parental warmth, involvement, and affection
3. Harsh discipline that is also inconsistent and lax; heavy use of psychological control
4. Low parental monitoring
5. Parental depression and anger
6. Low parental empathy for child
7. Strong parental valuing of aggression

Family Profile of Passive (Submissive) Victims

1. Parental overprotection/intense emotional closeness
2. Insecure-resistant attachment history
3. Low parent involvement/low family support
4. Poor parent-child communication
5. Harsh overreactive parenting

Source: From Curtner-Smith, M., Smith, P., & Porter, M. (2011). Family-level interventions with bullies and victims. In E. Vernberg & B. Biggs (Eds.), *Preventing and treating bullying and victimization.* New York: Oxford University Press, pp. 75–96.

Amelia middle and high schools in Ohio began a bullying prevention program that encourages bystanders to help put an end to intimidation and threats (Kranz, 2007). Developed in Norway, the Olweus Bullying Prevention Program (OBPP) is based on the pioneering work of Dan Olweus and is one of the most popularly used whole-school models today (Swearer et al., 2010). The program was begun with help from Child Focus, a nonprofit mental health agency located in the community. The emphasis of the program is on the bystander and trying to empower that individual to help the victim. Program components include developing policies and school rules against bullying, developing methods for reporting and recording bullying, identifying hot spots where bullying occurs, on-the-spot interventions by teachers, and weekly classroom meetings on bullying issues. Most research shows that bullying begins in the elementary school, slows in the middle school, and re-emerges in the ninth grade. OBPP (Olweus, 2003; 2013) is not a classroom curriculum but a whole-school, systems-change program at four different levels (see Table 5.3).

Table 5.3

General Requirements in the Olweus Bullying Prevention Program (OBPP)

School-Level Components	• Establish a Bullying Prevention Coordinating Committee. • Conduct committee and staff trainings. • Administer the Olweus Bullying Questionnaire schoolwide. • Hold staff discussion group meetings. • Introduce the school rules against bullying. • Review and refine the school's supervisory system. • Hold a school kick-off event to launch the program. • Involve parents.
Classroom-Level Components	• Post and enforce schoolwide rules against bullying. • Hold regular class meetings. • Hold meetings with students' parents.
Individual-Level Components	• Supervise students' activities. • Ensure that all staff intervene on the spot when bullying occurs. • Hold meetings with students involved in bullying. • Hold meetings with parents of involved students. • Develop individual intervention plans for involved students.
Community-Level Components	• Involve community members on the Bullying Prevention Coordinating Committee. • Develop partnerships with community members to support the school's program. • Help to spread anti-bullying messages and principles of best practice in the community.

Although some positive results from OBPP and other whole-school models have been found, research in this area has not been consistent (Swearer et al., 2010). Smith, Schneider, Smith, and Ananiadou (2004); Vreeman and Carroll (2007); and Merrell, Gueldner, Ross, and Isava (2008) conducted separate meta-analyses and found that positive results for whole-school models is mixed. Ttofi, Farrington, and Baldry (2008) reported in their meta-analysis that whole-school models seemed more effective in smaller European settings than in larger U.S.

schools. Educators need to accept that whole-school models to prevent bullying will be more effective in some settings and less effective others and that, regardless of the program, it is important to identify procedures that work in the individual school and then employ those procedures (Swearer et al., 2010).

There are critical issues that must be addressed if schools are to develop effective bullying prevention programs (Swearer et al., 2010). Due to lack of validity, researchers must stop relying solely on self-reported indices of bullying victimization and avoid studying programs that are not based upon a guiding theoretical base that provides inaccurate evaluation and development data. Interventions need to be directed to peers and family members who can prevent bullying behavior; incorporate factors such as race, disability, and sexual orientation; and focus special interventions for students who have been known to exhibit bullying behaviors instead of giving all students the exact same interventions.

Central to any schoolwide plan to address bullying behavior is the development of a defined, clear and easy-to-understand school policy or position statement on bullying. It is recommended that the following features be included in such a policy or position statement (Rigby, 2007).

- A clear statement of the school's position that bullying is inappropriate and will not be tolerated.
- A short, clear definition of bullying behavior that addresses both direct and indirect forms of harassment that includes cyberbullying.
- A statement that all people in the school community have the right to expect that the environment will be safe from bullying.
- A statement that defines the responsibilities of individuals who see other members of the community being bullied.
- General statements concerning what will take place to prevent bullying (e.g., instructional units and conflict management training) and how the faculty and administration will deal with those who bully others.
- A general statement outlining how the school proposes to interact with parents to address problems related to bullying.
- The description of a standard process to be used to assess the effectiveness of the process.

While schools address violence in a number ways, there is universal agreement that the best approach is to establish and implement procedures to prevent violence before it happens. As discussed previously, proactive procedures are extremely important when dealing with violence in school settings.

Illegal Drugs in Schools

Drug abuse has been seen as a major problem in and out of schools across the country for many years. Each year approximately 150,000 young people under the age of eighteen are admitted to drug abuse programs in the United States (Morral, McCaffrey, Ridgeway, Mukherji, Beighley, 2006). Like many other societal problems, substance abuse has a powerful negative impact in many ways. Drug use among young people remains at levels near or even above the peak years of 1979–1980 and has been shown to be particularly dangerous for African American males (Curwin & Mendler, 2004). One study that tracked a group of adolescents from ages nineteen to twenty-seven found that about 33% of the African American males who abused drugs died by age twenty-seven, compared to 3% for white males. The death rate for African American and white females was 1% (Clark, Martin, & Cornelius, 2008).

In a major survey of over 10,000 high school students, researchers investigated the relationship between school violence (i.e., carrying a weapon, being in a physical fight, damaging and stealing property, threatening with a weapon, and missing school due to safety concerns) and substance abuse (Lowry, Cohen, Modzeleski, Kann, Collins, & Kolbe, 1999). Just over 50% of the respondents to the survey reported drinking alcohol and approximately 25% reported using marijuana. Approximately 33% reported that they had been offered, sold, or given illegal drugs on school property in the last year. Nearly 60% indicated that they had used one or more of the substances listed in the survey in the previous month. The study also reported that the prevalence of school violence factors was greater for those students who had used at least one of the substances than for those who had not. More recently, Johnston, O'Malley, Bachman and Schulenberg (2011) found that 9.5% of eighth graders, 18.5% of tenth graders, and 23.8% of twelfth graders reported using an illicit drug in the last 30 days, with marijuana being the most popular. Marijuana use increased among teenagers from 2008 through 2010 with approximately 1% of eighth graders, 3% of tenth graders, and 6% of twelfth graders reporting they use marijuana daily. Researchers with the U.S. Department of Education and the Centers for Disease Control and Prevention in Atlanta, Georgia, suggest that drug abuse and school violence are so closely related that the problems associated with each one should be approached in a coordinated fashion. Addressing these problems in isolation or in a manner that separates one from the other risks less than optimum attention being given to either one.

A related study of high-risk elementary schools in Lexington, Kentucky, was conducted to determine knowledge levels, feelings, and attitudes of kindergarten students regarding alcohol, tobacco, and other drugs (Hahn, Hall, Rayens, Burt, Corley, & Sheffel, 2000). Results of the study indicated that approximately one in six kindergartners were able to identify marijuana, crack cocaine, LSD, injectable drugs, or other illegal substances. Although most of the children in the study voiced negative attitudes toward drug use, some of the students appeared to view drug use positively. The recognition of cigarettes and alcohol was not related to demographic factors. Minority children, however, were more likely to be knowledgeable about illicit drugs than nonminority children. How do such young children know so much about illegal substances? Young people are highly influenced by their close friends and their parents and this relates to their knowledge of and their likelihood of becoming involved in drug use (Curwin & Mendler, 2004).

There is evidence that solitary substance use can be related to poor academic achievement and educational attainment (Tucker, Ellickson, Collins, & Klein, 2006). Schools today are under tremendous pressure to improve the scholastic performance of students and much time and money is being dedicated to the academic preparation of students, teachers, and administrators. All feel accountable, and pressure, for reaching higher and higher levels of student achievement. Teachers must not forget, however, that many students have needs that go far beyond the academic concerns of the school, community, and even the state. In dealing with these issues, it is important to recognize that a coordinated program should be offered that will help to reduce the prevalence of problems such as drug usage and underage drinking (Wooley, Eberst, & Bradley, 2000). The strongest coordinated program will include and combine the resources of the school, family, and appropriate community agencies.

Many substance abuse programs have been developed in recent years in an effort to help control the drug use problem among young people. Jones (1997) described an evaluation of forty-seven such programs with only six earning high marks. The six programs rated most favorably were Alcohol Misuse Prevention Study (AMPS), Life Skills Training, the Michigan Model, Project ALERT, Project Northland, and Drug Abuse Resistance Education (DARE). Virtually all drug prevention programs, however, get mixed reviews. Adair (2000) evaluated fifty drug prevention programs and suggested that Jones' findings were correct only in the high rating of Project ALERT, believing that Project ALERT is especially good for middle school students. In their assessment of drug prevention programs, Elias, Gager, and Leon (1997) came to a different position on DARE, finding the program to have only two of what they considered to be the necessary characteristics of a good program. They identified QUEST as the best of the programs reviewed with Here's Looking at You, 2000, Growing Healthy, and Social Decision Making-Social Problem Solving (SDM-SPS) also being good programs. Providing information or using scare tactics, such as is felt by some to be the case with the DARE program, seem to have little positive effect and may even encourage curiosity and experimentation (Woolfolk, 2013). Some suggest that all drug abuse prevention programs fall short of meeting students' needs and that even the ones considered best lack complete usefulness because they do not focus strongly enough on student capabilities and do not provide complete and honest information to students (Brown, 1997).

While it is difficult to get agreement among the experts as to which prevention programs work best, it is clear that there is room for improvement in most programs. Factors have been identified that are important to acknowledge concerning the quality and completeness of any program (Jones, 1997). Successful programs help students with problem solving, social skills, and goal setting and provide training and support for teachers as well as family members and community involvement. Good programs also provide students with accurate information about drug use. In an effort to take a proactive stance, random drug testing of student athletes has become routine at study hall and lunch at many high schools across the country (Kansas Schools Take Drug Testing to Extreme, 2006). Acknowledging no quick fixes, efforts such as these to recognize the importance of engaging the problem, as well as its causes, are meant to address what has become a challenging and growing problem among school-age youth in the United States.

An important perspective on working with students who may be involved with illegal substances is that teachers and parents need to guard against accepting excuses and empty promises. Students who use drugs typically do not complete their schoolwork at the level of those who do not use drugs, and teachers must adhere to appropriate and consistent consequences for such behavior. When teachers notice changes in the behavior of a student that may indicate drug use, the student needs to be told about this observation. This should be done without accusation of drug use, but, as a caring teacher sharing an observation regarding a change in behavior with a student. If the teacher has tried to communicate this information to the student and the behavior goes unchanged, the teacher should then go ahead and approach the student with the suspicion of drug use. While taking this action, it is important for the teacher to listen to the student and interact in a caring, nonaccusatory and nonthreatening manner. Prior to any of this interaction, however, it is important for the teacher to share his or her concerns with the school principal or assistant principal, following whatever is in place as established school policy, and let that individual know what course of action is being taken.

SPECIFIC PREVENTION METHODS

Some methods used to prevent school violence are proactive. Requiring students to wear school uniforms is an example of this type of prevention. Some methods are less proactive and may be considered more punitive in nature; zero tolerance policies and school expulsion policies are examples of this type of prevention.

School Uniforms

One possible, and in some places popular, solution to school violence, gang activity, and difficult student behavior problems that received high interest beginning in the 1990s is having students wear school uniforms. The National Center for Education Statistics (2012) reported that in 2009–2010, about 19% of public school principals reported that their schools required students to wear uniforms, an increase from 12% in 1999–2000, and that approximately 57% enforced a strict dress code, an increase from 47% in 1999–2000. One view in support of this strategy has been that, if all students are dressed alike, unique gang clothing and symbols would be easier to detect and that this makes it more difficult for drug pushers and other undesirable persons to come on school campuses during school hours without being spotted by authorities. It also has been argued that the wearing of school uniforms is an effective strategy to lessen the differences of socioeconomic status that are often apparent in diverse schooling situations. A University of Houston study found that school attendance, academics, and behavior in middle and high school students improved once their schools adopted school uniforms with the biggest improvements being among female students (Emery, 2010). Lalwani (2011) reported that in 2009 some type of school uniform policy had been implemented in 21 states and, with respect to this implementation:

- overall crime rates dropped by 91% and rates of suspensions dropped by 90%,
- assaults on students from kindergarten through eighth grade decreased by 85%,
- number of sex offenses decreased by 96%,
- instances of vandalism declined by 69%, and
- 44% of parents reported that their children were more focused in school.

Many educators as well as noneducators favor requiring school uniforms. The third Phi Delta Kappa Poll of Teachers' Attitudes Toward the Public Schools (Langdon, 1996) indicated that 53% of the general public favored school uniforms while approximately 66% of the teachers favored them.

Although there are those who are not in favor of such policies, successes have been reported. A mandatory school uniform program was adopted with success in the elementary and middle schools of Long Beach, California (Stanley, 1996). After one year of the program being in operation, there were significant decreases in the reports of suspensions, assault/battery, assaults with a deadly weapon, fighting, sex offenses, robberies, extortions, charges of possession of both drugs and weapons, and vandalism. There also were fewer reports of classroom disruptions, overall unacceptable student behavior, bad attitudes, uncooperativeness, and poor work ethics. Parents felt that the school uniform policy led to positive results and were in greater support of the school. The students, however, were less than enthusiastic about wearing the uniforms and denied that the uniforms had led to positive results, though observed by others. In Anne Arundel County, Maryland, school uniform advocates reported that dressing uniformly eliminated the social pressures and the expense of buying fashionable clothes and encouraged children to behave better and get serious about learning (Butler, 2006). Some research indicates that a correlation exists between appropriate dress and academic performance and a greater sense of community. About 25% of public elementary schools in the country currently have some form of mandatory uniform policy, up from a handful in the mid-1990s.

Using his experiences as a former middle school principal in Los Angeles, California, Kommer (1999) added support to the development of school uniform policies in identifying the following positive results. School uniforms:

1. help to reduce gang influence,
2. create a more positive and businesslike atmosphere,
3. increase pride in the school,
4. reduce problems for students related to choosing what to wear to school,
5. reduce strife between students and parents concerning what to wear, and
6. lower the stress and expense for parents related to buying school clothes.

Further supporting the use of school uniforms, Wide (2013) more recently offered that school uniforms help:

1. prevent gangs from forming on campus,
2. encourage discipline,
3. students resist peer pressures to buy trendy clothes,
4. identify intruders in the school,
5. diminish economic and social barriers between students,
6. increase a sense of belonging and school pride, and
7. improve attendance.

Kommer advised those who may wish to institute a school uniform policy to make uniforms mandatory, not voluntary. Mandatory programs are felt to work better than those that are voluntary. It is wise, however, to provide an opt out option for parents who are adamantly opposed to uniforms or whose children transfer into the school after the beginning of the school year. A uniform policy will work if parents and students are involved throughout the decision-making process. If it is decided that a school uniform program is to be implemented, it is recommended that students be given the ultimate decision as to what the uniform will look like.

Hamilton (1999), a principal of an elementary school in Plainfield, New Jersey, had experiences similar to those previously described and stressed the importance of getting parents and students involved early in the decision making process. Parents who are in favor of the uniform policy can be encouraged to talk with those parents who are opposed to the idea. This positive support from parent peers, along with as much data as possible from the school, usually convinces those in opposition to at least try the new program. Parents who find buying uniforms a financial burden can receive assistance to ease this problem through local businesses or charitable organizations (Hamilton, 1999; Stanley, 1996).

Even with reported positive results, there are those who are opposed to school uniform policies (Caruso, 1996; Evans, 1996; Wide, 2013). Arguments against establishing school uniform policies include the view that:

1. uniform policies are an infringement on First Amendment rights,
2. having such a policy is a tool of power for school administrators,
3. uniforms represent an unnecessary cost burden given to parents,
4. gangs and violence still exist even with uniforms being worn,
5. uniforms do not do away with class distinctions between the "haves" and the "have nots,"
6. uniforms are simply a Band-Aid on the issue of school violence,
7. uniforms make students a target for bullies from other schools, and
8. uniform policies are difficult to enforce in public schools.

Each of these issues is important and must be addressed when the possibility of initiating a school uniform policy is being considered.

It has been suggested that the real push behind school uniform policies has been more political than research-based (Black, 1998). A study conducted by Educational Testing Service (1998) showed no apparent relationship between the use of school uniforms and student achievement or behavior. It may be concluded at this point that there is little significant research evidence to support that having students wear school uniforms improves discipline, increases student respect for teachers, promotes school spirit, raises academic performance, equalizes social status, or any other claims made by those promoting uniform policies. While some evidence exists to support school uniforms at the elementary and middle school levels, little evidence exists to support school uniforms for high school students. In spite of these acknowledged differing views, and in an attempt to address student management problems in their schools and make their schools safe, some education leaders and school boards still have instituted school uniform policies, and a number of the communities that have such policies do report positive results. Nevertheless, those who oppose such policies continue to note that there is little empirical data that support a link between the utilization of the policies and desired student behavior outcomes. The approach clearly deserves greater study.

Zero Tolerance

Since the 1990s, school systems have continued to adopt zero tolerance policies even though many researchers have reported that inherent problems exist in this type of solution to discipline problems (Martinez, 2009). **Zero tolerance** is *a policy for managing student behavior, usually adopted on a school district-wide basis, represented by the use of certain predetermined consequences when particular rules are broken; the consequences are applied automatically regardless of the circumstances surrounding the rule being broken.* Zero tolerance policies actually grew out of national drug enforcement efforts and later were used by public schools to address an array of unwanted student behavior problems that were frequently dangerous in nature such as the use of firearms (Skiba & Peterson, 1999). School systems began adopting tough codes regarding student behavior after Congress passed the 1994 Gun-Free Schools Act which required a one-year expulsion for any student bringing a firearm or bomb to school. Zero tolerance policies in many states, however, also are written to address such problems as fighting, drug or alcohol use, and gang activity, as well as more frequently observed offenses like possessing over-the-counter medications, disrespect of authority, sexual harassment, threats, and vandalism. In 1997, more than 90% of the public schools across the country had zero tolerance policies for fire-arms or other weapons and more than 85% had the policies for drugs and alcohol (Koch, 2000). Still significant, in 2010 more than 75% of public schools in the United States had some type of zero tolerance policy (Borum, Cornell, Modzeleski, & Jimerson, 2010). Even without consistent research supporting their use, zero tolerance policies seem to be prevalent across the nation based on the few studies that have been done (Ofer, 2011/12). Supporters of zero tolerance maintain that violence in schools has become lethal and must be addressed in a firm manner while critics of zero tolerance maintain that the approach affects a disproportionate a number of students at risk, as well as students who are poor and minority (Manning & Bucher, 2013).

Zero tolerance policies have become controversial in many areas. By 2004, the large number of reported cases where students were suspended for seemingly trivial offenses such as carrying legal, nonprescription pain killers (Advil, etc.), having small pocketknives in their cars, or having plastic knives in lunch boxes sparked broad public controversy (Zero Tolerance (schools), 2007). Yet, there are those who believe such policies help educators create the best environments for learning and that zero tolerance ensures that all students are treated equally. Others such as Skiba (2001) and his associates at Indiana University reported that such policies are typically overly harsh toward minority students. Still others hold the position that creating an environment where students know that minor offenses may be seen as reasons for suspension will make students more careful and, thus, better behaved. Many, however, take the position that this type of environment is neither good for learning nor good for student development (Ghezzi, 2006). Even though few adults have any tolerance for such behaviors as young people using drugs or drinking alcohol, all instances of student misbehavior are not as easily assessed. For example, a zero tolerance policy becomes much less clear if the word "using" is replaced with "possessing." Consider the following all-to-common scenario:

> a student in the elementary school was suspended from school because her mother put a butter knife in her lunchbox so that she could spread jelly on her sandwich.

The suspension took place because the school district had a zero tolerance policy against the possession of weapons (in this case possession of a knife) on any school campus. The student brought a knife to school in her lunchbox, and, therefore, the policy was applicable to her. While many argue that the little girl should not be suspended, they are still in agreement that knives should not be allowed on school property. Just this one simple illustration points to the complexity of the issue. In 2010, the New York City Civil Liberties Union, along with the American Civil Liberties Union, in conjunction with the Dorsey and Whitney Law Firm, filed a class action lawsuit against the NYPD's policy concerning the seizing and arresting of school children in violation of the Fourteenth Amendment (Ofer, 2011/12).

One of the major complaints voiced about zero tolerance policies is that minor, sometimes seemingly innocent infractions receive the same punishments as more serious violations as seen in the example with the butter knife. Curwin and Mendler (1999), two well-known educators who have written a great deal about behavior management and student motivation, support the validity of this complaint. They argue that the major problem with zero tolerance policies is that they treat all behaviors the same without allowing for a close examination of the motivation behind each individual behavior. Essentially, they are used too broadly as opposed to being individually applied to the specific situation. This creates an unfair system, they aver, which treats a student whose behavior may reflect only a minor problem with the same consequence of a student whose behavior is clearly antisocial.

Many educators have concern with the type of atmosphere felt to be created in a school where zero tolerance is practiced (Black, 2004; Ofer 2011/2012). It is observed that schools characterized by behavior controls such as zero tolerance policies are not as likely to develop attitudes and behaviors in students which are supportive of a productive democratic society (Hyman & Snook, 2000). The philosophy of zero tolerance, with its strong foundation on external rules and harsh punishments, tends to exacerbate youth violence, not abate it. Dwyer, Osher, and Hoffman (2000) indicated in their research that educators should avoid using techniques that label students or which oversimplify complex management and motivational issues. They caution that harsh penalties and zero tolerance policies are not the answer to problems of school violence. Instead of focusing on student behaviors in isolation, critics of zero tolerance policies recommend that schools should promote management policies that focus on the individual differences among students and the motivation behind given student behaviors. Management models that do this tend to include input from a variety of individuals including students, steps to correct unwanted behaviors through reflection, and interaction in a democratic, student-centered atmosphere (Curwin & Mendler, 2004; Dwyer et al., 2000; Skiba & Peterson, 1999; Wagner, Knudsen, & Harper, 1999/2000).

In spite of the fact that they enjoy a certain level of popularity, there is a lack of strong empirical evidence that supports the use of zero tolerance programs and their use may, in the view of many, be counterproductive (Skiba & Petersen, 2000). While supporters of zero tolerance policies credit recent declines in crime and school weapons cases to their use, there is little research data to support this claim. In spite of the lack of compelling statistics, 85% of principals, 79% of teachers, and 82% of students credit zero tolerance policies with keeping drugs out of schools (Koch, 2000). Those who support such policies believe that they promote safety in schools and give everyone involved more peace of mind while those who oppose the policies feel that they lack a sound rationale and are far too extreme (Grant, 2006).

There is no question that certain types of student behaviors cannot be tolerated in school settings. Likewise, there are important issues that must be addressed concerning the severity of the consequences associated with some misbehaviors, the motivation behind the behaviors, and the developmental characteristics of students exhibiting the behaviors. For example, a strong statement has been made for the development of zero tolerance policies in cases of sexual harassment (Essex, 2000). And yet, there must be differences between how such policies are applied across the PreK-12 grade span such as in kindergarten versus high school settings. It has also been argued that zero tolerance policies should exist to protect middle-level gay and lesbian students from being subjected to name calling and similar harassment (Taylor, 2000). In selecting any system of behavior management or consequences for these types of unwanted behaviors, at what point do students benefit more from sensitivity training and education to heighten social awareness as opposed to experiencing punishment for their behaviors? Is it possible that punishment will make harassing students even more aggressive toward gays and lesbians? Many believe that it will.

Research suggests that zero tolerance policies have been only moderately effective at best and frequently ineffective (Martinez, 2009). Four conditions have been identified that need to be present if the policies have any chance of making a positive difference in controlling student behavior (Blair, 1999). These conditions are that:

1. clear consequences for misbehavior must be developed and applied consistently,
2. all stakeholders (e.g., educators, parents, students, etc.) must collaborate in developing the policies,
3. those developing the policies must have a knowledge base of what has worked and failed in other school districts, and
4. there must be an integration of a comprehensive health and education program to help individual students with their problems.

Regrettably, today's world is one where some students bring guns to school and threaten or actually do harm to other students and teachers. Drugs are often found and sold within the walls of elementary, middle, and high schools. There are schools where young female students are frightened to walk down hallways because they are often touched and/or talked to in ways that are grossly unacceptable and where both young female and young male students are scared when they go into school restrooms. The challenge is how to establish an atmosphere within all schools that is safe, healthy, and educationally productive. A major question that must be dealt with when considering zero tolerance policies is, "how far should school policies go to protect students at the expense of certain democratic principles and rights that should permeate society?"

Expulsion

Tied closely to the concept of zero tolerance is the practice of expulsion (Wagstaff, 2004). **Expulsion** is *a process exercised by a school district's governing authority, generally the school board, of banning a student from attending school for the remainder of the school year or the remainder of the school year plus an additional period of time carried into the next school year.* An example of this would be when a student is expelled in May for the remainder of the school year plus all or a portion of the following school year. The enforcement of an expulsion and the determination of the length of an expulsion are made by the school board in a session where the student is allowed to have legal representation. Zero tolerance rules often result in either suspension, where the student is not allowed to return to school for a specific period of time (e.g., three or four days), or expulsion (Richards, 2004). The use of suspension and expulsion is a cornerstone of zero tolerance (Larrivee, 2009).

As with zero tolerance, a serious concern has been raised regarding the results of expulsion policies in that African Americans, as a group, are the recipients of a disproportionate amount of suspensions and expulsions (Townsend, 2000). Schools with higher numbers of African American and Latino students are more likely to have zero tolerance policies and, when students are suspended or expelled, they are more likely to enter the juvenile justice system (Jones & Jones, 2013). A survey of twelve large school districts showed that in some districts black students are three to five times more likely to be expelled or receive suspensions than white students. In Phoenix, Arizona, for example, while black students made up only 4% of the high school population, they received 21% of the expulsions and suspensions. White students received only 18% of the expulsions or suspensions but made up 74% of the total student population. Figures from the U.S. Department of Education identified that in 1997 black students represented 17% of the public school enrollment nationwide while also making up 32% of those suspended (Koch, 2000). An Allegheny County, Pennsylvania, 2006 report of students under court supervision identified that, of the 555 students under supervision between September and June, 463 (83%) were black and 90 (16%) were white (Grant, 2006). Expulsions add to the problems already experienced by many African American youths resulting in poorer educational opportunities and, ultimately, a greater rate of dropping out of school. The high rate of expulsions among African Americans is sometimes felt to be due to or at least influenced by cultural differences between these students and the predominantly white, middle class teaching work force. These cultural differences often lead to misunderstandings and misinterpretations of attitudes, behavior, tone, and working styles (Townsend, 2000).

For many, cultural differences are at the heart of the expulsion issue. Students who are most likely to be expelled and alienated from the system are the same students who often are already having problems in school and who arguably could benefit most from a quality public school education before entering the job market. Students who have difficulty learning and fitting into the middle class school society become unhappy, alienated, and less likely to comply with their teachers' expectations. Middle class children come to school to be educated and typically are reinforced for the values and mores of their society. Low socioeconomic status (SES) minority students come to school to be educated and, in the view of many, to get changed to the middle class social mainstream. This change is frequently painful and hard to accept. Many see the change as a misguided goal in the first place. In response to what is often interpreted as "forced change," many of these students rebel and some even threaten the safety and learning of others. They often fail, drop out, or are expelled and enter the world lacking the skills needed to support themselves, become nurturing parents and productive members of the community. Such children ultimately have their own children (before they become adults, they become parents) and these children often then come to school without the necessary parental and home support to be successful. The cycle continues and repeats itself seemingly *ad infinitum.*

Expulsion is the most serious strategy used by schools in student behavior management. When expulsion is used, the student's right to a public education is forfeited. In expelling a student from school, the position has been taken that the negative impact of having the student in the school setting is greater than the negative impact on the student's life when the student is removed from school. While some students have the financial means to attend a private school or pay tuition to attend school in another school district, many, if not most, expelled students do not have such options and spend their time out of school in unsupervised activities. This type of situation can lead to even greater problems. Research on school suspensions has found that up to 40% of school suspensions are due to repeat offenders (Skiba, 2001). Such practices may establish a downward spiral for both a student and the school. Many students offend and then re-offend. The punishment is disconnected from the student's needs, intent, and learning and the school ultimately denies its mission to teach (Larrivee, 2009). The decision to manage behavior through expulsion can have a profound negative impact on the lives of students and their families and should never be approached lightly. One study with students who had a history of prior drug use reported that separation from school and poor teacher-student relations were associated with subsequent drug use and other risky health behaviors. With young adolescents, being disconnected from school predicted their drug use two to four years later. One implication from these findings is that keeping adolescents in school, forming positive relationships, and connecting students to caring adults and peers can be critical in creating a protective environment for students who are already fragile in many ways (Fletcher, Bonell, & Hargreaves, 2008).

This is not an argument to abolish expulsion as an approach to behavior management. Schools cannot be allowed to become arenas for violence and bullying or sites for drug deals. It is an argument, however, for being especially careful and reflective before using expulsion as a management strategy. If used at all, expulsion should be the last resort to solve student management problems. Research shows that expelled students who do not attend alternative classes are less likely to re-enter school at a later point in their lives and more likely to get involved in gang activity, use drugs, and otherwise run afoul of the law (Koch, 2000). Expulsion should be used only when educators are certain that the impact of a student's negative behavior on the learning environment and safety of the school and other students outweighs the fact that the behavior of the student being expelled may deteriorate beyond help in the future after the expulsion.

SAFE ENVIRONMENTS FOR EXCEPTIONAL STUDENTS

Creating safe environments for exceptional students brings about the need for the development of a system that protects the rights of all students while ensuring that no group of students is given advantages beyond those of any other group. For example, it has been shown that many of the programs that have reported success in dealing with bullying have failed to address students with disabilities or create interventions for at-risk students (Rose, 2010; Rose & Monda-Amaya, 2012). Research suggests that students with disabilities are bullied more frequently when compared to nondisabled students; researchers have also found that students with disabilities are also more often the bully (Rose & Monda-Amaya, 2012; Van Cleave & Davis, 2006).

The management and motivation of exceptional students raises unique questions in the minds of many educators and parents regarding expulsion. The expulsion of exceptional or special students is an issue that creates its own set of complex concerns. If special education students are held to different disciplinary standards, they are not fully a part of the mainstream curriculum and procedures of the school. An effective disciplinary code that applies to all students can help create a more productive learning environment. The misperception that educators are expected to tolerate different behaviors for exceptional students, in fact, is largely the result of unclear administrative procedures and communications (Taylor & Baker, 2002). It has been suggested that there is a double standard with respect to the management of exceptional students vis-à-vis other students and a number of court cases can be identified that support the point that current laws place an inordinate burden on educators when questions of the management of exceptional students arise (King, 1996). Some feel that current laws may actually influence or encourage exceptional students to demonstrate a lack of responsibility for their behavior and respect for the system.

Before they are suspended or expelled, educators must offer evidence that the unacceptable behavior of an exceptional student is not a manifestation of the student's condition of exceptionality. Morrison and D'Incau (2000) studied special education students in California who had been referred for expulsion and identified that the causes of the unwanted behaviors were often triggered by events outside of the school. Even though students were performing poorly in school, it was often determined that the school system was not providing the services needed to help them deal with their deep-seated, unique challenges. Some educators actually believe that it should be easier to remove students with exceptionalities from the school setting when their behavior seriously interferes with the learning or safety of others (King, 1996). Others argue that schools need to do more to help exceptional students and support them within the regular school environment (Morrison & D'Incau, 2000). Decisions regarding expulsion, in particular when they involve students with exceptionalities, are extremely difficult to make and typically require expert legal guidance.

While there are obvious concerns about the rights of all students, special attention is given to the rights of students with exceptionalities under Public Law 94–142, the Individuals with Disabilities Education Act (IDEA) of 1975 (Eggen & Kauchak, 2013). This far-reaching law requires that educators working with students having exceptionalities do the following:

1. provide a free and appropriate public education (FAPE),
2. educate children in the least restrictive environment (LRE),
3. protect against discrimination in testing,
4. involve parents in developing each child's educational program, and
5. develop an individualized education program (IEP) of study for each student.

When managing students who have exceptionalities, there is more to be concerned with than just the legal, social, and educational ramifications of expulsion. Public Law 94–142 directs educators to ensure that students addressed in this legislation receive the most appropriate education possible in the least restrictive environment (LRE). Special students are diagnosed, an individualized educational program (IEP) is developed for each student by a team of educators, usually with parent participation, and the students are included as appropriate in a regular classroom setting (referred to by some as being mainstreamed) for either part of or the entire school day. Management and motivational problems associated with many exceptional students are related to the difficulty that they have in competing academically with other students, in receiving positive attention from their teachers and other students, and in feeling equal to and accepted by other students (Curwin & Mendler, 2004).

For the most part, the courts have supported school districts when their rights to expel individual students have been challenged. Even in cases where due process questions have arisen, the courts have consistently backed school district decisions (Zirkel, 1997; Zirkel & Gluckman, 1997). One reason given for this is that expulsion often takes place as a result of extreme circumstances such as violence, drug-related behavior, and general antisocial behavior which negatively impact the learning and safety of other students and which society strongly condemns. Little tolerance is shown for such behaviors when they are school-related.

If a teacher has a student with an exceptionality who is characterized by exhibiting unacceptable behaviors in a regular classroom setting, it is important that a plan or specific strategy be developed to help the student adjust to the setting in which he or she has been placed. If the teacher chooses to ignore the student's special needs and continues to teach as if the student were like all other students in the class, problems most definitely will occur and the student's rights will have been violated. If ignored, the student's unacceptable behavior will likely continue and possibly worsen. The teacher's behavior in not addressing the problem will be running contrary to federal law and, in fact, ethical practice. Teachers cannot let problems go unresolved, but must make adaptations in their instructional programs to accommodate the unique characteristics of exceptional students.

Four reasons why some students have difficulty fitting in the mainstream of American public education were identified following a study to determine if differences exist between students who are referred and those who are not referred for special education services (Gottlieb & Weinberg, 1999). The reasons include:

1. referred students come from families that are more transient than those of nonreferred students,
2. most of the students who were referred received a referral because they were behavior problems, weak academically, or highly unmotivated,
3. referred students were late to school substantially more often than nonreferred students, and
4. most referrals were made by a very small number of teachers who lacked training in the use of behavior management and instructional techniques that could be used as interventions that might reduce the need for the referrals.

Many students are referred for special education placements for reasons of being difficult to teach, presenting management problems for their teachers, and being different from the other students. When these students are included in regular classrooms, they many times are being sent back into environments where they already have shown a history of unacceptable behavior and poor performance. This can lead to increased management and motivation difficulties for their teachers as well as enhanced learning problems for the students themselves.

When principals and teachers work with special students, it is important that they have an understanding of the laws that protect their legal rights when behavior management techniques are being considered. Teachers and administrators need to be familiar with the basic features of IDEA, Section 504 of the Vocational Rehabilitation Act of 1973, the Americans with Disabilities Act of 1990, and the IDEA Amendments of 1997 (Smith & Colon, 1998). Since 1975, Congress has amended IDEA three times, 1986, 1997 and 2004. The Amendment in 1986 extended the rights and protections of IDEA to children aged three through five and held states accountable for locating young children who need special education. The 1997 Amendments, IDEA 97, brought about the features identified earlier in this chapter, i.e., FAPE, LRE, protection against discrimination in testing, the right to due process, and IEP. IDEA 1997 clarified much of the gray area that previously existed concerning the discipline of students with exceptionalities by expanding the authority of school officials when such students are found to have drugs or weapons in their possession (Osborne, 1998). The Amendments aided in the determination of whether or not a student's unacceptable conduct is related to the student's exceptionality and clarified that educational services must be continued for the student, even when the student has been suspended or expelled for misconduct unrelated to the disability.

The provisions of the IDEA Amendments of 1997 also impacted the behavior management responsibilities of IEP teams (Smith, 2000). The Amendments identified that a special education student can be placed in a 45-day interim placement in an alternative setting as a result of behaviors involving weapons, drugs, or dangerous activity (Dayton, 2000). When this 45-day interim placement is used, however, the IEP team must conduct an assessment of the behavior to determine if a link exists between the misconduct and the student's exceptionality. The team must also develop an intervention program, an IEP that addresses the unwanted behavior, and designate an interim alternative educational setting for the student.

In IDEA 2004 (Eggen & Kauchak, 2013), amendments included mechanisms to:

1. reduce special education paperwork,
2. create discipline processes that allow districts to remove students from classrooms who inflict serious bodily injury,
3. establish methods to reduce the number of students with diverse backgrounds who are inappropriately placed in special education,
4. make meeting the highly qualified teacher requirements of No Child Left Behind legislation of 2001 more flexible by allowing veteran teachers to demonstrate their qualifications by means other than a test, and
5. include students with disabilities in accountability systems (critics warn that testing students with exceptionalities in the standard ways harms more than helps them).

Many factors must be considered when regular classroom teachers, special educators, and school administrators manage the behavior of exceptional students. Weatherly (2000), an attorney who specializes in case work for students with exceptionalities, recommended that school officials follow specific guidelines in working with and providing services for exceptional students. These guidelines include:

- suggest appropriate individualized education services for each student,
- get all appropriate educators together with parents for IEP meetings,
- set all final decisions for education and placement in IEP meetings,
- do not let cost or availability of services interfere with decisions,
- avoid the inclusion of unnecessary details in the IEP,
- give due consideration to outside private evaluations of students,
- send parents written notice of any proposed changes in the educational program,
- develop a behavioral-management plan for disruptive students,
- show care when suspending or expelling disabled students, and
- remember that the right to a free and appropriate public education belongs to the student, not the parents.

Regular classroom teachers who have *included students* in their classrooms have much to consider regarding their approaches to management and student motivation. In preparing to work with such students, it is advised that teachers first address their own feelings toward the realities of working with exceptional learners. Teachers of students with exceptionalities must learn to deal with the frustrations and defeats that may come after long hours of planning and dedicated instruction. Teachers also need to be prepared to give an appropriate level of responsibility for behavior and learning to the special students themselves. Many teachers actually take too much responsibility for the behaviors of their students and need to recognize that they cannot accept excuses for behavior from students that are not legitimate and that they cannot solve all of their students' problems for them. Teachers can and should, however, set clear and appropriate limits and expect students to follow them. Exceptional students, as with regular students, must learn to take responsibility for their own behaviors and take an active part in their own problem solving and decision making. It is essential for teachers to be able to communicate with the special students in their classrooms, even if the students themselves have communication difficulties. In so doing, teachers need to be prepared to give special students honest feedback. This feedback might include praise but may need to also include constructive criticism. When carefully done, teachers actually can help an exceptional student by publicly acknowledging their own mistakes. This strategy of communication and openness tells the student that it is acceptable to try and sometimes fail. The classroom should be an inviting as well as structured environment. Many, if not most, students with exceptionalities perform best in environments that are highly structured and, therefore, predictable.

Safety in the school and classroom are of paramount importance and preventing bullying and the victimization of disabled students is dependent upon several variables (Rose, Monda-Amaya, & Espelage, 2011). Importantly, teachers must be aware of the specific characteristics of those students in the school environment who have disabilities and, at the same time, be cognizant of the prevalence and type of bullying that exists in the school. Schools must develop appropriate intervention strategies that address the needs of students with disabilities as well as focus on the social awareness of the entire school community (Swearer, Espelage, & Napolitano, 2009). Finally, it is especially important that educators, parents, and community agencies collaborate to create the best possible school environment for all students and accept that it will be impossible to create a safe environment for all students unless all members of this collaborative team believe it can be done.

Some identify that it may be better to focus on general guidelines that will be helpful in working with special needs students and other students who struggle with behavior instead of considering only specific behaviors or interventions for separate categories of special needs (Levin & Nolan, 2010). These guidelines assume that the teacher regularly modifies instruction to meet the student's needs and enable the student to experience success. Table 5.4 identifies twelve guidelines for working with special needs students in this regard.

ADDRESSING DIVERSITY

Many have suggested that achievement gaps and discipline gaps are opposite sides of the same coin (Gregory, Skiba, & Noguera, 2010). Considerable research has been dedicated to the investigation of the factors that might explain why there is a racial gap in school discipline where nonwhite students are involved in more discipline issues than their fellow white students. Gregory et al. (2010) examined the impact

Table 5.4

Guidelines for Working with Special Needs Students

1. Help the student develop a sense of belonging in the classroom. Model a positive attitude of welcome and acceptance and create opportunities for the students in the class to get to know each other and to work cooperatively.

2. Parents of special needs students typically have a better understanding of their child's behavior than their teachers do. This is especially true in the early part of the academic year. Parents understand what situations and contexts are likely to help the student maintain self-control and those that make self-control more difficult.

3. Use the expertise of other specialists as part of the problem-solving process. Read the student's IEP carefully and consult regularly with special education teachers, school psychologists and counselors, physical, speech, and occupational therapists, and therapeutic support staff and paraprofessionals who work with the student.

4. Your ability as a problem solver will be the most important tool that you possess to help students be successful and control their own behavior. Be a student of the student's behavior. Observe the student carefully and record as much information as possible about the student's behavior. Document those events and contexts that trigger inappropriate student behavior and those that lead to increased self-regulation.

5. Recognize and encourage positive behavior and effort whenever possible. Help the student to keep track of progress in his or her behavior over time.

6. Teach to the student's strengths whenever possible and gradually move from strengths to areas of weakness. The teacher's goal in maximizing student success should be to use the teaching modalities (visual, aural, kinesthetic, tactical, and so on) that match the student's preferred ways of learning as much as possible.

7. Make both instruction and your daily schedule predictable. Many special needs students function better when they are able to predict events that will occur and prepare themselves emotionally.

8. Keep instruction brief, clear, and to the point. If there is a long series of steps that students must follow to complete a given task, sequence the steps and introduce one or two at a time instead of giving all of the directions at once.

9. Hold appropriate but high expectations by focusing on the quality of work that the student does rather than the quantity. Help the student to clearly understand what high-quality work looks like by providing exemplars and rubrics, and by ensuring that students understand the criteria that you use to judge their work.

10. Work to make sure that students have the opportunity to learn the social skills that they lack. When students are lacking the social skills that they need to interact positively with classmates, it is important that they be given the opportunity to develop those skills.

11. Teach students self-management skills that they can use to gain or regain control when they experience problems. Breathing and relaxation techniques; anger management strategies, such as slowly counting to ten; or stop-relax and think, as well as nonpunitive timeout are tools that students can use to keep it together when things start falling apart.

12. Use functional behavior assessment (FBA) and positive behavior support to help students with special needs learn to control their behavior when appropriate. Certain states may require that FBA and positive behavior support be used before suspending or excluding a special needs student.

Source: From Levin, J., & Nolan, J. (2010). *Principles of classroom management: A professional decision-making model* (6th ed.). Boston: Pearson, pp. 249–251.

of factors such as poverty, neighborhood issues, achievement, differential selection, and processing issues to explain why nonwhite (especially black and Latino) students are involved in significantly more discipline problems than their white counterparts and noted that not one factor can be identified that accounts for this problem. In addressing this problem, a part of the solution needs to include school administrators becoming acutely aware of potential bias that takes place in disciplinary actions. Educators also need to try to understand why some students exhibit more misbehavior than others while, at the same time, improve practices designed to keep all students on task and engaged in learning.

Many schools and classrooms across the country are characterized by students of diverse socioeconomic backgrounds, skin colors, religious practices, and national origins. While this kind of diversity can form the foundation for rich and varied educational experiences for all students, it can also contribute to problems in communication and understanding between teachers and students, teachers and parents, and even students and students. These problems can be manifested through instructional challenges in making the curriculum relevant, interesting, and appropriately rigorous, and through classroom management and student motivation difficulties.

The majority of educators in schools today are from white, middle-class backgrounds. However, of the almost 50 million students in schools during academic year 2001–2002, 35% were from minority ethnic groups; this percentage is expected to increase to 44% by 2020 and to over 50% by 2040. In one of the nation's largest school districts, students come from 52 different countries and speak 52 different languages while the percentage of teachers from minority groups is about 13%. Nearly half of the schools have no minority teachers. This situation, predictably, can lead to misunderstanding, conflict, distrust, hostility, and negative teacher expectations. Students who come from a different segment of society, having different cultural backgrounds and life experiences, can quickly find it difficult to communicate and feel comfortable with many of their teachers and administrators. Some teachers have problems helping students of color for many reasons, including the fact that many teachers and administrators may actually hold negative perceptions of and expectations for their students (Banks, 1994). These negative perceptions and expectations generally emerge from a lack of understanding of the students' backgrounds and a difficulty in communicating openly and honestly with them. Nevertheless, behavioral expectations need to be high for all students (McEwan, 2003). If students come from difficult family situations with impoverished backgrounds and hold values different from those held by their teachers, they still must be expected to exhibit acceptable conduct as is expected of others. To expect less is to violate the student's right to an equal educational opportunity. If negative student behaviors are ignored by a teacher based solely on a student's background, in time the teacher will most assuredly be faced with a troublesome discipline problem. This was discussed earlier as related to teacher expectations and teacher efficacy. One of a teacher's greatest challenges is to hold appropriately high expectations for all students while meeting the unique needs that students from diverse backgrounds sometime bring to the school and classroom.

Even teachers who do not come from a white, middle class background, but who come from a background of a different culture, may not be prepared to deal with the challenges that they find in the classroom when called upon to serve students from a socioeconomic status or culture different from their own. Many have predispositions toward their students and hold stereotypes that unfairly label and characterize them. This lack of understanding of ethnic and cultural sensitivity on the part of some teachers and administrators can quickly lead to a total misunderstanding of student behaviors. Students coming from some cultural backgrounds, for example, may have adopted a set of behaviors which are accepted and considered appropriate in the home but which are considered inappropriate at school. A situation like this may lead such students to react in unanticipated ways to many of the traditional approaches to behavior management used by their teachers. Teacher expectations and procedures used at school in conducting classroom instruction may be very foreign to them (Zabel & Zabel, 1996). Teachers are advised to be cautious and not assume that just because children or families are from a specific ethnic or racial group that they necessarily share a common cultural experience. There are differences within cultures and within families. Students who are able to maintain comfort with behaviors that are valued in their home as well as those valued in the wider society, including the school, may be more likely to have positive views of themselves in both cultural contexts (Marshall, 2001).

Helping students from diverse backgrounds includes having an understanding and appreciation of the customs of these backgrounds and an understanding of why they have different values and behaviors than those traditionally found in and rewarded in schools. Inappropriate behaviors should not be ignored and change can be both difficult and slow. But, change can be positive if educators are informed, patient, and nonjudgmental. Students in underrepresented minority groups have culturally relevant knowledge and diverse cognitive abilities that schools can use to promote learning. When teachers teach and assess in ways that respect different student strengths, students learn and perform better (Sternberg, 2006). A part of the challenge includes getting students to know, accept, and respect each other (Wiest, 2003). Having students think critically about culture can help them toward achieving this end. To do this, students themselves must better understand the meaning of culture. Table 5.5 identifies opportunities that students could have in their schooling experiences to develop this cultural understanding. By exploring these different aspects of culture, students will understand each other better, and, through the instructional experiences that bring this understanding about, teachers will also understand their students better, in particular those of different cultural backgrounds.

There is no doubt that socioeconomic factors have a major impact upon the quality of education any student receives, regardless of the school. A 1994 report from the Children's Defense Fund identified that almost one-fifth of all school children live in poverty and over 40% of

Table 5.5

Schooling Experiences to Develop Cultural Understanding

1. Contemplate the value of diversity.
2. Define culture.
3. Take another individual's perspective.
4. Analyze social behavior.
5. Speculate on the meaning of observed actions and interactions.
6. Interpret language.
7. Analyze and compare cultural customs.
8. Explore change in and alternatives to habitual behavior.
9. Examine sociotypes and stereotypes.
10. Identify sources of intercultural conflict.
11. Propose solutions to intercultural problems.
12. Devise social action measures.

Source: From Wiest, L. (2003). Twelve ways to have students analyze culture. *The Clearing House,* January/February, 136–138.

that group come from families whose income is less than one-half the poverty level (Children's Defense Fund, 1994). Children from such backgrounds are at risk of failure, especially in the present day world of high-stakes accountability and standardized testing. They also are at risk of being misunderstood, not having their personal and learning needs met, and subject to higher levels of disciplinary actions, suspensions, and expulsions from school (Townsend, 2000). The program *Raising Healthy Children* is designed to help reduce the problems associated with adolescence for at-risk students (Cummings & Haggerty, 1997). Emphasis in the program is placed on developing a bond between students, their family members, and the school. *Raising Healthy Children* offers teachers training in proactive classroom management strategies, motivation skills needed for at-risk students, and techniques for teaching social skills and reading. Through the program, parents participate in workshops designed to help their children (students) socially and academically while collaborating with their teachers. Programs such as this that offer specific skills to teachers while developing a strong parenting component represent positive approaches to dealing with problems that may result from social and cultural diversity.

Many disadvantaged students who attend high schools in urban communities come from difficult home and community circumstances and face unique challenges (Matus, 1999). For example, many adolescents from such communities hold full-time jobs, making it virtually impossible for them to consistently complete the homework that their teachers assign. Because of their work schedules, they also are often tired and easily distracted at school. Teachers and administrators need to use a humanistic approach to management with such students, including peer mediation programs and flexible scheduling of classes and assignments to help them adjust simultaneously to school and work expectations. Conflict Resolution, an example of a peer mediation program, was introduced in Chapter 3. The importance of treating students with respect, not yelling or speaking harshly to them, and rewarding them when they do well cannot be overemphasized. Teachers must be sensitive to the needs of all of their students and make every effort to understand the reasons for their students' behaviors when some of these behaviors may be unacceptable, and be informed by these reasons when seeking solutions to their problems.

As previously noted, public schools are institutions built upon middle class values and mores and run by a teaching work force that comes largely from a predominantly white, middle-class background. Many students in the public schools, however, are neither middle class nor white, resulting in a greater chance for miscommunication and misunderstanding between teachers and students. Efforts at behavior management, which can create tension in any situation, can bring about especially unique classroom problems in this context where miscommunications and misunderstandings can prove to be particularly damaging. While all students need to be held to high standards of conduct in the school setting regardless of their personal backgrounds and circumstances, teachers and administrators need to be knowledgeable and appreciative of the unique characteristics and needs of a diverse student body and of each individual student in the student body. This type of sensitivity in teachers and administrators can come only from an understanding of the reasons for certain behaviors that students exhibit. Having this understanding will enable all educators to be more effective in helping all students conduct themselves in acceptable ways. Lack of sensitivity can quickly create a "me against them" attitude or feelings of pity for students on the part of teachers and administrators. Either of these attitudes will lead to feelings of alienation on the part of at-risk students. All students can learn, and a student's culture is a significantly important part of the learning package and potential that each student brings to school. To engage students from diverse cultural and linguistic backgrounds, teachers must see them as capable learners (Villegas & Lucas, 2007). Teachers need to hold the view that all students can learn and, in the case of culturally different students, have a specific framework for addressing their learning needs. In working with such students, teachers must be prepared to: (1) understand how their students construct knowledge, (2) learn about their students' home lives and communities, (3) be socioculturally conscious, (4) hold affirming views about diversity, (5) use appropriate culturally response instructional strategies, and (6) be advocates for all students.

THE FIRST YEAR OF TEACHING

The first year of teaching is a time of great challenge, complexity, and adjustment, as beginning teachers must be able to face many new and different demands and respond to them effectively. In a review of a large number of studies focusing on important challenges faced by beginning teachers, classroom discipline heads the list and motivating students is second (Tauber, 1999; Veenman, 1986).

Martin and Baldwin (1996) studied how beginning teachers are different from experienced teachers in the way they perceive classroom management and how school counselors can help them develop better learning environments in their classrooms. They found that teachers who had taught three years or less had more controlling attitudes toward students than did those who had taught more than three years. It is suggested that this controlling attitude toward students can result in less favorable learning conditions, damage to student self-esteem, and that school counselors should be used to coordinate mentor programs between experienced and novice teachers. School counselors could also lead support groups where new teachers can brainstorm solutions to shared problems and provide consultation to new teachers concerning best practice techniques for managing and motivating students. While the first year of teaching poses difficult challenges for many teachers, equally challenging is determining ways to support and assist beginning teachers as they enter the profession. Understanding the phases that many beginning teachers go through can be helpful not only to the beginning teachers but also the administrators and veteran teachers who are there to assist them. Table 5.6 identifies five phases of transition found in the first year of teaching.

Table 5.6

Phases of Transition in the First Year of Teaching

Phase	Characteristics of the Phases
Anticipation	The anticipation phase begins during the student teaching portion of preservice preparation. The closer student teachers get to completing their assignments, the more excited and anxious they become about their first teaching positions. New teachers enter with a tremendous commitment to making a difference and a somewhat idealistic view of how to accomplish their goals. This feeling of excitement carries new teachers through the first few weeks of school.
Survival	The first month of school can be very overwhelming for new teachers. They are learning a lot and at a very rapid pace. They are instantly bombarded with a variety of problems and situations they had not anticipated. Despite teacher preparation programs, new teachers are caught off guard by the realities of teaching.
	During the survival phase, most new teachers struggle to keep their heads above water. They become very focused and consumed with the day-to-day routine of teaching; there is little time to stop and reflect on

Phase	*Characteristics of the Phases*
	their experiences. Particularly overwhelming is the constant need to develop curriculum. Although tired and surprised by the amount of work, first-year teachers usually maintain a tremendous amount of energy and commitment during the survival phase, harboring hope that the turmoil will subside.
Disillusionment	After six to eight weeks of nonstop work and stress, new teachers enter the disillusionment phase. The intensity and length of the phase varies among teachers. The extensive time commitment, the realization that things are probably not going as smoothly as they want and low morale contribute to this period of disenchantment. New teachers begin to question their commitment and their competence. Many new teachers get sick during this phase.
	During the disillusionment phase, classroom management is a major source of distress. The accumulated stress of the first-year teacher, coupled with months of excessive time allotted to teaching, often brings complaints from family members and friends. They express self-doubt, have lower self-esteem, and question their professional commitment. Getting through this phase may be the toughest challenge that new teachers face.
Rejuvenation	The rejuvenation phase is characterized by a slow rise in the new teacher's attitude toward teaching and generally begins in January. Having a winter break makes a tremendous difference for new teachers. It allows them to resume a more normal lifestyle, with plenty of rest, food, exercise, and time for family and friends. This vacation is the first opportunity that new teachers have for organizing materials and planning curriculum. This breath of fresh air gives novice teachers a broader perspective with renewed hope.
	Through their experiences in the first half of the year, beginning teachers gain new coping strategies and skills to prevent, reduce, or manage many problems they are likely to encounter in the second half of the year. During this phase, new teachers focus on curriculum development, long-term planning, and teaching strategies.
	The rejuvenation phase tends to last into spring with many ups and downs along the way. Toward the end of this phase, new teachers begin to raise concerns about whether they can get everything done prior to the end of school. They also wonder how their students will do on the tests, questioning once again their own effectiveness as teachers.
Reflection	Beginning in May, the reflection phase is an invigorating time for first-year teachers. Reflecting over the year, they highlight events that were successful and those that were not. They think about the changes that they plan to make the following year in management, curriculum, and teaching strategies. The end is in sight, and they have almost made it; but more importantly, a vision emerges as to what their second year will look like, which brings them to a new phase of anticipation.

Source: From Moir, E. (2011, August). *Phases of First-Year Teaching*. Retrieved February 24, 2013, from http://www.newteachercenter.org.

It is critical that new teachers are assisted in easing the transition from student teacher to full-time professional. Recognizing the phases new teachers go through provides a framework for the design of support programs to make the first year of teaching a more positive experience. Beginning teachers need a well-planned, extensive, and continuous induction program with a strong mentoring component with master teachers that lasts for at least the entire first year of teaching if not longer. Experienced teachers need to be encouraged to assist first-year teachers by providing them with practical information, political *savoir-faire*, and professional support (Morgon, 1997). Practical information involves important, everyday matters such as how to fill out purchase orders, the location of preferred parking places, and even which copy machine to use. Political *savoir-faire* deals with how certain things are perceived and what may or may not be acceptable behavior in certain situations such as dealing with parents and colleagues. Professional support could involve sharing lesson plans, guidance on ways to motivate certain students, and methods of classroom management. When inexperienced teachers receive this type of advice from supportive, experienced teachers, they typically become less frustrated and more likely to remain in the teaching profession longer. The more comprehensive induction support that a new teacher receives, the more likely the teacher is to remain in the profession (Strong, 2006). In a study where 72 teachers were examined six years after they were enrolled in an induction support program that provided them with veteran teachers released full-time as mentors, 84% of the teachers were still teaching after four years. This compares to a nationwide figure of 67% after the same period of time. These numbers suggest that comprehensive induction support is effective in increasing teacher retention.

Principals also must be key figures in the mentoring of new teachers. Brock and Grady (1998) reported findings from a study conducted with principals and first year teachers that explored the needs of beginning teachers and how principals can assist them. The study showed that most principals offer new teachers some type of orientation program, assign mentors to new teachers, and spend time working with new teachers on an individual basis. Although the new teachers in the study felt that the orientation and mentoring programs were helpful, most of them indicated that they would have preferred to have had more time with the principal to get clearer perspectives on the principal's expectations for them and more immediate feedback on their performance.

Although there are many teacher education programs throughout the country that prepare candidates for initial certification, there is often a wide variance across these programs in the abilities of their graduates, even among graduates of the same program. In spite of its agreed upon importance, many teacher education programs fail to require students to take specific courses in the area of classroom management (Tauber, 1999). This is no doubt surprising to many given the repeated high rating of concern that teachers give to working with student behavior problems. Much of what teachers learn with respect to classroom management techniques comes through school district efforts in in-service training and what some offhandedly refer to as "on-the-job training." Because district programs vary in their approaches to preparing teachers, and because individuals are naturally different in many ways, all first-year teachers are not equally prepared to teach, manage, and motivate their students. This is especially true since the level and ultimate effectiveness of their preparation may be relative to the type of school in which they are teaching. For example, a first-year teacher who might be well prepared to teach in a rural school setting may find it difficult to be successful in an inner-city setting. Likewise, teaching in a suburban school site near a large metropolitan area like Chicago or Miami would present a different set of challenges from teaching in a school located on an Indian reservation in Oklahoma or one in the Appalachian area in North Carolina. Teacher training institutions must continue to improve the preparation of their graduates to teach in present-day, standards-driven, diverse school settings. Principals also must understand the significant role that they have specifically in the development and success of beginning teachers and, at times, teachers-in-training. Many of the frustrations that drive young teachers out of the profession could be significantly reduced by more real-world initial preparation; effective instructional leadership; strong induction programs; and supportive, experienced colleagues willing to share with and support their first-year teacher colleagues. Professionals already in the field should see it as their responsibility to do everything in their power to ensure the success of beginning teachers. High rates of teacher attrition are well documented with one report citing 14% of teachers leaving after only one year and 46% leaving before the end of the fifth year (Auguste, Kiln, & Milller, 2010). The top five reasons that beginning teachers identify for leaving the teaching profession are: (1) poor working conditions, (2) testing pressure, (3) low wages, (4) threat of lay-off, and (5) burnout.

The following checklist represents advice given by first-year and veteran teachers to assist those entering their first year of teaching (What to Expect Your First Year of Teaching, 1998).

- Plan relentlessly; create back-up plans for teaching students of varying abilities.
- Set high, consistently reinforced expectations for behavior and academic performance.
- Show and require respect in the classroom at all times.
- Reach out to parents and your administration, preferably early on and before a problem arises.
- Consider participating in an extracurricular activity which strengthens relationships with students and can be enjoyable as well.
- Seek mentors, team teaching assignments, and regular exchanges with fellow first-year teachers.
- Be flexible and ready for surprises.
- Work closely with counselors or other school personnel authorized to respond to children's social problems.
- Take care of yourself physically and spiritually.
- Love learning, love kids, and love teaching.

TEACHER STRESS

It seems as though each academic year the demands on teachers increase and the reports of teacher stress increase proportionately. Educators are continually subject to higher levels of consistent stress than are professionals in most other fields (Crute, 2004). Problems managing and motivating students, pressure to produce high student test scores, increasing amounts of paperwork, and anxious parents and students are some of the factors that contribute to stress-related problems in the teaching workforce. Teacher job satisfaction has declined to its lowest point in 25 years and has dropped five percentage points in the past year, from 44% very satisfied to 39% very satisfied (*The MetLife Survey*, 2013); overall teacher job satisfaction has actually dropped 23 percentage points since 2008. Teacher job satisfaction has dropped while stress among teachers has increased significantly. Thirty-six percent of teachers in 1985 reported that they felt under great stress at least several days a week. That number today has increased to 51% of teachers indicating that they feel under great stress at least several days a week. Elementary teachers (59%) report greater stress than middle school teachers (44%) and high school teachers (42%). This level of stress has resulted in many young teachers leaving the classroom in only their first years of teaching. National Education Association data indicate that one-third of new teachers leave the profession in the first five years of teaching often because of stress-related issues.

Dealing with disruptions and students who are unmotivated are consistently identified as two of the primary sources of stress for classroom teachers. If this stress is sustained over long periods of time, the result can be teacher burnout. A teacher who suffers from **teacher burnout** is characterized by having reached a *point of extreme stress where the teacher has lost his or her enthusiasm for teaching and has little energy to focus on helping students learn.* Coming to work is difficult for such teachers who often complain of headaches, exhaustion, frustration, irritability, outbursts of anger, and many other similar symptoms including depression (Curwin, Mendler, & Mendler, 2008; Hendrickson, 1979). There is no doubt that discipline and stress go hand in hand. Some of the greatest sources of stress for teachers can be found in problems of interacting with students, addressing lack of student interest in school, and handling students with problem behaviors. These are essentially problems of motivation, management, and discipline. Although understanding conflict and stress is the first step toward developing successful coping behaviors, teacher preparation programs rarely include skill development, at least in-depth skill development, to help teachers deal with overwrought individuals. Reducing stress for all parties allows teachers to focus on the more important aspects of their jobs. Stress undermines physical, emotional, and intellectual energies precisely when strength in these areas is needed most (Morris, 1998). A teacher under stress is unlikely to be a good manager or motivator of students.

Although related, teacher burnout and attrition (i.e., leaving the profession) are not the same thing. Some teachers leave the profession because they are experiencing symptoms of burnout, but many others leave for other reasons. Too, all teachers who burn out do not quit. Some remain in the classroom though they have lost virtually all zest for their work (Zabel & Zabel, 1996). If the negative effects of being burned out cannot be reversed, it is in the best interest of the students, the schools, and the communities they are there to serve when these teachers leave the profession.

Certain identifiable factors exist in a teacher's world which can augment the possibility of burnout (Zabel & Zabel, 1996). The number of students assigned to a teacher can be seen by the teacher as creating an unfair burden, though in some cases this feeling may be more a result of perception than reality. Such a feeling is important, however, if it is real to the teacher. Stronger feelings and actual support from parents, other teachers, and especially administrators can ease the perception of being overburdened. The students assigned to teachers also can be a determiner of teacher stress. Students with exceptionalities, for example, especially those with emotional or behavioral problems, can behave in ways that are stressful to their teachers as well as their classmates. Additionally, teachers can become burned out if the expectations that they have for their jobs are greatly different than the realities of their jobs. Most teachers enter the profession for the intrinsic rewards that come with teaching, not an extrinsic reward such as salary. However, if a teacher does not receive intrinsic rewards from working with students, parents, or colleagues and teaching in general; if sufficient external rewards are not present; or if teaching in some way disappoints a perhaps overly idealistic view of the profession; job-related stress may be the end result. Disparity between expectations for teaching and the reality of teaching can be a real cause of stress. Many teachers become frustrated and develop feelings of inadequacy as a result of poor student performance. In the current era of high-stakes testing and accountability, increased expectations for student achievement have placed considerable stress on teachers and students alike. Because of these and other complex factors, many teachers are caught in a cycle of unfulfilled expectations and negative feelings, behaviors, and reactions from students, parents, colleagues, and administrators. In the end, they become frustrated because circumstances are not as they had expected which, ultimately, can lead to negative behaviors in the classroom. Negative teacher behaviors in the classroom often result in increasingly negative behaviors on the part of students. Increased levels of discipline problems, in turn, bring about increased levels of stress and frustration for teachers and the cycle continues.

In responding to their job-related stress, teachers can enter into either a Burnout Cycle or Renewal Cycle as a result of the approach they take in responding to stressful problems with students (Larrivee, 2009).

In the Burnout Cycle, the teacher responds to student misbehavior in one of two ineffective ways. The teacher either avoids the misbehavior by retreating (overlooks, ignores, denies, rationalizes, surrenders, or pleads) or attacks the misbehavior (orders, interrogates, blames, puts down, threatens, argues, provokes, punishes, or seeks revenge). As a result of either approach, there typically is no improvement in the student or the student's behavior worsens, and the teacher is often hurt or humiliated. The teacher's anxiety increases and the teacher often withdraws or acts out in some way. As a result, student misbehavior increases (Ratcliff, Jones, Costner, Savage-Davis, & Hunt, 2010). When the cycle becomes repetitive, burnout is the predictable end result. Teachers may suffer both physical and mental side effects, be preoccupied with negative thoughts, lack motivation to go to work, be fatigued and irritable and even experience muscular tension, high blood pressure or ulcers.

In the Renewal Cycle, the teacher responds to student misbehavior in one of two effective ways. In the first way, the teacher is proactive and initiates action (expresses feeling, clarifies teacher expectations, accepts ownership, provides rationales, invites participation, solicits information, enlists cooperation, or requests help). In the second way, the teacher is reactive in responding to something the student has initiated (validates student feelings, acknowledges student needs, respects student perspective, asserts teacher needs, provides options, offers assistance, mutually explores resolutions, or negotiates a plan). Through either of these approaches, student behavior typically improves and there is less confrontation. In this cycle, the teacher feels valued and respected. Through effective use of the Renewal Cycle, teacher self-efficacy improves, the teacher remains engaged and enthusiastic, and there is increased appropriate student behavior. The Renewal Cycle clearly is the desirable path for the teacher to take in that it produces positive results, not only for the teacher and his or her own health and effectiveness, but also positive results for the student in terms of student behavior and learning.

If the stress cycle is to be broken, teachers need to be able to examine their own feelings and emotions as an important first step toward stress reduction. In so doing, teachers must be prepared and capable of assessing how their feelings and behaviors affect their relationships with their students and colleagues (Rizzo & Zabel, 1988). The following suggestions are offered to teachers as effective approaches to deal with teacher stress (Nissman, 2009, p. 108).

- Recognize that stress is not a problem, but a symptom. Focus on what is causing the stress, e.g., classroom management, administrative pressure, lack of community support, home responsibilities, or lack of sleep, and take action.
- If stress is extreme, seek professional assistance.
- When experiencing a stressful situation, write down in a log the situation and how you are dealing with it. After a period of time, evaluate the log and see if a pattern develops. This information will assist you in making appropriate changes in your teaching.
- When experiencing anxiety, share your feelings with the people with whom you are dealing. This may lower your level of stress after an incident.
- Make a concerted effort to separate your stress-producing problems and handle them one at a time. Once you have coped with one situation, that success often alleviates other situations that have led to a stressful reaction.
- Evaluate your reactions and be sure you are not overreacting to the responsibilities placed on you. You cannot solve everyone's problems.
- Be open to investigate other professional areas in and out of education. Such an investigation or change can bring back the enthusiasm you once felt as a classroom teacher.

Since behavior management problems are a primary cause of stress and burnout, special attention to the way teachers' own behaviors affect their students is required if stress is to be reduced and brought under control. A teacher who dislikes or is feeling dissatisfied with his or her teaching quickly conveys these feelings to students who, recognizing this, often exhibit unwanted behaviors that then create more stress for the teacher. For this situation to improve, teachers must confront their feelings of stress and do something proactive to appropriately cope with them. Teachers who avoid holding back their emotions by finding safe ways to vent their feelings are much less likely to become overly stressed. Withheld emotions often lead to negative and depressing thoughts. Teachers who are able to think and act positively are more likely to project an acceptable image to their students, which then improves life in the classroom for everyone concerned (Curwin, Mendler, & Mendler, 2008).

Among other characteristics and strategies, a good sense of humor is a wonderful aid when combating burnout and stress. Though easy to say yet sometimes difficult to do, if a person can simply learn to laugh at himself or herself and not take too many things on a personal level, stress can be reduced. However, at times, too much stress can lead to dangerous depression or seriously aggressive acts. When serious problems of this nature are identified, it is advisable for the teacher to seek professional assistance from someone who specializes in issues dealing with job-related stress.

Administrators can and need to help teachers who are having stress-related problems (Pawlas, 1997). Nearly 7 in 10 (69%) of principals report that the responsibilities and expectations of the principal are not similar to those of the job just five years ago and that working with teachers and their stress-related problems has become an especially difficult challenge, although an important part of the principal's leadership responsibilities (*The MetLife Survey*, 2013). More principals identify that it is a challenge to maintain an adequate supply of effective teachers in urban schools (60% vs 43% in suburban schools and 44% in rural schools) and in schools with two-thirds more low-income students (58% vs 37% in schools with one-third or fewer). Principals should always take time to listen to a teacher's frustrations. A problem that may sound trivial to the principal can be truly stressful to the teacher who took the first step to visit the principal to talk about the problem. Principals need to be supportive and, whenever possible, make a point of looking for something good to share with a frustrated teacher. Giving reassuring advice or help to a teacher who seems to have encountered a particularly frustrating situation can be especially beneficial. The principal, for example, might speak to a disruptive student or request a meeting with the student's parents as a strategy to be of special assistance. Supportive, reassuring behavior by the principal can do a great deal to lift a teacher's morale. Some principals have created special support groups within their schools as a strategy to help teachers get help in stress reduction. Activities such as yoga, meditation, breathing exercises, and dance have been used successfully as strategies to make the work place more enjoyable and reduce the stress related to the responsibilities of teaching.

CONCLUSION

Chapter 5 provided a discussion of the importance of creating and maintaining a safe learning environment followed by an examination of key factors that educators should examine when trying to establish such an environment. Central to any concept of safe learning environments is the prevention of violence in schools explored here with an emphasis placed on the topic of bullying. Bullying, presented as an all-to-common form of violence among students, is discussed along with the topics of violence control and prevention focusing on the practices of zero tolerance, expulsion, and the requirement of school uniforms. An in-depth discussion of special concerns associated with providing safe environments for exceptional students as well as all other students in diverse learning communities is included.

The last two topics discussed in this chapter are of a slightly different nature. Special concerns of beginning teachers and the impact of stress and teacher burnout are seen as having special importance in any investigation of issues of best practice in classroom management and student motivation. Management and motivation concerns are uniquely related to both of these topics as issues of management and motivation are tightly intertwined with many of the problems related to the first year of teaching and the ongoing pressures of working in the profession. Consequently, they, in turn, are potential causes of teacher stress and burnout. This chapter has sought to extend the understanding of management and motivation in the classroom with respect to identified special problems while reinforcing the important need for educators at all levels to continue their study in these critical areas.

QUESTIONS/ACTIVITIES FOR REFLECTION

1. What is your personal assessment of zero tolerance policies related to student behavior management? Do you see zero tolerance positively or negatively? If you were a building administrator interested in adopting such a policy, how would you begin the process? What would be important questions that need to be answered?

2. Many teachers hold the view that expelling certain chronic misbehaving students from school is needed for the greater good of helping other students who exhibit positive behaviors. Others see ex-

pulsion as an act of discarding a human being into a world of little hope or positive future. Evaluate the strategy of expulsion as a means of dealing with student misbehavior and explain why you have made the evaluation you have made.

3. The practice of including exceptional students in regular classrooms has resulted in greater diversity in classrooms than ever before. Many regular classroom teachers are strongly in support of this practice while some believe that having exceptional learners in regular classrooms helps neither the regular students nor those that are exceptional. If you were a teacher in a regular classroom with exceptional learners, what important information would you need to know to be able to maintain a well-managed classroom with highly motivated students?

4. If you were a teacher new to the profession, what personal plan would you put in place to address the potential problems of teacher stress and burnout? What would be the key elements of the plan and how would you go about ensuring that the plan was successful?

5. A number of early warning signs related to potential student violence were introduced in the chapter. Interview three teachers working in classrooms today and review the signs on the list with them. What is their assessment of the problem of violence in schools and classrooms today and the accuracy of the warning signs on the list?

Chapter 6

RESPONDING TO STUDENT MOTIVATION AND BEHAVIOR PROBLEMS

> Future teachers and teachers alike would do well to model their practice on what we observed strong teachers doing: being alert and redirecting off-task behaviors, avoiding retreating, using appropriate praise and rewards, and being aware of pacing and keeping children engaged. (Ratcliff, Jones, Costner, Savage-Davis, & Hunt, 2010, p. 313)

The ability to respond to specific classroom behavior problems so that the problems are effectively addressed represents a special skill, or perhaps more accurately a set of skills, that requires development and refinement over time. Effective teachers as reflective practitioners must individually analyze unacceptable behaviors exhibited by students to develop acceptable ways to address each behavior and manage and motivate those students who are not conducting themselves in ways appropriate to the classroom.

This chapter will examine several instances of student conduct that are seen by most teachers as representing motivation and behavior problems (Charles, 1976; Hunt et al., 2009). The use of the Model for Reflection and Inquiry, introduced in Chapter 1 to help analyze and address problems of classroom management and student motivation, will be illustrated through the use of behavior management scenarios as practical examples of typical classroom problem situations.

TEACHER REACTIONS TO STUDENT MISCONDUCT

Teachers can and do prevent many problems from occurring through the effective use of managerial and motivational techniques that they regularly incorporate into their teaching. Researchers have identified that the most effective teachers spend less time addressing student behavior problems than teachers who are considered to be not as effective (Ratcliff, Jones, Costner, Savage-Davis, Sheehan, & Hunt 2010; Rimm-Kaufman, La Paro, Downer, & Pianta, 2005; Savage-Davis, Costner, Ratcliff, Jones, Sheehan, Scott, & Hunt, 2011)). In his initial research, Kounin (1983) compared the behavior of effective and ineffective teachers as classroom managers and concluded that the primary difference between the two groups of teachers was not in how they handled disruptive behavior, but in their dispositions to quickly and accurately identify a problem behavior and act on it. As previously discussed in Chapter 3, a key teacher disposition is the quality of *withitness*. **Withitness** is *the ability to have an ongoing awareness of events throughout the entire classroom and not just one area of the setting.* Even with the ability to display this and other key dispositions, the occasion will occur in virtually any classroom when a student acts in an undesirable manner. Undesirable behaviors may be represented by a minor infraction of rules such as talking too loudly or not waiting for others to finish talking before speaking. Or, the problem could be of a more serious nature such as a student endangering the safety of other students or doing something that directly interferes with the learning of classmates. It is critically important that teachers react immediately when a student openly fails to follow expectations for proper classroom conduct. *When a teacher is aware that a student is violating a rule governing student conduct yet does not react to correct and extinguish the behavior*, the teacher is said to be exhibiting **retreating behavior**. This behavior can lead to a vicious cycle that contributes to more unwanted student behavior in the future (Jones & Jones, 2013; Ratcliff, Jones, Costner, Savage-Davis, & Hunt, 2010). Teachers need to always be prepared for the potential need to alter (some might say correct) the behavior of some students and to correct those students who do not respond to their instructional, motivation, and management plans.

It has been suggested that any one of three different approaches to classroom leadership (i.e., management) can be used by teachers to modify student behavior (Schlechty, 1976). Influenced by the earlier work of social psychologists such as French and Raven (1959), the position is taken that, to be effective, teachers must earn or otherwise gain a type of social power or leadership over the students in the classroom. If the teacher does not maintain leadership of the group and all individuals in it, leadership will be gained by someone else, in this case one or more students. Teachers are felt to manage their classrooms through the use of one of three strategies: *normative, remunerative,* or *coercive.* **Normative strategies** are *behavior strategies used by the teacher in maintaining a well-managed classroom based on all involved doing what is traditionally expected of them because each person knows his or her expected role;* teachers are expected to direct or ask students to do certain things, and students are expected to do what their teachers direct or ask them to do. **Remunerative strategies** are *behavior strategies used by the teacher that are based on the power of rewards.* Rewards can take the form of special privileges, extra time to participate in enjoyable activities, or more tangible rewards such as candy or tokens (Borich, 2011; Borich & Tombari, 1997). **Coercive strategies** are *behavior strategies used by the teacher that are based on the power of punishment.* If students do not behave properly, they will be punished. Some educators believe that an over-reliance on coercive strategies may alienate students to the point that they withdraw from the learning process. Even with this potential concern, many teachers attempt to manage the learning environment through the use of coercive power. Such strategies, however, clearly can produce short-term gain coupled with long-term loss.

Normative power is dependent on the teacher's ability to gain respect from students. When teachers are seen as knowledgeable, trustworthy, fair, and concerned, students more readily respond to their requests (Goodlad, 1984). When teachers treat students with respect, students develop a greater sense of belonging or psychological membership in the classroom. Students respond more consistently to a system of management based on normative strategies when a respectful and trusting environment has been established. Such a relationship between students and their teachers is essential if effective management is to be realized (Glasser, 1986). Normative power is positional in that the role of *teacher* carries with it, by its very nature, a high degree of influence and authority. If teachers conduct themselves the way students feel teachers should conduct themselves, students typically will respond positively to their teacher's use of normative strategies and do what their teachers ask, simply because it is their teachers who are making the requests.

Operant conditioning forms the foundation of remunerative management. Chapter 4 included a discussion of the Applied Behavior Analysis management theory based on B.F. Skinner's theory of operant conditioning. The basic purpose that drives remunerative management is the motivation of students by the use of rewards so that they will continue to exhibit, and even intensify, acceptable conduct. The parent who gives money to a child for every "A" on the report card, the teacher who shows a special film because the students all made good grades on a mathematics test, or the principal who hosts a pizza party for all students who make the Honor Roll each represent uses of remuneration to motivate and manage students. One of the most important aspects of remunerative management is that it focuses on the positive, not the negative aspects of students' behaviors. In spite of this, many educators criticize management and motivation by the use of remuneration approaches suggesting that students should not be expected or motivated to exhibit appropriate behavior only for the purpose of receiving rewards (Kohn, 1993).

Coercive management relies on the use of physical or psychological pain or discomfort, taking away belongings or privileges, or threatening either of these measures to persuade (i.e., motivate) students to discontinue unwanted behaviors. An important concern regarding the use of coercive strategies is the fear that their use may increase student antagonism and lead to students becoming alienated from their teachers and the learning process. Since coercive strategies focus on the negative aspects of student behavior, it is important that teachers avoid the use of consequences that belittle, embarrass, or attack the character of a student. When consequences are given for undesirable behavior, teachers should focus on just that, the undesirable behavior, not the student as an individual. What should be emphasized in efforts to extinguish a student's unwanted behavior is that it is the behavior that is unwanted, not the student. Comments such as, *I don't know what you get away with at home, but you cannot do that in my room,* or *Stop acting so immaturely,* can come across as attacks on the student's character or that of the student's parents. Attacks such as these can result in hurt and embarrassment with the end result being alienated, angry, or otherwise disenfranchised students. In some cases, such attacks may also produce alienated and angry parents.

If a student does something that is considered inappropriate, the teacher should deal with the misbehavior and the consequence swiftly.

Identifying the consequences for undesirable behavior early in the school year emphasizes to students that they have an important responsibility for their own self-control (i.e., self-regulation) and forewarns them of the end result if they do not take this responsibility seriously (Emmer, Evertson, & Worsham, 2006; Evertson, Emmer, & Worsham, 2005; McCormick & Pressley, 1997). Early identification helps make clear in the communication process between the teacher and his or her students just what is considered as unacceptable and what is not. In establishing these ground rules, the teacher will have taken an important proactive and preventive step in dealing with potential management problems.

Greater emphasis has been given in recent years to observational research that is felt to provide a better understanding of specific teacher classroom behaviors related to student behavior, time-on-task, and academic success (Bracey, 2009a; 2009b). Pianta (2006) along with a group of his colleagues at the University of Virginia (see for example Rimm-Kaufman, La Paro, Downer, & Pianta, 2005) has been a leader in this research field. Another group of researchers following this same line of exploration are at Coastal Carolina University in South Carolina. These researchers have examined classroom climate with particular emphasis on teacher and student instructional interactions, teacher and student behavior management interactions, and student time-on-task behavior. These interactions were analyzed to determine if they had an impact on teacher effectiveness and student academic performance. The research results strongly suggest that the major variable that separates effective teachers and ineffective teachers is the teacher's ability to effectively manage student behavior in the learning environment (Ratcliff, Jones, Costner, Knight, Disney, Savage-Davis, Sheehan, & Hunt, 2012; Ratcliff, Jones, Costner, Savage-Davis, Sheehan, & Hunt, 2010; Ratcliff, Jones, Costner, Savage-Davis, & Hunt, 2010). Specifically, teachers who spend more classroom time dealing with student behavior problems spend less time providing instruction and their students, in turn, spend less time exhibiting on-task behavior. Recent research in high school settings (Ratcliff, Pritchard, Costner, Knight, & Hunt, 2013) also suggests that, as the amount of classroom behavior problems increases, student performance on standardized, end-of-course tests can be predicted to decrease. These researchers note that retreating behavior, previously discussed, is characteristic of teachers who have difficulty in managing student behavior. Using regression analysis (a statistic that allows a researcher to predict the likelihood that an increase or decrease in one variable can be used to predict an increase or a decrease in another variable), it was identified that an increase in teacher retreating could predict an increase in student off-task behavior at the p <.001 confidence level (Ratcliff, Jones, Costner, Savage-Davis, Sheehan, & Hunt, 2010). In a study at a public high school designed to educate academically gifted students, the researchers found that the major difference between the classroom environments of this school and regular public school settings was the lack of behavior management problems (specifically teacher retreating and student rebellion) and the presence of student on-task behavior, not the teacher methodologies or levels of questions asked by the teachers (Ratcliff, et al., 2012). Research is currently being conducted to determine the degree to which classroom climate factors related to specific teacher and student interactions may also be related to the achievement gap among students in the categories of gender, race (white/nonwhite), special needs, and poverty. Building on this foundation, the remaining sections of the chapter will focus on best practice as it relates to appropriately addressing management problems when they occur and being proactive in the avoidance of behavior problems before they happen.

THE PROACTIVE TEACHER

Being characterized as proactive as opposed to reactive in teaching says a great deal about how the teacher approaches meeting his or her responsibilities. The **proactive teacher** is *a teacher who has the ability to "head off" most management problems before they occur and respond to management problems when they do occur in such a way that sets the stage for learning to continue in the future.* Given that there will be cases of student misconduct from time to time in all classrooms to which teachers will need to respond, it is important that teachers remain appropriately focused on the purpose behind any use of their power. The teacher's primary purpose in reacting to student misconduct is to change the behavior of the student so that the school environment will be safe and conducive to learning for all students, including the student(s) exhibiting the misbehavior. The purpose is not simply to react to a disturbance or unacceptable behavior so that the disturbance or behavior is eliminated. In reacting to student misbehaviors, the teacher's emphasis should be on eliminating the unacceptable behaviors so that students displaying these behaviors, and their classmates, will gain the greatest benefit from their schooling experiences. Additionally, effective teachers see their responses to student misbehavior as opportunities to teach their students what proper behavior, in some ways proper social behavior, i.e., pro-social behavior, is and how they can exhibit this behavior. In this process, they also teach and reinforce which behaviors are considered to be improper, i.e., antisocial. Their responses to student behavior problems focus specifically on the undesired student behaviors while avoiding personal attacks on students. Teacher responses that can be interpreted as personal attacks on students increase the probability of future disruptive behavior. More importantly, such responses can result in a decrease in student learning. Teachers who concentrate their efforts on motivating students to do better, as opposed to policing them to not misbehave, establish more productive learning environments and fruitful relationships with their students.

A number of teacher behaviors have been identified through educational research that are associated with a behavior management system and a learning environment that encourage students to conduct themselves appropriately (Cotton, 1999). The behaviors and system also decrease the likelihood that students will misbehave in the future. The following behaviors are recommended in establishing an effective behavioral management system.

1. Set behavior standards that are similar to the standards set in the building conduct code.
2. Tell students that there are high standards for conduct in the classroom and clearly explain rules and consequences for their behavior.
3. Have standards that are conscious of cultural influences on conduct.
4. Give students a written set of behavior standards and review the standards periodically.
5. Establish clear and specific rules at the beginning of each school year or semester.
6. Allow students to help establish rules and procedures in grades 4-12.
7. Provide appropriate amounts of review and re-teaching of rules in PreK-3 settings.

8. Link discipline sanctions to the students' inappropriate behaviors and avoid using or threatening to use corporal punishment.
9. Focus on teaching positive, pro-social behaviors, especially when students consistently repeat inappropriate behaviors.
10. Quickly stop students who are disruptive (i.e., do not retreat) to avoid loss of learning time and maintain student on-task behavior).
11. Focus on inappropriate behaviors and not the students' past offenses or personalities.
12. Handle disciplinary problems themselves with referrals to administrators only in rare situations.
13. Actively seek new methods and strategies to improve students' behavior management skills.

Teachers who exhibit these behaviors are considered proactive in their approaches to student motivation and classroom management. Instead of waiting for a disruption to occur before acting or being reactive, they use behaviors and strategies designed specifically to create an environment that decreases the potential for inappropriate conduct occurring in the first place; thus, the opportunities to retreat are lessened greatly. Hunt et al. (2009) discussed eight behaviors that characterize teachers who create environments designed to promote positive student behavior and diminish student misbehavior. In exhibiting these desired behaviors, the teacher:

1. prepares thoroughly so that all students stay on task with activities suitable for their individual rates, styles, and abilities of learning,
2. develops classroom routines that help students get through non-instructional times when behavior problems are most frequent,
3. communicates with parents to develop a strong support system to work with specific management problems,
4. maintains a professional demeanor when carrying out their duties and responsibilities,
5. recognizes inappropriate student behaviors and deals with them quickly while ignoring insignificant conduct,
6. exhibits calm, confident behavior when correcting inappropriate student conduct,
7. follows up immediately on directives when students do not respond positively, and

8. focuses on preventing problems instead of reacting to problems.

These behaviors focus on the development of classroom learning environments where teachers can rely mainly on a normative management system with the teacher and students together forming a positive learning relationship founded on trust and respect. They also reinforce the need for the teacher to utilize effective teaching practices that keep students focused and involved in constructive learning activities and reduce "down times" when most misbehavior occurs.

Maintaining a professional demeanor, exhibiting calm and confident composure, and reacting only to truly inappropriate and not minor student misbehaviors are all ways for teachers to earn the trust and respect of students. Following through with appropriate consequences when students fail to respond to directives is an essential behavior used by effective teachers to develop consistency in their management. Schlechty (1976) and Hunt and Bedwell (1982) noted that teachers who retreat and ignore students who do not respond positively to their requests greatly increase the chance of having more management problems in the future. The need to know how to prevent problems has similarity to the need for the teaching profession to become more science than art and for teachers to recognize their need to know what works specifically and in what situations (Marzano, Pickering, & Pollock, 2004). For this to occur, teachers must have a desire and commitment to change. Knowing how to prevent problems requires being willing and able to learn from past mistakes as well as accomplishments and to seek and utilize the assistance of other professionals. Freiberg and Driscoll (2004) used the term **advancework** in referring to *the process of preventing problems before they begin rather than reacting to problems after they have already occurred.* Advancework requires teachers to gather information needed to develop a better understanding of their students, the community and school, and the impact the content being taught has on the behavior of their students.

One further aspect of effective management not yet discussed to this point is that teachers who desire to minimize their management problems set as a goal the development of inner self-control in students (Good & Brophy, 2007). It is not sufficient for teachers to be satisfied merely in being able to manage their classrooms and students. A major part of the enculturation needed in any school is for students to learn to manage how to live and function in a supportive environment with others. Without self-control, an aspect of being a self-regulated learner, it is difficult if not impossible for students to resolve the various conflicts that may develop in their lives on any given day.

The first days of the school year or the beginning of a semester are critical for the teacher to develop a system of rules and procedures for effective classroom management. Various research studies have identified that one important quality that characterizes effective teachers as managers is that they establish their expectations for student behavior early and consistently reinforce them thereafter (Emmer et al., 2006; Freiberg & Driscoll, 2004). It is recommended that teachers use the first weeks of the school year to clearly communicate their rules and procedures to their students, observe student attitudes and work habits, and begin instruction with a high level of energy and enthusiasm (Evertson et al., 2005). This will help greatly to establish a foundation upon which the teacher's academic program can be built. Such clarity is also needed in working with parents to ensure a positive approach to developing good classroom management at the beginning of the school year (Wong & Wong, 2009).

Effective teachers project themselves as leaders in the classroom while creating a learning environment based on concern, trust, and respect. Students maintain a high level of productivity because they are regularly engaged in learning activities (i.e., exhibiting on-task behaviors) appropriate for their learning styles, interests, and abilities. Students have a clear understanding of the rules and procedures for classroom behavior and the consequences that accompany the breaking of rules or not following procedures. They observe that the teacher quickly and consistently takes action to ensure that all students follow established rules and procedures, that there is a high standard for conduct, and that they must assume responsibility for their own behavior.

Teachers who aspire to meet these expectations and who follow these guidelines will have students who more regularly conduct themselves in an appropriate fashion. As this discussion has made clear, student misbehavior in the classroom can be a symptom of ineffective teaching which can lead to a cycle of student misbehavior, followed by teacher retreating, followed, in turn, by increased student misbehavior that has the potential to challenge the teacher's ability to regain control (Ratcliff, Jones, Costner, Savage-Davis, & Hunt, 2010). Because effective teachers accept that it is unrealistic to believe that all student misbehavior can be prohibited and that problems can occur even in what may appear to be the best of classroom situations, as a result of their study and prior planning they are prepared to handle these problems swiftly with minimum interruption to the learning process. Table 6.1 organizes effective teaching concerns related to motivation and management into three categories: *personal considerations, instructional considerations,* and *environmental considerations.*

Table 6.1

Teaching Concerns as Personal, Instructional and Environmental Considerations

Personal Considerations	*Instructional Considerations*	*Environmental Considerations*
Teachers should conduct themselves in a calm, confident manner.	Able students must be challenged.	The classroom should be a clean, comfortable setting.
Teachers need to be prepared for unexpected events.	Low ability students should not be placed in unduly frustrating situations.	The classroom should be void of major distractions to learning.
Positive student behavior should be praised.	Instruction should be both exciting and enjoyable.	A few rules for acceptable conduct should be clearly stated.
Teachers should show respect and affection for students and ensure that student ideas are valued.	A variety of questioning patterns should be utilized including low and high cognitive questions that are broadly distributed.	Parents and administrators must offer support and understand the roles that have been established for them.
Students should be treated in a consistent fashion.	All students should experience success on meaningful tasks.	The atmosphere should be one of acceptance.

Source: From Hunt, G., Wiseman, D., & Touzel, T. (2009). *Effective teaching: Preparation and implementation* (4th ed.). Springfield, IL: Charles C Thomas Publisher, p. 204.

ADDRESSING SPECIFIC MANAGEMENT PROBLEMS

The teacher's role in student motivation and classroom management should be examined in the context of the ideas and recommendations presented throughout the entire body of this text and not in any one chapter. As emphasized, the most productive learning environments are those where high levels of motivation and an absence of student misbehaviors are found. Teachers are encouraged to keep in mind that student misbehavior is typically the symptom of some other problem occurring in the classroom or perhaps in the personal life of a student. While the teacher must address the misbehavior, he or she must also be proactive by identifying the source of the misbehavior and taking the necessary steps to prevent the problem in the future.

What is unacceptable behavior? It is important for both teachers and students to have the answer to this question clearly in mind as effective teachers do not react to just any student behavior that appears undesirable. Consider the following four definitions of unacceptable behavior. Unacceptable behaviors are behaviors that:

1. disrupt the learning of one or more students,
2. threaten the safety of one or more students,
3. are in direct violation of written schoolwide or classroom rules, and
4. are a violation of accepted social mores (e.g., the use of profanity, inappropriate touching, etc.).

In addition to these four definitions, teachers often identify rules for student behavior specific to their individual classrooms as part of their own individual management and discipline plans. That which is unacceptable in one teacher's classroom may be acceptable in another teacher's, while some behaviors are always unacceptable in every classroom. For example, some teachers may have the expectation that students should speak only after first raising their hands and being recognized while other teachers may encourage more open discussion and actually expect and desire spontaneous participation from their students. However, if there are schoolwide rules for certain behaviors, such as that no candy is to be eaten in classrooms or no hats are to be worn inside the school building, all teachers are expected to enforce these rules.

The number of rules a teacher has influences how much time the teacher will spend monitoring and managing student behavior. The more rules there are the more time will be spent in seeing that they are followed. It is recommended that teachers have only those rules considered to be most important and which relate specifically to promoting the instructional program of the classroom. The fewer rules the better with no more than five or six being considered maximum by many teachers. Not only do greater numbers of rules create added monitoring problems for teachers, they create greater problems for students in trying to remember them and the consequences that will occur when they are not followed.

Many authors have identified and categorized various kinds of student misbehaviors found in classrooms and made suggestions concerning strategies teachers can use when confronted with them. It is important to recognize that student misbehavior needs to be analyzed and then addressed in a situational manner as such behaviors are contextual. What may prompt a behavior in one student may not in another. What may prove to be an effective remedy to one problem in one situation may or may not be as effective in another (Gootman, 2008). The following section of the chapter examines eight frequently observed student misconduct behaviors and provides suggestions for teacher intervention strategies. Misbehaviors that students repeatedly display are referred to as chronic misbehaviors and teachers need to take actions to minimize their presence in the classroom. Even with this information, teachers are advised to analyze and evaluate each situation independently and then apply the most suitable solution. The behaviors included here are: *inattention, disruptive talking, attention-seeking, chronic avoidance of work, dishonesty, unruliness, defiance,* and *aggression.*

INATTENTION

Inattention behaviors are defined simply as *students not paying attention when the teacher is conducting instruction or when participation in an instructional activity is expected (i.e., they are not exhibiting on-task behavior).* Common inattention behaviors exhibited by students are daydreaming, staring into space, doing unrelated work, doodling, or even playing with some object, e.g., calculator, toy, ruler, during instructional time. Inattention is often seen as one of the least severe management problems, typically because the inattentive student tends not to disturb other students in the classroom. However, this can be a serious problem because inattention is off-task behavior, and off-task behavior has been shown to be related to ineffective instruction (Baugous & Bendery, 2000; Ratcliff, Jones, Costner, Savage-Davis, Sheehan, & Hunt, 2010; Waxman & Huang, 1997). If not addressed, one student's inattention can be adopted by other students in the classroom if the inattention is seen as being acceptable to the teacher.

Working with Inattention Problems

If a teacher's lesson is progressing well, the teacher who has twenty-five students in a classroom is advised to not interrupt the instructional process that is effective with twenty-four students for one student who may be inattentive. While it is important that all students attend to the teacher's lesson, there are more subtle ways to effectively address the problem of a student being inattentive than to disrupt the learning of the rest of the students in the class to eliminate the inattentive behavior of one or even a few students. Moving physically closer to an inattentive student will usually help bring the student's attention back to the learning task or to what the teacher is saying. This use of proximity control will allow the teacher to modify the student's behavior without ever having to say a word. When teachers are physically close to students, the likelihood of student misbehavior diminishes.

Teachers can do a number of things to be proactive in preventing student inattention with the first step being to evaluate the physical arrangement of the classroom. Researchers established years ago that students sitting in certain parts of the classroom get less teacher attention than other students and are more likely to be inattentive if they are so inclined (Adams & Biddle, 1970). It is recommended that seating arrangements be developed so that those students most inclined to be inattentive sit as near to the teacher as possible. The corners of the classroom farthest from the teacher are areas to avoid for students prone to inattentiveness. The distance between the student and the teacher is an important variable when determining the likelihood of a student being inattentive.

Another important physical factor affecting inattention is spacing. Students who are seated too closely to one another automatically have greater opportunities for distractions. When students are seated at tables, adequate space must be provided so that each student has a comfortable work area that does not encroach on the area of other students. It is best when space is provided away from the student's immediate work area for the storage of excess books and supplies that can become distractions. Lack of adequate space and comfort increases the probability that distractions and inattentiveness will occur.

Room temperature is another physical factor that affects attention. While comfort level as far as temperature is concerned varies from individual to individual, it is generally better to have the room temperature slightly cool rather than warm. If the room temperature gets too warm, activity may slow down and some students are likely to become sleepy.

A final physical factor affecting inattention is the presence of distractions in the classroom. Most elementary school students sitting beside a window overlooking a playground are almost certain to be distracted. Similarly, many students at the secondary level sitting beside an open door leading to a busy hallway may lose their focus on the teacher's lesson. Although there are some distractions over which teachers have little control (e.g., construction workers, the first snow of the year, the onset of important events, etc.), to the degree possible, distractions should be eliminated or at least minimized to help students stay on task.

Beyond physical factors, the teacher's own instruction can be an important factor impacting student attentiveness. Student inattention will increase when the teacher's instruction lacks excitement and enthusiasm. Though some may say that teachers cannot be exciting every minute of the day, this is little consolation when students are inattentive or exhibiting some other form of unwanted behavior. Instruction that is not stimulating may reflect insufficient preparation on the part of the teacher in preparing for instruction, motivation, and management at the same time. Effective teachers are enthusiastic and often animated. They think about their students individually when they plan their lessons in terms of how a particular activity will draw students into the center of the instructional process or leave them on the edge. Teachers who have inattentive students are often characterized by doing the same thing over and over, lacking spontaneity and excitement, teaching subject matter that students see as having little importance or meaning to them or as being too difficult for them to master, and not engaging students actively in the learning process. Teachers are encouraged to use a variety of different instructional strategies, vary stimuli to encourage student interest, and use multi-media presentations and hands-on activities to add excitement to their instruction. Even though quiet, sedentary activities have a place in the classroom, many students, especially younger students, have difficulty maintaining attention when involved in activities that do not require their involvement for extended periods of time. Classrooms where students are given the opportunity, and are expected to actively participate in the learning activities, as well as the actual planning of the activities as appropriate depending on their age, constitute environments that foster student attentiveness. Students who are involved in learning activities that are meaningful to them are seldom inattentive.

Beyond questions of classroom environment and instruction, certain personal characteristics of the teacher may augment student inattention. The monotonic voice that drones on has become a symbol of the uninteresting, stereotypical bore. Teachers who talk in this manner should not be surprised if their students become inattentive or even disruptive. Use of voice inflections is recommended along with complementary gestures to enliven the teacher's instructional delivery. The use of humor at the moment students' minds are starting to wander also is an effective strategy. Teachers should never underestimate the effectiveness of an appropriate joke or humorous anecdote with students of all ages.

The source of some attention problems also can be found in the students themselves as opposed to the teacher or the physical environment. Some students may be inattentive even though the teacher is doing an excellent job teaching a dynamic curriculum due to personal problems either at school or outside of school that are so severe that it is difficult, if not impossible, for them to attend to their class work. Too, students who have been allowed to be inattentive at other times in other classes or during other lessons may have developed a pattern of behavior of not attending to the lessons that their teachers present. They may have developed shorter attention spans simply because they have never been required to be attentive. To help a student become attentive, the teacher first must understand the reason why the student is inattentive. Gaining this understanding will require problem solving and analysis on the part of the teacher. If the cause of the student's inattention is a personal problem, counseling may be needed. If the student simply has poor learning habits, it is the teacher's responsibility to reinforce the student when good attention is shown and not give reinforcement when it is not.

Developing an effective questioning technique can be a very effective strategy to help students be more attentive (Good & Brophy, 2007). Teachers are encouraged to ask a variety of questions and direct these questions to a variety of students. When a teacher asks a question first and then calls on a student for an answer, this questioning approach encourages all students to listen to the question, in case they may be called on to answer it. It also helps the students focus on the answer that is eventually given to the question. Teachers should remain aware of to whom they have directed their questions to make sure that their questions are uniformly delivered throughout the classroom. This strategy was discussed in Chapter 4 in reference to the equitable distribution of the teacher's questions. It is easy to fall into a pattern of directing questions to only a few students, typically to those who are more normally responsive and attentive. This pattern of question asking allows students who are not involved in the questioning process to become inattentive as they become disconnected from the lesson. Asking questions has the potential to draw students into the instructional process and strengthen the students' active connection to the teacher's lesson. Asking questions also has the potential to embarrass students publicly in the classroom. A teacher who calls on a student knowing that the student is being inattentive, thinking that putting the student "on the spot" in front of his or her classmates will cause the student to be more attentive in the future, can be making a major error in judgment. Not only may the student not be attentive in the future, the student may resent the teacher for the public embarrassment and be motivated to be involved in more serious forms of misbehavior than inattention.

Teachers are encouraged never to reinforce or reward student inattention; unfortunately, this is an error that is easy to commit. When a teacher gives directions and students do not pay attention, the teacher is actually reinforcing this unwanted behavior when the directions are regularly repeated or when students are allowed to ignore the directions that have been given. This teacher behavior sends the message to the other students in the class that being attentive is not necessary. Good listening habits are learned behaviors, and students who habitually fail to be attentive will improve their abilities to pay attention only if their behaviors are shaped by the teacher to do so. This will take time. Teachers must be patient yet firm.

DISRUPTIVE TALKING

Disruptive talking is *talking that interferes with the learning process by interrupting the teacher while teaching or students as they are listening to the teacher or as they are involved in completing activities that the teacher has assigned.* Different teachers set different standards for acceptable student talk in the classroom, and this fact itself can cause confusion for students who move from teacher to teacher during the school day. There may be no other standard for unacceptable student behavior that varies as much from teacher to teacher as the one that defines acceptable talking in the classroom.

Working with Disruptive Talking Problems

Different teachers invariably have different views of what is an appropriate level of student talk in the classroom. Individual teachers may even vary during the school day or from day to day as to what they consider to be a permissible level of student talk. This variance could be determined by many things, even the type of lesson that is being conducted. For example, a teacher normally will accept a greater amount of student talk when a cooperative group activity is taking place than when students are involved in a more traditional teacher-led discussion. All students can understand and adjust to these differences when they know what the teacher expects. This is, when the ground rules are clear. Problems arise for students when they do not know just what teachers expect or when expectations are changed based on reasons unknown to the students. It is confusing to students when teachers fluctuate from situation to situation for no apparent reason. Teachers need to be consistent with their standards and expectations and avoid punishing a student one day for a behavior that was considered acceptable on another.

Students become involved in disruptive talk for many reasons. Although the need to talk with peers is a strong drive for many students, teachers can take steps to prevent or eliminate such unwanted interaction when it is disruptive to the instructional process. One strategy to address this type of problem is for the teacher to be certain that initial directions and instructions are stated clearly. Students often talk to classmates as they try to figure out what the teacher wants them to do. Teachers should observe students for nonverbal indications of confusion and ask questions to be certain that their directions are clear to everyone before having students start an activity or before moving on to the next segment of a lesson. Idle talk also can be a result of lessons that are not felt to be motivating. As is true with inattention, much unwanted talk will disappear if students are involved in lessons that require their participation and that hold their interest.

The prevention of disruptive talk begins with the teacher. Students who are given an assignment that is stimulating and meaningful enough to hold their interest and adequate to occupy them for the entire instructional period are not likely to become involved in unwanted talk. This is an important point to remember as disruptive talk can occur when students have been given work that is too simple and which results in an abundance of idle time just as it can develop when they have been given work that is too difficult. This type of situation leads to frustration as students do not see themselves as being able to be successful on what the teacher wants them to do. It is critical that teachers understand the abilities and interests of their students in planning and delivering their instruction, in particular as this relates to student talk and attention.

Additionally, it is not uncommon for certain special events in the school or classroom to lead to unwanted talking and teachers must be prepared for this. For example, teachers should explain to students what they consider to be appropriate behavior when guests come to the classroom, when the class goes to an assembly, or when students go on field trips. Teachers should talk to their students about these and other similar events before they occur and review with them what they expect. These are all important proactive and preventive measures on the teacher's part. Students have a natural curiosity and will want to ask questions and talk when special events such as these occur. If the teacher prepares for this beforehand, instead of waiting until the level of student excitement is at its highest, there will be less unwanted talking, confusion and frustration on the part of the students as well as the teacher.

Certain instructional activities also will naturally stimulate what may initially seem to be unwanted talking, especially with younger students. If issues of excessive student talk develop, teachers are encouraged to discuss the problem and its causes with the entire class. While it is difficult for students to objectively examine their behavior when they are excited, it is possible for them to look back at a later time and reflect on what they did that may have been considered inappropriate and discuss ways to avoid previous unacceptable behavior. Teachers who lead by example instead of bossing students, and who work to develop positive relationships with their students, will have positive results from class meetings that can be used to address an issue such as this (Glasser, 1998).

Although some undesired talking can be explained by unexpected events or the use of certain instructional activities, some students have problems with excessive talking regardless of what is taking place in the classroom. In many cases, these students can be better controlled through the classroom seating arrangement and teacher movement during instruction. Some students will talk excessively if they are allowed to set together and simply separating their seats can reduce if not eliminate this behavior. As with inattentiveness and the use of proximity control, nearness to the teacher can act as a preventive measure for unwanted talking. Teacher movement will also add an additional dynamic to the lesson that will increase the likelihood of students attending to the teacher rather than to each other. The following strategies should be considered when working with students with disruptive talking problems (Nissman, 2009, p. 105).

- Use proximity to get in the middle of the classroom, possibly touching a noisy student's shoulder to keep class discussion flowing without bringing peer attention to the student.
- Allow students free time to chat. This may cut down on the talking out of turn.
- Confer with parents and possibly help them establish a reward system for their children for having good days.
- Allow students to communicate during seatwork time through writing notes or whispering. However, abuse of his privilege should result in some predetermined consequence.
- Give a warning or warning signal (e.g., flicking the lights on and off); if talking persists, use a predetermined consequence.

A word of caution is important with respect to student talk. Teachers are encouraged to rethink their goals in teaching if they desire to teach in classrooms where student to student talk is discouraged or considered inappropriate. Instructional settings are social settings and student interaction with peers as well as teachers is essential if optimal levels of achievement are to be reached. While some teachers may have strong views concerning problems of excessive student talk, the ability to appropriately communicate ideas is one of the most important life skills an individual can develop. It would be regrettable to think that any teacher's classroom was structured to discourage the development of open, clear communication. Conversation can be contagious and teachers cannot allow students to talk and chatter freely to the extent that they and their peers have problems learning and the teacher has problems teaching. At the same time, it is important not to let the classroom be represented by unrealistic expectations for a level of silence which may be more appropriate for a library than for an environment where active student exploration is to be desired and encouraged.

ATTENTION-SEEKING

It is commonly understood by teachers at all grade levels that some students misbehave simply to get the attention of their classmates or the teacher. **Attention-Seeking** behavior is *a student misbehavior problem often manifested in tattling by younger students to get their teachers' attention or by older students acting as the class clown or the show off as a way to get attention from the teacher as well as other students.* Due to peer pressures and other social considerations, tattling tends to become less frequent as students grow older.

Working with Attention-Seeking Problems

Regardless of the method chosen by an attention-seeking student (i.e., tattling, clowning, etc.), attention-seeking behavior should not be reinforced by the teacher or other students in the class. As with any form of misconduct, for some reason important to them, attention-seeking students need special attention in the social setting of the classroom. Teachers should not doubt that some students have a special need for attention and should provide such students the opportunity to receive the attention that they need in an appropriate manner. Instead of clowning to get the attention desired, an attention-seeking student might be given the opportunity to receive attention by helping the teacher in some meaningful way or by sharing ideas, stories, or reports to the class at an acceptable time.

Some attention seekers are characterized by insecurity because they do not receive the attention that they need at home, in the peer group, or from the teacher. Demeaning or publicly chastising an attention-seeking student for his or her behavior should be avoided. Effective teachers make the effort to learn more about the cause of the undesired behavior and ways to appropriately satisfy the student's need. Such students might benefit from receiving praise in front of the group when they conduct themselves properly or in private just between the teacher and the student.

It is best to redirect the inappropriate behavior of an attention-seeking student through private, not public, conversations. Although it may be a temptation for some teachers when dealing with chronic attention seekers to tell them to "act their age" or "stop acting silly," these responses only serve to harm more than help the situation. The best procedure to follow is to ignore unwanted attention-seeking while channeling the student to a way of getting attention in an acceptable manner. Teachers should make every effort to give attention to students when possible, but only reinforce them when their behavior is appropriate (Good & Brophy, 2007).

In terms of being proactive, it is important for the teacher to prepare the environment to prevent problems with attention seekers as it is with other forms of student misbehavior. This can be done by communicating the guidelines for appropriate behavior early in the school year and then consistently following those rules and procedures that have been established (Levin & Nolan, 2010). Some student tattling can be prevented simply by telling students early in the year what kinds of information they should and should not report to the teacher (Evertson et al., 2005). This is also true for other forms of student attention-seeking. When students know what is considered as proper behavior in the classroom, the attention-seeking student can often be quickly cut off and redirected to an appropriate activity by being reminded of what has and what has not been identified as acceptable behavior.

A part of preparing the environment to eliminate or reduce attention-seeking from certain students could involve special consideration of the teacher's instructional program. If teachers closely monitor the unwanted behaviors of their students, they might discover that some students are seeking attention when they have nothing else that seems meaningful or interesting to do. If this is the case, it provides important information for the teacher regarding the importance of ensuring that all students are actively involved in high-interest and meaningful learning activities. When this is established, the frequency of students using attention-seeking behaviors, and likely all student misbehaviors, will be reduced.

CHRONIC AVOIDANCE OF WORK

All teachers are aware that some students habitually do not complete the assignments that they have been given. **Chronic Avoidance of Work** is *a misbehavior demonstrated by a student who consistently fails to complete his or her assigned work following repeated teacher effort to get the work completed.* This can represent a serious problem if students find that when they fail to do their assigned work, no negative consequence results. If not completing assigned work has no meaning, students will become less inclined to complete their assignments as the school year progresses. Teachers need to have a management system in place to regularly follow up on the assignments they give to students to make sure that the assignments are being completed in the manner and time frame expected (Evertson et al., 2005). While perhaps not openly disruptive to the class, avoidance of work is a serious matter since students not completing their assignments are not taking part in important learning activities. Too, if one student does not finish assignments as expected with no consequence, other students are apt to follow suit. This is an example of what Kounin (1970) referred to as the *ripple effect.*

Working with Chronic Avoidance of Work Problems

In a situation where assignments are not completed in a timely manner, the teacher needs to first determine if the student's ability to complete the assignment is the primary cause of the problem. The teacher should know this before any interaction with the student takes place. This actually should be known before the assignment is given; if a student lacks the necessary prerequisite skills or knowledge to complete the assignment, an adjustment in what is assigned needs to be made. Students should not be held responsible for work that they are not able to complete if the problem of completing the work is based on a basic lack of ability on their part. Assignments that teachers give need to be made with an understanding of student ability in mind. In cases where a student is overwhelmed by the totality of an assignment, but yet has the ability to complete the work, the teacher should consider breaking the assignment up into smaller units.

Where a student has the ability to do the assigned work but is for some reason choosing not to do so, early intervention on the teacher's part is needed. Before taking any action, the teacher will benefit from additional information about the student to be able to determine why the assignments are not being regularly completed, especially in a classroom where other students are successfully completing the same assignments. This normally requires collecting and checking student work while carefully maintaining and recording the results. This activity represents an application of the third step in the Model for Reflection and Inquiry. Using these records, the teacher can determine to what degree a student is not completing homework and/or classroom assignments. Follow-up conversations with the student and possibly with other teachers who are familiar with the student and the student's work may then be used to determine why the work assigned is not being completed.

It has already been identified that some students do not finish their work because an assignment may be too challenging for them. Personal problems may also interfere with a student's ability to do what the teacher desires. Death or illness of a loved one, divorce or separation of parents, difficult home environment where a student has neither the time nor place to complete assignments, homelessness, and abuse are examples of the many types of problems that can interfere with a student completing his or her schoolwork. A teacher who discovers that a student has such a problem should work closely with the student, giving help and support until the situation has improved or until the student is more in control of the situation. The school counselor can often help such students deal with their personal problems and meet their responsibilities at school and in the classroom.

After inquiring into the situation, it may be discovered that neither personal problems nor learning problems are the causes of the student's incomplete work. Some students simply choose not to complete their assignments because they are not appropriately motivated to do so. A parent conference sometimes is one of the best techniques to use in intervening to change the behavior of students who elect not to finish homework and classroom assignments (Evertson et al., 2005). When this strategy is used, it is important to be able to show parents the records that have been kept of the student's past performance. What students are telling parents at home may be different from what is actually taking place in school. A record of past homework or classroom assignments that were never completed may be important evidence to show a parent who has been told by the student that no such assignments were made or that assignments were turned in. A monitoring or recording system should be developed where the teacher can send a list of homework assignments with needed materials home on a regular basis (e.g., daily or weekly) for the parents' review. An important part of the teacher's role includes working with parents. Students' attitudes about school are influenced by their parents and, when they feel good about their teachers and school, the students are more likely to receive reinforcement for desirable behavior (Jones & Jones, 2013). Parents need to be informed about student academic performance and behavior so that they can be involved in their child's school experience. Parent involvement can have a positive impact on students' attitudes toward school, belief in the relationship between effort and school performance, and persistence at schoolwork.

Parents and teachers together might want to explore the development of a reward system to encourage a student to regularly complete in-class or homework assignments. A behavior contract, discussed earlier in Chapter 3 as recommended by William Glasser, can be an effective tool to use in a situation such as this. Teachers need to be careful, however, not to decrease penalties or increase grades simply because the student may make a slight improvement over time. It is easy to send a message that doing only some of the work is acceptable when this is not the case. If a reward system is to have the optimum effect, it must encourage students to put forth the maximum effort. Teachers are advised to assign homework on a regular basis so that students come to expect that homework is a regular part of the classroom routine. Assignments should be of reasonable length and seen as being manageable by the students.

DISHONESTY

Dishonest behavior represents *one of the most serious forms of student misconduct often exhibited through cheating and/or stealing and telling untruths or lying.* Cheating and stealing generally have a more devastating impact on the entire classroom as they automatically affect others and are more difficult to deal with in a positive, proactive manner. In an international study where students gave themselves high marks for ethical behavior, around 60% of American high school students reported having cheated on a test, 28% admitted stealing from a store, and 23% said they had stolen from a parent or other relative (Sixty Percent of U.S. High School

Students, 2006). Ninety-two percent of the students indicated that they were satisfied with their personal ethics and character, and 74% agreed with the statement, *When it comes to doing what is right, I am better than most people I know.* Following high-stakes school testing and accountability discussions sweeping the nation, some lawmakers say they want to make sure that testing results are credible. Much of this is a reaction to reports of cheating where some high test scores have been reported to be the result of "adult interference" (Kummer, 2006). Tens of thousands of students were found to have cheated on the Texas Assessment of Knowledge and Skills (TAKS) test including thousands on the state's graduation test (Benton & Hacker, 2007). The analysis conducted found cases where over 50% of students had suspicious answer patterns that researchers say indicate collusion, either between students or with school staff. More recently, the Fulton County grand jury in Atlanta, Georgia, indicted 35 educators from the school district, including principals, teachers, and testing coordinators in a cheating scandal. The former superintendent of Atlanta Public Schools was among the educators who surrendered to authorities. Investigations had been made into the remarkable improvements on standardized test scores in the district. About 180 teachers were implicated initially. According to the indictment, cheating is believed to date back to early 2001 when standardized testing scores began to turn around in the 50,000-student school district. For at least four years, between 2005–2009, test answers were altered, fabricated, and falsely certified (CNN Staff, 2013). Dishonesty has been rated as one of the most serious problems that teachers must deal with in the management of their students (Charles, 1976; Hunt et al., 1999).

Working with Dishonesty Problems

One problem that teachers encounter when dealing with dishonesty in the classroom is that children and adolescents, at least young adolescents, are still in the formative stages of their moral development. What is right and wrong for many students is often very much determined by the situation. Certainly at young ages, students are still learning right from wrong, appropriate from inappropriate, etc. Because of this, teachers are advised to focus on the intent as well as the impact and results of such behavior. Children in the early elementary grades, for example, often do not have a clear understanding of *truth* and *own-*

ership as would be expected of them if they were older. Young adolescent students may decide to steal a test paper from their teacher's desk as much for the excitement of the adventure and the accomplishment as from a desire to cheat and improve their grades. The advent of modern technology has only served to acerbate the problem. As technology makes it easier than ever to cheat, educators are combating the intractable problem on at least three fronts: (1) setting clear standards and consequences, (2) using technology to fight back, and (3) talking with students and parents about ethics and pressure (Noguchi, 2006). Also at issue is the actual definition of dishonest behavior. With more and more encouragement for the use of cooperative learning strategies and students-working-together instructional activities, teachers need to clearly define just what honest or dishonest behavior is when students are encouraged to work together and to share their work products in route to completing assignments.

Regardless of the motivation, teachers have the responsibility to guide students in their learning of acceptable standards of conduct and cannot condone dishonesty. No matter the age of the student, dishonesty should always be cast in an unfavorable light. Nevertheless, teachers must remember that many students do not come from backgrounds that reflect and promote middle class standards of behavior that are common to teachers and school environments. Many students must learn acceptable behavior at school, in this case honesty, though the home and community should and no doubt will play an important role in this learning process. Such behavioral development can be long-term in nature.

It is important to minimize the temptation to dishonest behavior by discussing with students the difference between helping a classmate and cheating, demonstrating desired behaviors for various activities and having students identify appropriate as opposed to inappropriate behaviors (Burden & Byrd, 2013). When dealing with a student who has possibly been dishonest, the teacher must be cautious not to label the student when approaching the student being suspected of having committed the misbehavior. If a student is labeled as a *cheat, thief,* or *liar,* the possible ill effect on the student's future behavior and self concept is a consequence that needs to be avoided. If a student is caught cheating, for example, the teacher is advised to talk to the student in private, present the reasons for suspecting cheating, express concern and try to find out why the student cheated, explain the consequences and be sure that the consequences fit the situation, and then discuss the consequences for subsequent cheating (Weinstein, Romano, & Mignano, 2011). Telling students they are bad or dishonest may cause them to genuinely think of themselves this way and begin to consistently assume these roles. Students would then be following the teacher's prophecy for or about them as was discussed earlier in this text. As with confronting students with other forms of misbehavior, the teacher should never publicly accuse a student of having been dishonest with other students or teachers serving as an audience.

Since it is important to help students understand the importance of honest behavior, there needs to be consequences for dishonest behavior. For example, the student could lose valued privileges or a grade could be lowered if the dishonesty was of an academic nature. Teachers need to realize that what is dishonest for mature adults may not be for some students and their peers. It could be helpful to plan activities that improve the students' perception of honesty and how to show it in everyday situations. It also could be helpful to use activities that will build feelings of mutual respect with peers and adults such as having group projects that involve working in the community. Finally, it is recommended that the teacher discuss with the class the consequences of stealing in the outside world, instruct students to keep valuables in a safe place, and discourage bringing valuable items to school.

Beyond trying to determine appropriate consequences, it is important to determine the cause of the misbehavior. If a student cheated on an assignment because the assigned work was at a too difficult level, a new assignment should be made in the future that will allow the student to achieve success without cheating. The need for the teacher to have an accurate understanding of a student's ability and make appropriate assignments based on this understanding has been previously emphasized under the heading Chronic Avoidance of Work. One characteristic of students who have a history of failure is a reliance on getting help from others (perhaps through cheating) as opposed to relying on their own ability to study and learn. If a part of the problem, feelings of learned helplessness and low self-concept must be overcome before a meaningful and long-lasting change in behavior can be expected (Weiner, 1985).

UNRULINESS

Unruliness is *a state of general student misbehavior characterized by a lack of self-control which may be exhibited by such behaviors as talking loudly, running in hallways, using unacceptable language, getting out of seats without permission, and playing practical jokes.* Unruly students are not generally aggressive or defiant but habitually break school and classroom rules. One reason why this behavior syndrome is considered less severe than other behaviors is because unruly students typically do not desire to hurt others or be disrespectful but just lack personal self-control. They often seem out of control to teachers and other students alike.

Working with Unruliness Problems

Some students are unruly because unruly behavior has been modeled around them on a regular basis. They have copied and adopted this behavior and may have even been rewarded for it. A child growing up in a family where the adults there disregard manners normally looked upon as acceptable, show constant criticism of mainstream values, curse, and question authority, will often go to school and display some of these same types of behaviors. Over time, this unruliness becomes ingrained in the student and represents an adopted personality trait. Unruly students, however, also come from family backgrounds that do not model such traits. This fact reinforces that a student's home environment should not always be looked upon as the determiner of a student's behavior. Whatever the origin of a student's unruliness, if nothing is done to correct the behavior, the behavior will augment over time. To accent the problem, unruly students can become negative role models that other students may choose to emulate if the teacher does not intervene and respond to the problem.

Many students find the social and academic adjustments expected in a school setting difficult and uncomfortable where they do not receive satisfaction from academic and social activities. This lack of satisfaction can trigger unruly or even rebellious behaviors. If they have not investigated the situation thoroughly, when teachers react to unruliness, they may be dealing with the symptom and not the true cause of the misconduct. Students who are unruly generally need closer supervision than other students, and an effective technique to use with them is close monitoring. Close monitoring is important but can be a challenge un-

der certain conditions such as field trips, laboratory work, and other activities where consistent teacher supervision is more difficult.

Unruly students need to experience success in school as do all students. Repeated failure increases the likelihood of repeated misconduct. Although there needs to be consequences when students break established rules, teachers must be certain to separate their reaction to a
negative behavior from a reaction to the student as a human being. Unruly students are often unpopular with many of their peers and, unfortunately, many of their teachers. Because of this, it is important to build
within them a sense of self-worth and belonging. Such students need to
be in controlled situations where they have an opportunity for success,
are reinforced when success is achieved, and not be overly stimulated
to a point where they will lose self-control. When encountering an unruly student, teachers should have the frame of mind that they are dealing with someone who needs support and nurturing more than discipline and control.

It is recommended that student isolation be given serious consideration when it becomes necessary to discipline an unruly student. If isolation is used, it needs to take place in a non-stimulating area. Students
should see the isolation as an opportunity for them to calm down and
regain their self-control, rather than as punishment, and it should be
clearly explained to them why they are there. Though it should not be
seen as a punishment, neither should it be seen as a reward. A student
who sees being isolated as a reward may be saying volumes about how
he or she sees being in the teacher's regular classroom environment.
After the prescribed period of isolation is over, and a student who has
been isolated is back in the normal classroom setting, the teacher
should guide the student to exhibit desired behaviors and reward these
positive actions appropriately. The behaviors of unruly students will
change in positive ways when they begin to experience more success,
in particular on activities that are meaningful and of value to them. This
change in behavior will also result in greater social acceptance by their
peer group.

It is advised that the teacher privately let the student know how his
or her behavior is impacting the classroom and what is expected in
terms of desired behavior. Success will be built on establishing a trusting relationship. The teacher should listen carefully to what the student
has to say and try to channel the student's talents into a more productive direction. Regardless of the motivation, the teacher should make it

clear that the student's solution to his problem is both his and his teacher's responsibility. It may also be helpful to identify some aspect of the curriculum in which the student is interested and capable and provide him with independent work in this area and observe carefully for any change in behavior. This could allow the teacher to utilize a high interest area of the curriculum to motivate and engage the student and to then reward the student accordingly.

DEFIANCE

Defiant behavior is *a serious form of student misbehavior where a student refuses to do what the teacher asks of him or her or boldly talks back to the teacher in a hostile or threatening way.* Defiance is a serious type of misbehavior because it threatens the leadership position of the teacher. If a student is allowed to be defiant to the teacher, with no meaningful consequence to follow, it is possible that other students will act similarly, resulting in a total loss of classroom control. This is one of the worst possible things that could happen to a teacher; teachers must think and be prepared to act quickly when faced with student defiance.

Working with Defiance Problems

Teachers are encouraged to use caution when dealing with any defiant or hostile student because such a student is not likely to comply to normal verbal commands. A student who challenges a teacher usually realizes that serious, deviant behavior has already taken place and this may cause his or her emotions to intensify. Rather than take offense at what has been said or done, it is recommended that the teacher stay calm and, if possible, direct the student out of the classroom into an area where a teacher-to-student conversation can be held privately. Removing the student from the immediate classroom setting has three major advantages: (1) the student is given time to get his or her emotions under control, (2) the peer audience in the classroom will not be able to stir emotions and reinforce further defiance, and (3) the student's need to keep face in front of the rest of the students in the class will be gone.

Following are recommended guidelines to follow when students become defiant (Burden & Byrd, 2013).

- Stay in control of yourself.
- Direct the rest of the class to work on something while you speak to the student in a private area away from the rest of the students.
- Stand a few feet away from the defiant student (i.e., don't get in his or her face).
- Acknowledge the student's feelings by saying something like, "I can see that you are really angry."
- Avoid a power struggle in the conversation. For example, don't say something like, "I am the boss here, and I am telling you what to do."
- As a means to defuse the situation, offer the student a choice of actions for what the student needs to do next.

In rare situations, some students may become so emotionally hostile that they refuse to leave the classroom. With a younger or smaller student, the teacher can simply escort the student from the classroom. If the student is larger and refuses to leave the classroom, it is advisable for the teacher to send another student for an administrator or another teacher for help. It is not advisable that the teacher risk having a physical confrontation with a defiant student.

When talking with defiant students, the teacher is encouraged to exhibit as much openness as possible. Rude remarks from students should not be taken personally and definitely should not be followed by similar remarks from the teacher. Sarcasm is never warranted and its use can quickly cause the situation to worsen. The teacher is advised to not participate in an argument with a defiant student and to try to separate the student as a person from the student's undesirable conduct. The teacher has a responsibility to explain to the defiant student that the behavior that has been shown will result in consequences and that these consequences will be carried out in a just and timely manner (Evertson et al., 2005).

Kazdin and Rotella (2013), leading scholars in the area of working with defiant students, suggest that when working with deviant children, teachers should:

- notice and reward good behavior immediately,
- tell the student what he or she should be doing instead of dwelling on the bad behavior,
- be enthusiastic when students exhibit good behavior,
- use reward systems to change the behavior of students who exhibit repeated defiant behaviors,

- stay calm when students exhibit defiant behavior,
- when punishment is necessary, make it brief and immediate; dwelling on the misbehavior can actually reinforce it, and
- use 90% of behavior interactions to reinforce good behavior.

Causes of defiance are often deep-seated and defiant behavior is frequently accompanied by a level of anger and frustration that may have reached a point that can no longer be contained. This hostility could be a result of problems at school, both academic and social, as well as problems found in the student's home life. In cases where students have chronic problems with these types of outbursts, professional help may be warranted. Regardless of whether the student displays frequent defiance or has simply had a momentary loss of control, an understanding teacher who is willing to listen and help can be an important support for the student. A private teacher-to-student conference may allow the student to see the teacher as being fair and concerned when this may not have been what was initially thought. Through this building of rapport and trust, the teacher may be able to understand why the student acted the way he or she did. Since the teacher is encouraged to interact with defiant students on a one-to-one basis and not in the public setting of the classroom, the teacher also may feel freer to admit mistakes, if they were made, and discuss ways to improve the classroom climate to lessen stress and frustration. While a teacher cannot afford to ignore a defiant act since it challenges the teacher's authority, it is important for the teacher not to react to defiant students in a confrontational way.

AGGRESSION

Aggressive behavior is *a serious student misbehavior often represented by fighting although lesser forms of aggressive behavior are not uncommon such as name-calling or other verbal attacks, pushing and shoving, and overly physical play.* Because when aggressive behaviors are displayed, there is the possibility that one or more students may be injured, aggressive behavior in schools and classrooms is a serious problem. Since even nonfighting aggression can result in physical combat if allowed to escalate, teachers must be prepared to deal with aggressive behavior in a quick and decisive manner.

Working with Aggression Problems

An important initial strategy to use in working with students who have been fighting, name calling, or pushing and shoving is to allow them to "cool-down" before any interaction with them or teacher follow-up takes place. It is best to keep students who have been fighting away from one another and from their peers when possible immediately after the fight has taken place. Classmates have a tendency to fuel an already volatile situation when emotions are running high. When the students are mature enough, having each student write his or her version of why the fight or aggressive behavior began is a good "cooling-off," defusing activity. After the students have calmed down, the teacher then can meet with each student individually to discuss whatever problem precipitated the aggression. The teacher should stress the inappropriateness of the behavior, the need to solve problems in a more acceptable way, and discuss with the students how the problem could have been resolved differently. If the teacher finds it difficult to get an accurate explanation of why the problem started from the students involved, it is appropriate to ask uninvolved students for additional information. It is best not to do this in front of the combatants, however, as this will only increase the likelihood of further emotional outbursts.

Virtually all schools and school districts have established procedures to follow when handling student fights and aggressiveness. Teachers need to understand the policies and procedures that are in place in their schools and districts and these procedures should always be followed. Typical procedures involve school administrators, parents, and guidance personnel and are designed to ensure the safety of all students on the school grounds. Conflict resolution and peer mediation programs, presented in Chapter 3, have been successful in dealing with this type of student behavior on a schoolwide basis at the middle and high school levels.

Many teachers are concerned about whether or not they should try to step in and physically break up a fight that is underway. Only if the teacher feels that it is safe to do so, perhaps with younger and smaller students, is it recommended that the teacher try to separate students who are fighting. In a situation where a fight occurs, the first step should be to have all other students leave the immediate scene so that they will not be injured. Such an environment is not safe for spectators and may tend to spur on the combatants. If the teacher does not feel safe separating the fighting students, a loud command to stop fighting, i.e., a desist, should be issued, and someone should be sent to quickly bring help (Evertson et al., 2005). One difficulty in dealing with aggressive behavior is that aggressive behavior situations can escalate quickly giving the teacher little time to react. Through their own alertness and *withitness* in being aware of what is taking place throughout the classroom, however, effective teachers can deter many problems and certainly diffuse many situations before they become violent or physical encounters. When violent outbreaks do occur, teachers need to remain calm in facing such situations and, through their prior planning, know just what they are going to do.

Although most aggression in the school setting is manifested in momentary outbursts as a consequence of frustration, some students have problems that may need to be addressed through professional assistance such as would be provided by a medical doctor or psychologist. At times, trained professional help is needed to work with teachers and parents to develop an individual plan to help the specific student involved (Zahrt & Melzer-Lange, 2011). There may be times when a student needs help beyond that which the teacher can provide. Some students come from homes and communities where they see aggression modeled frequently and believe that the use of aggressive behavior is an acceptable way to solve problems. Other aggressive students have histories of academic failure and frustration at school and have become alienated from the mainstream and norms of the school environment. They can display aggressive behavior as a type of defense mechanism. Finally, situations where students have been physically or emotionally abused, or perhaps seen a parent and/or sibling abused, can represent the background of a student who behaves aggressively. Such students all too frequently become aggressive and abusive themselves as a reaction to what they have experienced at home. Regardless of the reason, aggressive behavior cannot be allowed to exist in the classroom. A display of aggressive behavior that the teacher does not respond to represents a true threat to the safety in the classroom, the teacher's ability to teach, and the teacher's authority as classroom leader.

Long-term solutions to aggressive behavior require that teachers make it clear to students that such behaviors are unacceptable. Teachers need to listen patiently when discussing problems with aggressive students and refrain from verbal chastisements and emotional outbursts as this will only further arouse their aggressiveness (Brophy & Mc-Caslin, 1992). As with all forms of student misbehavior, it is necessary to understand the sources of the motivation and frustrations of aggressive students to be able to help them regain and then maintain their self-control.

APPLYING THE MODEL FOR REFLECTION AND INQUIRY

As discussed in Chapter 1, the Model for Reflection and Inquiry is a recommended process for the teacher to follow when dealing with student misbehaviors and/or motivation problems. Applications of this model will be examined in the following section of the chapter where teachers are confronted with some of the common problems that have been previously discussed.

Janice's Problem

Janice is a sixth grade student in a middle school organized through the use of integrated instructional teams. During the first six weeks of school, Janice's performance was very much like what would have been expected based on the grades she received in school prior to this year. On her first grade report, Janice received a "B+" in mathematics and an "A" in all other subjects. However, soon after the next grading period began, Janice's behavior began to change. Her teachers all noticed that she no longer completed all assignments and often failed to even attempt much of her homework. These problems were discussed at a team planning meeting, and it was determined that Janice was likely to receive a "D" in language arts and no grade higher than a "C" in all other courses on her next report card.

At least one problem in this case is easy to define. Janice, who in the past has been an excellent student, no longer completes her in-class and homework assignments. This has had a major negative impact on her performance in all subjects. Since there seemed to be no obvious or apparent problems in her classes at school that the team members who served as Janice's teachers could identify, they hypothesized that perhaps the change in Janice's behavior was due to a new boyfriend (not an uncommon problem with sixth grade pre-teens) or to some problem at home. Ms. Greene, Janice's mathematics teacher, called Janice's mother to share insights. Janice's mother was certain Janice did not have a boyfriend, though interest in the opposite sex was certainly increasing, and assured Ms. Greene that Janice was getting along fine at home. She did comment that Janice had said that school didn't seem very interesting to her anymore and that she saw little purpose in most of her school work. She preferred to spend her evenings on the phone or listening to music while reading magazines rather than studying or completing assignments for school.

Upon learning this, Janice's teachers changed their hypothesis; it was now believed that Janice simply had lost her motivation and interest in school. Perhaps school was no longer purposeful, challenging, or fun for her. Ms. Greene was now able to talk with Janice with a more complete background of information gained from the parent conference, and collective teacher observations and discussions. Janice admitted that she had lost interest in school and actually disliked many of her assignments. In her opinion, they took her away from more interesting thoughts and activities. With this new information providing a better understanding of the problem, the teachers decided to challenge Janice with more sophisticated assignments that they hoped would pique her interest while helping her to see the importance of learning to her future. By working with Janice's mother, they were able to develop a system to motivate Janice through rewards related to her interests when she successfully completed her schoolwork.

George's Problem

George is a first-grade student who had his kindergarten experience through home schooling. Early on, Ms. Williams, his teacher, observed that George had difficulty in his relationships with other students. Even during the first weeks of school there had been complaints from other students about George hitting and biting other students. Ms. Williams talked with George and used isolation in the "Timeout" area as a consequence. However, during the fourth week of school, George lost his temper on the playground and threw a rock that barely missed hitting another child. George was so upset he had to be physically restrained until he calmed down so that he would not hurt the other child or himself. Ms. Williams realized she had a more serious problem to deal with than she had first thought.

Like Janice, George's problem can be easily identified. George has bouts of aggression that can disrupt the instructional environment and endanger the safety of others. Ms. Williams, George's teacher, has a serious problem that must be addressed immediately. Since George had been home schooled up until this time, there were few school records that could provide helpful insight into his previous schooling experiences and behaviors. Through her observations of George, her experiences with other children, and her consultations with Ms. Langston, the principal, Ms. Williams hypothesized that George's problem with aggression was not just a simple problem of adjusting to school. Ms. Williams wondered if George's staying home the previous year might not actually be related to this problem. Additional information was gained through a conference with Mr. and Ms. Cobb, George's parents. Ms. Williams learned that George had shown signs of aggression early in life and that there was a history of problems at church, in day care, and with other children in the community. George was kept home the previous year in hopes that he would "grow out" of the problem. Unfortunately, the problem did not lessen and the Cobbs admitted that they were anxious to get help. Ms. Williams' hypothesis had been correct. Through the resources of the school system, the Cobbs were able to get professional help for George so that he could function in the least restrictive environment in his schooling. In dealing with a problem of this nature, George's parents, teacher, administrators, counselor, and psychologist all recognized that they needed to patiently but deliberately work together as a team to achieve the results that they desired.

Monica's Problem

Monica is a senior in high school who has always made above average grades in her classes with the exception of French I which was a struggle for her to achieve a "C-", her final grade last year. Monica made a very respectable score on the SAT and has been accepted to the state university where both of her parents graduated. Monica's parents, Mr. and Ms. Pepper, teach at the high school she attends and are very proud of her. They promised to buy Monica a new car for graduation so that she can more easily visit home from the university next year. One day, the Peppers were called by Mr. Long, the principal, to come to the office at the end of school. When they arrived Mr. Long told them that Mr. Davis had caught Monica cheating on a major French II examination.

The problem identified is that Monica has cheated on a test and this cannot be treated as a minor infraction. Neither Monica nor her classmates can be allowed to think that cheating goes without consequences. Mr. Davis, Mr. Long, and Monica's parents all hypothesized that Monica cheated because she needed the two units of French to graduate from high school and to complete her admission to the university. She did not want to disappoint her parents and ruin her plans for next year but felt that she could not be successful without cheating. Mr. Davis was wise enough to also hypothesize that Monica had a low level of self-confidence and a self-efficacy problem that left her feeling helpless to pass French II through her own individual efforts. Mr. Davis realized that, as long as Monica held such an external locus of control, she would continue to have problems with motivation and confidence and that this could also cause serious problems for her after she completed high school and began taking classes at the university. After talking with Monica's French I teacher from the previous year, Mr. Davis met with Monica and developed a program of study where, through her own efforts, Monica would be able to pass French II. Monica did face the consequences of her serious misconduct. She would have to accept a lowered grade on the test, re-take a different version of the test, and do additional work in the class. However, due to her teacher acting in a proactive manner and as a caring and reflective educator, she came out of a difficult situation a stronger, better person.

In each of these cases just presented, the teachers involved, with help from others, systematically identified the problems they were dealing with, planned workable solutions, and were able to help their students. The students were able to become more successful in school through the use of reflection, inquiry and genuine concern on the part of their teachers. Instead of simply reacting to misbehaviors in isolation, the teachers collected data from a variety of sources that helped them make more informed decisions to effectively address the problems with which they and their students were dealing. When faced with problems of classroom management and student motivation, reflective educators do not enter into "me against you" arguments with their students. They seek to eliminate their students' misbehaviors with an eye on their students gaining needed skills and motivation so that such misbehaviors will not hamper their learning or adjustment in the future.

CONCLUSION

Chapter 6 has provided information and recommended strategies to be used when responding to specific types of student misbehaviors. The recommendations reinforce the teacher's role in establishing a strong management system and included the teacher giving special attention to specific personal, instructional, and environmental considerations. As has been the case in other areas of the text, the need for the teacher to be proactive and well planned in dealing with issues of student motivation, classroom management, and instruction, and being able to address problems when they occur, was emphasized.

The chapter also addressed types of student misbehaviors felt to be both common and serious in challenging the teacher's ability to effectively teach students and manage the learning environment. These misbehaviors were: *inattention, disruptive talking, attention-seeking, chronic avoidance of work, dishonesty, unruliness, defiance,* and *aggression.* Each of these misbehaviors represents a threat to teachers in carrying out their instructional responsibilities and maintaining their roles as classroom leaders. The information provided defined the misbehaviors and then gave guidance as to possible ways to respond to them.

The chapter concluded with three problem situations for analysis and illustrated the use of the Model for Reflection and Inquiry as a tool to guide teachers in logical problem solving with respect to responding to the student misbehaviors illustrated. Two important aspects of dealing with problems of student motivation and management are evident. First, teachers must understand each of their students and their issues in these areas and have a broad knowledge of motivation, management, and instruction to be able to effectively address the problems that they encounter in the classroom. Second, beyond understanding, teachers must have the ability to use their understanding of their students and knowledge about motivation, management, and instruction to successfully solve those problems that they encounter. Teachers will fall short of what is needed in effective teaching if they have knowledge about their students, motivation and management and do not know how to use this information. Likewise, having knowledge about reasoned decision making and logical problem solving without a solid understanding of pertinent information on which to base problem solutions will also cause the teacher to not achieve what is needed in effective practice. The knowledge base of information presented here on student motivation, classroom management, and effective teaching practices, along with illustrations of the use of the Model for Reflection and Inquiry, will enable the teacher to effectively resolve most problems encountered in the classroom related to these areas.

QUESTIONS/ACTIVITIES FOR REFLECTION

1. Analyze the statement, "teachers can frequently prevent most problems before they ever occur." In your opinion, what does this statement mean? Do you agree with it? Explain.

2. Though criticized by some, coercive management strategies are used by many teachers every day. How do you assess their use in terms of whether they should or should not have a place in a teacher's management plan?

3. How do you think that a teacher can truly prepare to react only to a student's misbehavior and not to the student as a person?

4. How would you go about helping a student understand the difference between sharing information with the teacher to be helpful, or even prevent a problem from occurring, and tattling?

5. If you were a teacher who recognized that a colleague was having problems in getting students to complete their work primarily because the work that was being assigned was too difficult, how would you help your colleague understand that this was the case? How can a teacher maintain high standards in teaching and in assignments given and respond to a variety of ability or knowledge levels in the classroom at the same time?

Chapter 7

CASE STUDIES FOR ANALYSIS IN STUDENT MOTIVATION AND CLASSROOM MANAGEMENT

The intensity of an experience is a critical element in effective learning outcomes. Are children and young people fully and often intensely engaged in their school experiences or are they psychologically detached? Do they think of the school experience as something in a textbook or a recitation that is over there while they are over here? Are they spectators or participants? Learning cannot be a spectator sport. (Dale, 1972, p. 9)

While effective teaching can be defined in different ways, as presented here effective teaching is teaching that brings about increased levels of student achievement. For increased student achievement to occur, teachers must be informed reflective decision makers. To engage in reflective decision making and to bring about increased levels of student achievement, the information that teachers possess must include knowledge and/or abilities in the following areas:

1. understanding the abilities, interests, and background characteristics of students,
2. understanding what is known through educational research about student motivation,
3. understanding what is known through educational research about student behavior management in the classroom,
4. understanding what is known through educational research about best practice in teaching, and
5. the ability to use information as a reflective decision maker who

applies relevant knowledge in a systematic approach to solve problems of student motivation, student behavior management, and instruction.

Detailed information has been presented throughout the previous chapters in this text regarding each of these five areas of knowledge and/or ability. Of special importance has been an introduction to the use of the Model for Reflection and Inquiry in Chapter 1. The model has been referred to throughout the text to reinforce the importance of effective teachers being logical problem solvers. It is included here in Figure 7.1. An important focus of this chapter is on using the model to explore specific student behavior situations that represent problems of student motivation and/or classroom management.

The Model for Reflection and Inquiry

1. **Statement of the Problem**

   The problem is identified and clarified; the problem should be meaningful and manageable.

2. **Development of a Hypothesis(es)**

   A hypothesis or educated guess regarding a solution to the problem is formulated; there may be more than one hypothesis.

3. **Collection of Relevant Data**

   Data or pertinent information relevant to the problem is collected and/or identified; references or sources of information are considered and reviewed.

4. **Analysis of Data**

   Clarifications are made as to information collected; sources of data are considered and perhaps reconsidered. Relationships should be identified among data collected and data should be clearly organized and analyzed as to how this information relates to the problem.

5. **Interpretation and Reporting of Results, Drawing Conclusions, and Making Generalizations**

   Conclusions should be drawn and relevant generalizations made related to the accuracy of the original hypothesis.

Figure 7.1. Model for Reflection and Inquiry.

While it is not always possible to outline a linear process or define a specific step-by-step procedure for reflective practice, there are important teacher actions and behaviors that are fundamental to being a reflective educator and that characterize a reflective practitioner. These include the following: (Larrivee, 2009).

1. **Solitary Reflection**: The teacher makes time for thoughtful consideration of his or her actions and critical inquiry into the impact of teacher behavior on instruction and student behavior. This helps to keep the teacher alert to the consequences and impact of his or her actions on students and the dynamics in the classroom.

2. **Ongoing Inquiry**: The teacher continually questions the status quo and conventional wisdom as a way to further develop his or her understanding of best practice in teaching, motivation, and management. The quality of this questioning and critical inquiry can be enhanced through the involvement of collegial support.

3. **Perpetual Problem Solving**: In becoming a perpetual problem solver, the teacher involves synthesizing experiences, integrating information and feedback, uncovering underlying reasons, and discovering new meaning in the problem solving process. Solving problems and looking upon the classroom as a laboratory for purposeful experimentation characterizes the teacher's regular operation of behavior.

Reflective educators are able to use information in a logical manner to solve the problems that they encounter in working with their students. In cases where additional information is needed for the problem to be solved beyond that which is immediately available, reflective educators have the ability to acquire this additional information and appropriately apply it to the decision-making process. Teachers are confronted on a daily basis with numerous problems needing resolutions. It is the ability to solve these problems efficiently and effectively, and learn from the problems that have been solved, that in large measure determines the teacher's overall effectiveness.

The remainder of Chapter 7 focuses on the application of the Model for Reflection and Inquiry as a systematic problem-solving approach recommended for use in addressing nine different types of student misbehavior commonly found in schools today. Eight of these misbehavior types were introduced and discussed at some length in Chapter 6. The misbehavior of bullying was introduced in Chapter 5. Vignettes are provided that represent the following student misbehaviors: *inattention, disruptive talking, attention-seeking, chronic avoidance of work, dishonesty, unruliness, defiance, aggression,* and *bullying.* Two vignettes for analysis are presented for each type of misbehavior. The first vignette introduces the problem as it might be encountered at the primary-elementary grade level; the second vignette illustrates the problem at the middle-secondary level. Looking upon logical problem solving as representing a reasoning process that involves asking and then finding answers to a series of guiding questions, the following questions are offered to facilitate the analysis of each vignette. Consider the following questions that a teacher should ask, and possible answers to them, when faced with student motivation and classroom management problems.

Guiding Questions for Student Motivation and Management Problem Analysis

1. Exactly what is the problem that I am dealing with?
2. What might be a possible solution that I could use to effectively address the problem?
3. What additional information do I need to have that will impact the effectiveness of my solution? For example, what information do I need:

   a. about my student(s)?
   b. about my teaching?
   c. about the specific problem that I am facing?
   d. from other teachers?
   e. from my student's family?

4. How will I know if my solution was effective?
5. What should I do if my solution is not effective?
6. How can I decide when or where this particular solution will work in the future?

After reading each vignette and keeping the questions listed here in mind, apply the Model for Reflection and Inquiry to develop an acceptable solution to each of the following problem situations.

INATTENTION (PRIMARY-ELEMENTARY GRADES)

Suki's Inattention

Suki is a fourth-grade student who does not care for school; school seems boring to her. At least that is how Ms. Graves, Suki's teacher, sees it. According to Ms. Graves, what Suki appears to do best is sit next to the window and watch other students on the playground as they play games and enjoy other activities. She likes going to the playground in Ms. White's physical education class, and Ms. White says that Suki has good physical abilities. When the students select teams, she is usually one of the first ones chosen. She also enjoys arts and crafts class taught once a week by Mr. Brown. Mr. Brown indicates that Suki has a kind of "creative flair" in art. She is especially good in sketching with her pencil and working with clay. Mr. Brown says that she has the ability to envision things on her own rather than only do the assignments that she is given.

Ms. Graves, however, sees Suki as someone who just cannot stay focused in class. This is especially the case when she is talking to the entire class. In her opinion, a fourth-grade student should be acting more maturely. Besides looking out the window, sometimes she just draws or doodles at her desk. She also has an annoying habit of tapping her pencil on her desk and humming quietly to herself. Suki has a history of poor grades and lately has shown some behaviors that are not acceptable to Ms. Graves. Suki's inattentive behavior can also be distracting to the other students as well. She is sorry to admit it, but she has come to a point where she prefers Suki's daydreaming rather than some other misbehaviors that she might exhibit. At least she is not being disruptive when "she is in her own world."

Still, Ms. Graves has become especially concerned with Suki and a few other students like her as her school district has become very focused on the importance of raising test scores. Her principal makes more and more frequent visits to her classroom to see how things are going and to check up on whether or not everyone is on task. Suki, sadly, is often not on task.

Ms. Graves spoke to Suki's mother about her inattention at the last parent conference, and she said that she would speak to her about it. So far, though, Suki's inattentive behavior has not changed at all. Ms. Graves just doesn't know what she should try next, but she knows that she has to do something. What should she do?

INATTENTION (MIDDLE-SECONDARY GRADES)

Javier's Inattention

Ms. Thomas, Javier's seventh-grade math teacher, finds Javier to be a polite young man. Javier is always well dressed in the current fashion and quite popular with his classmates. When he answers questions in class, which isn't all that often, he speaks clearly and uses correct grammar. While she sees Javier as a pleasant student, she feels strongly that he doesn't pay enough attention to what is going on in the classroom to get the most out of it. She often notices him looking at magazines that he has brought with him to school or writing short poems or song lyrics in his notebook rather than paying attention to what she is saying. She has heard him play his guitar in the lunchroom and, in her opinion, he is quite talented.

Sometimes, when she is teaching, she observes Javier just staring out into space. He often doesn't seem to know what is expected of him. She doesn't think that he is really misbehaving badly in class, but she does see his inattention as a definite problem. Up to this point Javier's behavior hasn't proven to be a problem for other students, although she is worried that some of them might begin to do what Javier is doing. He is very popular and some of the other students even seem to look up to him. She has seen other occasions in the classroom where, when one student began to do something, others then began to follow.

She is aware that Javier has lived in the United States for about four years and that he and his parents moved to this country from Mexico. He has one older brother in the twelfth grade and a younger sister in the second grade. Javier's older brother has received an academic scholarship to attend the local university next year. It is a very prestigious scholarship, and he plans to major in government in preparation to one day become a lawyer. Javier has made average grades all through elementary school, not excelling or doing poorly in any one subject. In her class, however, he is barely keeping up. Javier's mother stays at home and is not employed. His father works as a salesman at a local automobile dealership. Ms. Thomas has never had a conversation with Javier's parents, but, she has seen them at some of the Parent-Teacher Association meetings.

Although Javier's not paying attention isn't the greatest problem in the world, it is creating difficulty for Ms. Thomas, and she is sure that he isn't learning as much as he can from her teaching. She, however, wants to reach all of her students but isn't sure just what to do in this situation. What should she do?

DISRUPTIVE TALKING (PRIMARY-ELEMENTARY GRADES)

Sierra's Disruptive Talking

Sierra is a third-grade student in Ms. Jackson's classroom. Sierra is an excellent student who has never made a grade below "A" since she began school. She is very proud of her record and seems to be pleased that other students are aware of it as well. She has indicated that her parents always give her a special reward for getting good grades on her report card. Getting good grades in school seems to come easy for her.

Her best friend is Beth who is also a good student, yet not as excelled as Sierra. Although Beth is a good student, her grades have been getting worse in recent weeks. She often does not complete the assignments that Ms. Jackson has made and often does not follow the instructions and examples that Ms. Jackson provides. Ms. Jackson has noticed that Sierra usually finishes her work before anyone else in the class and then spends time talking to Beth. She feels that this has been a part of the reason for the drop she has seen in Beth's performance. When it got to the point that Sierra was consistently talking while Ms. Jackson was explaining lessons to the class, she changed their seating arrangement so that their seats were as far from each other as possible. This bothered Beth a good deal because Sierra now has become best friends with Rachel, who she now sits beside. In fact, Sierra now spends much of the class time talking with Rachel whose work is beginning to suffer. In turn, Beth now has begun talking in class with Clifford instead of completing her own work.

Ms. Jackson's effort to help Beth's grades improve by moving her away from Sierra has not been effective. Rather, Beth has begun her own disruptive talking behavior and is now having a negative impact on Clifford. Sierra's disruptive talking has actually continued even with the new seating arrangement as she now talks to Rachel after she completes her assignments.

Ms. Jackson has spoken to her about her problem with talking, and Sierra has promised to stop. She told Sierra that when she talks that it is distracting to her when she is teaching, and this is frustrating. She also thought about lowering Sierra's grade because of her talking but decided not to mention this possibility to her at that point. Ms. Jackson was prepared to speak to Sierra's parents about the problem at the last parent-teacher conference that they had scheduled, but they didn't show up for the conference as planned. She isn't sure what step to take next. What should she do?

DISRUPTIVE TALKING (MIDDLE-SECONDARY GRADES)

Kelli's Disruptive Talking

Kelli is one of those students who seems to be happy one day and sad the next. One day she is prepared with her homework, and the next time homework is due she hasn't done it. The one thing that Mr. Howard, Kelli's tenth grade science teacher can predict, however, is that he can tell every time Kelli is in the classroom because she seems to be constantly talking when she is there. He has spoken to her about her talking on more than one occasion because he finds it to be quite distracting to his teaching. Sometimes, she talks to other students when he is trying to teach and often just calls out answers to questions that he is asking, even when he is about to call on another student for an answer. She even makes remarks about what he is talking about during his lesson to seemingly no one at all. It is as though when an idea comes into her head she just says whatever comes to mind. When she talks, he focuses on her talking, and loses track of where he is. This upsets him, and he thinks that Kelli and the other students can tell when he gets upset.

To Mr. Howard, Kelli hasn't outgrown a behavior that he thought was more common to elementary school students. One thing that adds to his frustration is that Kelli almost always receives some of the highest grades in the class. He really can't figure out how she does it when he knows that she isn't giving his teaching her undivided attention. Kelli's talking is also distracting to the other students who sit near her. Some students don't want to be her lab partner because they know that it is difficult for them to concentrate and get their work done when she is nearby.

He has heard that Kelli is from a large family, but he really doesn't know anything specific about her home life. He can't recall ever speaking to anyone from her family. The more he thinks about it, she is actually somewhat of a mystery to him. He can't remember if he has ever seen Kelli with any other students outside of class on any regular basis.

He knows that he has to do something about Kelli's disruptive talking. He just isn't sure, though, how he can find out what he needs to know and what to do to make things better. What should he do?

ATTENTION-SEEKING (PRIMARY-ELEMENTARY GRADES)

Bridget's Attention-seeking

Bridget, although she comes from a disadvantaged background, makes very good grades in her fifth-grade classroom. Yet, Ms. Wilson, her teacher, is very concerned about Bridget's behavior problems. While it is easy for her to recognize that Bridget has what many call a "sound mind," she also often acts in a manner that Ms. Wilson feels is immature for a child her age. For example, Bridget is known by her classmates as a "tattler" who frequently goes to Ms. Wilson to tell her of some instance when a classmate broke a rule while the teacher was not watching. Not only does this make her classmates angry, this constant behavior, more common to younger children, has started to get on Ms. Wilson's nerves. It certainly interrupts her instruction when Bridget does this. Moreover, Bridget tries to dominate Ms. Wilson's time, even pretending to not understand things just so Ms. Wilson will come and sit beside her desk. At the beginning of the school year, Bridget "clowned around" and tried to be funny in class seemingly as a way to get attention. She hasn't done this for some time, though, as many of the other students laughed at her in a way that was not the "type of laugh" that she was seeking.

Ms. Wilson finds it difficult to give the necessary attention to the other students in the class because of Bridget's constant demands. During a conference, Ms. Wilson found that, although Bridget is living with an aunt who seems to care for her very much, she has been in three different homes over the past five years. Bridget's birth father, who didn't live with her long, has now left the area and has not been heard from for over a year. Bridget's birth mother has four other children and has asked her sister, Bridget's aunt, if she could care for her. She has tried to care for Bridget, but her circumstances are also difficult as she is away at work in the late afternoons and evenings during the week. In all, Ms. Wilson has discovered that Bridget is one of those many children who, in large part, are raising themselves. It is no wonder that Bridget craves attention from her as she gets little positive attention away from school. Still, Bridget's behaviors are interrupting to her instruction and she feels that they are not age-appropriate for a student in the fifth grade.

Ms. Wilson wants to help Bridget as she does all of her students, and she recognizes her learning potential. However, she cannot continue to accept Bridget's attention-seeking behaviors. She is uncertain about how to approach the problem. What should she do?

ATTENTION-SEEKING (MIDDLE-SECONDARY GRADES)

Jennifer's Attention-seeking

Jennifer is in Mr. Winslow's tenth grade Spanish II class. This is an unusual class because, of the twenty-four students in the class, only five are females. Mr. Winslow noticed early on in the term that Jennifer frequently did things to bring attention to herself. Sometimes she would just act out in a disturbing way and other times she would do something to try to look funny. Once or twice, she even came to Mr. Winslow to tell him something that seemed unnecessary about another student in the class. Not only is her behavior annoying, it is also disturbing to him and the rest of the students.

Mr. Winslow thinks that Jennifer is really struggling to keep up with the other students in the class and wonders if maybe this could be a reason for her attention-seeking. Maybe, she is trying to hide that she isn't doing very well. But, when he asked some of the other teachers in the school who had Jennifer in class, he learned that this was how she acted in their classes, too. One of the other teachers added that Jennifer lived with her mother and a younger brother who attended the middle school.

Mr. Winslow is worried about Jennifer for a number of reasons. First, her clowning around and drawing attention to herself is distracting to him and other students. Second, he thinks that Jennifer coming to him and telling him things about other students is not a typical or appropriate behavior for a student her age. It certainly isn't earning her any friends in the class. Finally, he is concerned that Jennifer isn't being successful as a student. Except for trying to draw attention to herself, she is friendly, attractive, well dressed, communicates clearly, uses good grammar, and gets along fairly well with the other students. Through some of his investigation, he learned that Jennifer is a cheerleader and that she has been in some of the school plays. On the surface, she seems far better off, at least financially, than some of the other students that he is teaching. But, he has been teaching long enough to know that what might be apparent on the surface might not represent the complete situation. He knows that when students seek attention on a regular basis that there may be additional problems that need to be dealt with in addition to attention-seeking.

He wants to help Jennifer, but he just doesn't know how to go about it. One thing he knows for sure is that he needs to know more about her. What should he do?

CHRONIC AVOIDANCE OF WORK (PRIMARY-ELEMENTARY GRADES)

Tabitha's Chronic Avoidance of Work

Tabitha, at times, can be one of the most cooperative students in the class and other times she can just act as though nothing in the class has any importance to her. Mr. Waverly is Tabitha's fifth-grade teacher, and he has observed her behavior with interest. Lately, what has become especially bothersome for him is that Tabitha seldom turns back in to him the work that he has assigned. He does a lot of whole group instruction as well as cooperative learning activities, and it doesn't seem to matter. For the past two months, it has been virtually impossible for him to get any schoolwork from Tabitha. It seems that almost weekly he asks her about her work that is due, and she always has some comment to make about it. Sometimes it is in her mother's car. Other times she and her parents had gone out to eat the night before, and she didn't have a chance to get it done. Frequently, she just shrugs her shoulders and says that she has simply forgotten to do it, but that she will bring it in the next day. The next day, Tabitha never seems to have her work.

Mr. Waverly is very concerned about Tabitha's behavior; it has happened before but has not lasted so long. At this point, Tabitha is falling further and further behind the rest of the students in the class. The school has a parent-teacher conference scheduled in about two weeks, but Mr. Waverly isn't sure that he can wait that long to speak to Tabitha's parents. He knows that both of them work and that it might be hard for them to help her regularly with her schoolwork. He has spoken to the teachers who had Tabitha in class in the third and fourth grades, and they indicated that this was not typical behavior for her. Although they did not remember Tabitha as being a high performing student, they did remember her as a student who was solidly in the average range and who was cooperative and helpful in class. She also got along well with other students.

This description of Tabitha doesn't remind Mr. Waverly of the Tabitha that he knows. His Tabitha is neither cooperative nor dependable. Sometimes, she seems downright moody. He also doesn't see her getting along well with other students or even regularly associating with them. Even with just this brief history, Mr. Waverly knows that he has a problem that he needs to deal with. Tabitha's behavior needs to change in terms of her schoolwork, and, if she is having other problems, he needs to be prepared to help her there as well. But, what should he do next?

CHRONIC AVOIDANCE OF WORK
(MIDDLE-SECONDARY GRADES)

Jay's Chronic Avoidance of Work

Ms. Davis is Jay's ninth-grade English teacher. She has been closely following his progress, or perhaps his lack of progress, for the past three weeks. It is difficult for her to know just what Jay is able to do because he so seldom completes and turns in the work that she has assigned. To reinforce the high expectations that she has for her students, she regularly gives writing and some other question-completion assignments each week. Jay hardly ever turns in the work that she has given.

Ms. Davis knows that things have been pretty rough for Jay. He is in the ninth grade when most of his friends are in the tenth grade. Jay repeated seventh grade. That had been a difficult year for him as his mother died that year. She has thought about pulling his record to see how he did in school before that year, but she hasn't had the time. Jay lives with his father and three younger sisters. She hasn't visited his home, but she knows that Jay's father works at the local electronics plant. It has to be hard for him raising three young girls and Jay.

Still, Jay is behind the other students in the class and falling further behind with each assignment that she gives. She asked him a couple of times why he hadn't completed his work, and all that he said was that he hadn't had the time. Once he said that he didn't understand what he was supposed to do and really didn't see the point in it anyway. She doesn't understand how he can't know what she wants. She gives her assignments in a very regular and predictable way. He has many chances to ask questions if he is not sure what she wants.

Fortunately, Jay's outward behavior in class doesn't seem to be a problem. He is quiet and keeps to himself. She isn't sure if he has any real friends in the class or not. She usually teaches the class as a large group and hasn't seen him talking to any of the other students for any length of time. She has so many students in her classes throughout the day that she hasn't been able to get to know Jay very well. She feels bad about this, but that is just the way it is.

She doesn't want to give Jay poor grades, but she can't ignore his not completing his work. After all, she has her standards to think about. She does recognize that she has a problem. But, she isn't sure what to do. What should she do?

DISHONESTY (PRIMARY-ELEMENTARY GRADES)

Thom's Dishonesty

Ms. Gore has been teaching fourth grade for ten years and is considered an excellent teacher by both parents and fellow educators. However, never in her ten years of teaching has she had the type of problem that she has had this year. The problem began when Terry reported that he had some money missing from his desk. He said that it was a couple of dollars. Two days later, Lakisha said that part of her lunch had been taken. Within the next week, almost every student in the classroom reported that they had been the victim of something having been taken. Ms. Gore knows that some of the reports are not factual. Some children are simply mistaken, and others have gotten caught up in the moment. However, she is certain some things are being taken; in fact, someone went so far as to steal money from her own desk. But now, students are accusing other students without having any proof.

Ms. Gore finds it amazing that a fourth-grade class can take on all the primary characteristics of what she thinks of as an unruly mob. Fingers are being pointed and innocent students are being hurt by false accusations. She even got two calls one evening and one email last week from parents asking what was going on in the class. Their children had told them that some things had been taken from them. While the parents didn't seem angry, she could tell that they wanted to know more about the problem and what was being done about it. All she could say was that she was looking into it. Getting calls from parents makes her think that things are truly getting out of control.

Then, a most amazing thing happens. She finds some of the things that have been taken in Thom's desk. When confronted in private, Thom admits to taking everything. Ms. Gore is very confused because Thom's parents are known to be wealthy and generous people. Thom does not "need" to steal. Thom tells her that he is sorry he has stolen and that it will never happen again. He also begs her not to tell his parents about what he has done.

Ms. Gore, although an experienced teacher, is not sure just how to handle the situation. It won't take long for the other students in the class to find out that it is Thom who has been taking things. After that, their parents will soon know. She has a lot to think about and some important decisions to make. What should she do?

DISHONESTY (MIDDLE-SECONDARY GRADES)

Shekiah's Dishonesty

Mr. Gallagher sees himself as someone who can handle most any problem in the classroom. He teaches eighth-grade social studies and tries to have his class operate as though it is a small, democratic community. Everyone has a chance for input into making the "rules" and deciding how the community will operate. He has the class meet regularly to talk about how things are going. Communities are governed by laws, and he thinks that having his students meet on a regular basis will help reinforce this fact. This also helps him see what is on the minds of his students and shows them that he cares about their ideas and their lives. He is glad that he has a positive relationship with his students because he is facing a difficult problem. Over the past month, some students have told him that they have had things missing. Some of the missing items have been pens and pencils, but some have been make-up kits, perfume, and even money. He also thinks that he has had some cheating on his last two tests. The students who told him about the stealing even named another student in the class, Shekiah, as the thief. He also believes that Shekiah has been cheating on his tests. Stealing affects other students in that their property is lost. Cheating also affects other students in that it can make a difference in the grades that they receive. Cheating also may be symptomatic of other, deeper problems.

Mr. Gallagher doesn't know much about Shekiah except that she doesn't seem to him like someone who would steal and cheat. She has only been in his class for about two months as she has just recently started attending the school. She interacts well with the other students and seems bright and alert. He has seen both of her parents at school functions, and they both came for the parent-teacher conferences that had been held just two weeks ago. Stealing and cheating are very serious problems. The class meetings that he has held so far have not gotten into anything like this. Should he bring up the problem of stealing and cheating to the students at a class meeting? Maybe, he is wrong about Shekiah. But, what if he is right, and she really is doing these things? This is a problem that has to be dealt with.

There are issues here that are important not only because of the acts that have been committed but also because they have been formally brought to his attention by some of the students. The problem is pretty much out in the open and needs to be dealt with. He has to take action, but it has to be the right action. What should he do?

UNRULINESS (PRIMARY-ELEMENTARY GRADES)

Billy's Unruliness

Billy is a second grade student who has little self-control. One of his favorite things to do is run down the hallway at school making motor sounds with his mouth while pretending to shift gears with his right hand. Although Billy thinks this is great fun, Ms. Lee, his teacher, finds this behavior unacceptable. So do other teachers in the school. Billy's classmates often find Billy annoying because he frequently gets too loud and out of control when the class is involved in one of Ms. Lee's many fun activities. Actually, Ms. Lee views Billy as the kind of child who usually means to please; in fact, Billy is a good learner and makes above average grades as a rule. However, more than once Billy has embarrassed her by his behaviors like running and talking too loudly in the cafeteria and knocking on each teacher's door as he goes by on his way to the restroom.

At first, Billy's behavior seemed as though it might just be the behavior of a very energetic boy. Billy almost always seems happy and alert when he comes to school. The fact that he does make good grades has indicated to Ms. Lee that he has a sound mind and is able to comprehend what is expected of him. He seems to be one of the stronger students in the class in science and math. His repeated behaviors that just seem too loud, too physical at times, and too much playground-like, however, have proven to be a problem for what Ms. Lee is trying to accomplish in her teaching. His behavior, she feels, also has impacted negatively on the learning of the other students in the class.

Ms. Lee has spoken to Billy on more than one occasion about his overly rambunctious behavior, and his response has always been that he will try to do better. In fact, Ms. Lee feels as though Billy has tried to do better, but has simply been unsuccessful in his attempts. Her view is that, if he can learn science and math, then he can learn to act properly in the classroom and school. She has even thought about having Billy meet with the assistant principal, hoping he might be able to offer assistance. So far she hasn't done this nor has she spoken to Billy's parents about his behavior.

Ms. Lee has always been the kind of teacher who desires to "solve her own problems" whenever they occur. Billy's behavior, though, seems to be getting worse and not better. Ms. Lee needs to try something else, but what?

UNRULINESS (MIDDLE-SECONDARY GRADES)

Kendrick's Unruliness

Kendrick is a handful for Ms. Singh. Ms. Singh is Kendrick's eleventh-grade social studies teacher, or at least tries to be. She has all but given up on Kendrick ever being well behaved in class or being a good student. He is too loud and boisterous. He probably thinks that he is funny, but she thinks that he is trouble to have around. About every time that she seems to have things going well, he does something to distract her and the rest of the class. Sometimes, he will just get out of his seat and walk around the room; other times, he will talk to the other students who sit near him. She doesn't think that he knows how to whisper. She can hear him talking all the way from the back of the room where he usually sits. She doesn't use assigned seats for her students as it is her opinion that students this age should be able to pick where they want to sit in the class.

Ms. Singh considers herself to be a dedicated and flexible teacher, but her way just isn't connecting with Kendrick. She knows that he is popular in school and thinks that this is because he is on the basketball team. She has never been to one of the games, but she has heard other students talk about how many points he always scores. She has even heard that there may be some college scouts looking at him for a basketball scholarship. Her view of him, though, is that he simply is undisciplined.

As a student, Kendrick is struggling. His work is below average, and his mind really appears to be "somewhere else" when she is teaching. Ms. Singh has become very frustrated because she believes that Kendrick is getting the best of her. His behavior is distracting to her and to the other students; to her he seems immature when compared to the rest of the class. She has looked in his file and knows that he lives with his mother and four brothers and sisters. He has had a poor track record in school over the years and is barely making the grade to be able to play basketball. As she sees it, basketball is one of the only things that keeps him coming to school and doing any work at all.

Ms. Singh feels that, when Kendrick acts out in class, this makes her look bad in the eyes of the other students. If she allows him to "get away with it," other students eventually will try to do the same thing. She knows that a lot of students aren't interested in social studies, and that surprises and disappoints her as she finds social studies very interesting. He certainly hasn't learned very much from her teaching up to this point. In her opinion, the situation has to change. What should she do?

DEFIANCE (PRIMARY-ELEMENTARY GRADES)

Maggie's Defiance

Maggie is a second-grade student who has had a personal problem during the current school year. Mr. Ray, her teacher, is aware that Maggie's parents recently divorced and that Maggie has become very upset by the fact that her father has moved to a new dwelling with another women and her children. Maggie continues to live with her mother and her older sister who will graduate from high school at the end of the year. The source of Maggie's frustration seems obvious. Immediately after the divorce, there appeared to be little change in Maggie's behavior. Over the past month, however, her behavior has changed significantly in a negative way.

Mr. Ray is concerned that on three occasions in the last two weeks Maggie has refused to do as he has requested and has told him in front of other students that she did not have to what he told her to do. These incidents have taken place in such a way that he feels his ability to control his class has been threatened or at least definitely challenged. The public nature of this challenge has been especially bothersome to him. At first, he was shocked at Maggie's behavior and her remarks and just tried to coax her to do what he had asked. Fortunately, she did. On another occasion, when he asked his students to work together in pairs, Maggie and the student that she was paired with got into a big argument about who was going to do what on the project that he assigned. When he talked to them about it, the other student said that Maggie didn't want to cooperate and share the materials that he had passed out.

Mr. Ray feels sorry for Maggie and knows that she is suffering. The changes in her home conditions must be traumatic for her. Still, he does not feel that he can continue to allow her to talk to him as she has and challenge his authority, especially in front of other students. With Maggie's parents' divorce being final, there is no chance that her lifestyle will return to the way it was. Mr. Ray, who is a first-year teacher, is uneasy about going to his principal for advice because he wants to appear as though he can manage his own classroom problems.

He recalls some discussions in college that dealt with managing classrooms, but doesn't remember that this particular kind of situation was presented. He recognizes that he has a problem. Now, he must find the solution. What should he do?

DEFIANCE (MIDDLE-SECONDARY GRADES)

Eric's Defiance

Ms. Hutton is in her first year of teaching. She feels fortunate that she has been able to get a job given that she graduated in December and that there are not as many teaching positions open in the middle of the school year as there are at the beginning of the year. The part that she doesn't feel so fortunate about is that the position that she has accepted is at the high school level when she wanted to teach younger students. The school is also in a rather rough neighborhood. Still, she pledged to herself that she was going to be the best health teacher that she could be. One thing that she learned early on is that some of the students in the school come from very difficult home backgrounds. At times, some of them are hard to manage.

Eric is one such student. Up to this point, Ms. Hutton has not had any major problems with Eric though she has made every effort to avoid them too. Eric appears to be one of those students who tries to push the envelope as the popular expression goes. He seldom acts as though he wants to be involved in the activities that she has planned and almost dares her to see if she can get him to participate. Once or twice he even has made what she thinks are "smart remarks" about what she is having the students do. Even though she has a good relationship with most of the students, she still feels very new to being a teacher. Maybe things have gone fairly well up to this point only because she has shown a lot of flexibility in what she asks her students to do and when she asks them to do it. From listening to some of the other teachers talk, she wonders if she is being too flexible.

Today, Ms. Hutton has given her students what she thinks will be an interesting assignment that her students will enjoy doing. When Eric gets the assignment sheet, Ms. Hutton can tell that he doesn't want to do it. As she is walking by his desk, he just wads it up and drops it on the floor. He says, "this is the most stupid thing I have ever been asked to do, and I'm not gonna do it." Ms. Hutton knows that she is facing one the most difficult moments in her short teaching career. She can't let Eric talk like this in the classroom, and she also knows the problem is bigger than just this one assignment.

How can she best deal with the problem of the moment as well as help things be better in the long run? What should she do?

AGGRESSION (PRIMARY-ELEMENTARY GRADES)

Julian's Aggression

Julian is a kindergarten student whose behavior has been a concern to both his parents and his teacher, Mr. Woo. Julian seems to be advanced in his learning as compared to some of the other students in the class. His mother, a former first-grade teacher, spent a great deal of time with him before he began school which resulted in his being a very good reader when he started kindergarten. He also does well in beginning writing and in certain computation skills activities. In fact, Julian's parents wanted to have him placed in the first grade this year with children a year older because of his advanced learning abilities. They both value education highly, and as Julian is their only child, they are very focused on his development and eventual accomplishments. The accelerated placement to first grade, however, was not made.

Although Julian's academic skills are much like a student in the first grade, Mr. Woo recognizes that Julian's social and emotional characteristics are actually less developed than those of even the average kindergarten child's. When playing on the playground with other students, Julian often becomes angry and hits or bites his classmates. When Mr. Woo tries to control Julian, Julian frequently screams and even kicks at him. Additionally, Julian's aggressive behavior is not relegated only to the playground. He displays similar behaviors in the cafeteria, the hallways, and sometimes even in the classroom. While there is room for other students to avoid him on the playground, this is not the case in the classroom. On more than one occasion, classroom activities have had to be adjusted because of his behavior. Over the past month, some parents have even complained to the principal that they did not want their children in the same class with Julian because they feared for their safety.

When in a conference with Mr. Woo, Julian's parents voiced their opinion that Julian gets frustrated because the other students are not as advanced as he is which results in his angry outbursts. Since the beginning of the school year, they have continued to feel that Julian should have been placed in the first grade. Mr. Woo shared with them that he has tried to talk to Julian and work closely with him, but that his aggressive behavior is a definite problem for him and the other students.

Mr. Woo isn't sure just what to do next. He likes Julian and recognizes that he definitely has learning potential, but his behavior needs to change and this represents a real problem. What should he do?

AGGRESSION (MIDDLE-SECONDARY GRADES)

Sebastian's Aggression

Mr. Allen is embarrassed to say it, but he has come to the point where he is glad when Sebastian is absent from school. Mr. Allen teaches seventh-grade math, and Sebastian is one of his students. The school year started out all right, but it started without Sebastian. It is now early December, and Sebastian joined the school and his class in late October. It has been a rough month and a half. Sebastian is a very aggressive person. He has already been in two fights and come close on a number of other occasions. When Sebastian is around, the tension in the class seems to rise.

Sebastian is physically smaller than many of the other students and has had a difficult time catching up to them academically. Mr. Allen hasn't had a chance to see the file that has been sent from Sebastian's last school, but, at least in math, Sebastian is far behind. Sebastian also has had a difficult time adjusting to the rest of the students in the class as well as to his teaching style which Mr. Allen sees as being very straightforward.

He doesn't believe that Sebastian is a bully in that Sebastian doesn't regularly start fights with other students. But, he is quick to say things that offend other students or something that most people consider uncalled for and inappropriate. He sees Sebastian as a loner; he doesn't appear to have any friends in the class. Sebastian was always eating by himself the few times that he saw him in the school cafeteria. The more he thinks about it the more he really feels sorry for him. He is in a new community and a new school and is behind the other students in his class. This must make him feel very out of place. Maybe, he is doing the best that he can do.

One day, all of the good feelings that Mr. Allen had about reaching Sebastian seemed far away as he saw Sebastian and another student standing face to face, perhaps squaring off, in the back of the room. Class hadn't started, but it was supposed to in just a few minutes. Mr. Allen's attention was attracted to the back of the room when he heard two students say "Sebastian shouldn't have said that to him," and "I'll bet Sebastian is gonna get it good."

Mr. Allen knows that he has at least two problems to deal with. First, what is he going to do about the fight that is about to take place in his classroom? Second, what can he do to help Sebastian not be involved in such situations in the future? What is the answer to each of these questions?

BULLYING (PRIMARY-ELEMENTARY GRADES)

Jose's Bullying Problem

Ms. Howard is a third-grade teacher in a mid-size elementary school. While she has encountered different and sometimes difficult problems in her teaching each year, she has been able to resolve them satisfactorily. This year, though, she has been confronted with a new problem, at least new to her, that she has yet to resolve. Ms. Howard's school year began with 23 students in her classroom but now that number has grown to 24 with the addition of Jose about a month ago. Her initial impression of Jose was quite positive as he was polite, quiet, completed his work, seemed cooperative and generally kept to himself. Now, however, Ms. Howard has developed another view, one that has become troublesome.

As she has observed Jose in her classroom and in other areas of the school, she has seen more closely his relationship with other students. In particular, this has involved two of her other students, Marcus and Charles. She has been both troubled and surprised by what she has observed. Marcus and Charles have been two of her favorite students. Now she thinks that she may be seeing a different side to them.

Over the last three weeks, she has seen one or both of them tease and make fun of Jose. At times they have walked by his desk and knocked his books, papers and pencils to the floor. At other times they have shoved him out of line in the lunch room. At still other times they have actually punched him at recess when they thought that no one was looking. One of the other third-grade teachers who was on playground supervision said that she had heard them call Jose some very ugly names and say some very mean things to him.

The end result has been that Jose has become quieter than usual, missed days of school, and become inconsistent and sloppy in his school work. To make things worse, she has heard some of the other students in the class laugh when the two boys played their tricks on him. Ms. Howard had come to think of her classroom as a small community where all of the members got along and watched out for each other. Now she isn't so sure. Marcus and Charles come from what she thinks of as good homes. They have grown up together in the same community and moved through the grades in the same classes. Why would they be doing these things?

Ms. Howard is well aware of many of the issues in schools that involve bullying, but she has never encountered it firsthand. Obviously this situation cannot continue and she knows that she has a responsibility to take some action. She is not sure, however, just what that action should be. What should she do?

BULLYING (MIDDLE-SECONDARY GRADES)

Keith's Bullying Problem

Keith is in the tenth grade and very anxious for the school year to end. Actually, he is anxious for his high school years to end so that he can get away from one particular student, Junior. Junior also is in the tenth grade, and, for some reason that Keith can't understand, Junior has taken it upon himself to make his life miserable. Junior stands about 6'2" and weighs around 200 pounds. Keith is a modest 5'9" and barely 150 pounds.

Although Keith and Junior only have one class together, it seems that each day Junior has something in store for him. So far, Junior has trashed his gym locker as well as his locker in the main part of the school, let the air out of the tires on his car in the school parking lot, and in the lunch room walked by and dropped a dirty rag onto his plate of food. Sometimes he just walks by and bumps into him, hard, and makes comments about the way he dresses, how he smells, or how he has his hair cut. Junior has also made threatening remarks to him such as "I'm looking forward to finding you alone some day after school." Keith is even afraid to go into the restroom alone. School is no longer a place for learning but merely a place for surviving.

Keith's favorite teacher is Mr. Jeffries, his social studies teacher. He has shared some of his concerns with him, but Keith isn't sure just what will come of it. Mr. Jeffries said that he should tell a school administrator, but he doesn't want a reputation of telling on other students and getting another student in trouble. He knows that other students have seen how Junior has been after Keith, but no one seems to be interested in getting involved. Most just look on for the entertainment or turn their heads and walk away.

Last Friday, when he was ready to leave school for the weekend, he saw Junior in the parking lot just leaning on his car so he decided to stay in the school until Junior went away. That took about an hour. Some teachers walked by while he was waiting, including Mr. Jeffries, but no one said anything. He has decided that when he comes back to school on Monday, if he comes back, it might be a good idea to bring something to protect himself.

In all, he simply doesn't know what to do. He thinks that Mr. Jeffries understands his situation, but he doesn't believe that any help will come from him. He doesn't know if he should try to stand up to Junior or just try to stay out of his way. In the meantime, his grades are terrible and he is a nervous wreck. What should Keith do? What should Mr. Jeffries do?

CONCLUSION

In spite of the many classroom rules and procedures that teachers may have established, many of the problems that they face each day have no one right answer or resolution. Most are specific to a particular situation, to the student or students involved, and require analysis within individual contexts. Through guided problem solving based on a strong knowledge base of information related to best practice in teaching, student motivation, and classroom management, teachers can identify patterns in the various problems that they encounter and learn from one problem to another. While each situation needs to be analyzed individually, over time, common patterns and plausible solutions will emerge. It is because of this that it is critical that teachers learn from each situation that they encounter so that they can more quickly find effective solutions to the problems that they will be faced with in the future.

The vignettes presented here for analysis serve to illustrate this point. Teachers can learn from their successes, as well as from their failures, if they are willing and able to analyze them in a systematic, informed, and objective manner. Whether the teacher is dealing with a problem of dishonesty in the second grade or defiance in the tenth grade, a logical approach needs to be followed to address the problem. Chapter 7 offered a number of realistic problems for review. By addressing each problem as a situation where certain questions must be asked and answered for the problem to be resolved effectively, the positive impact of using a logical problem-solving model in problem resolution can be seen. Through the disciplined use of the model in these hypothetical situations, the transfer of possible effective solutions can more easily and successfully be made to the real-life problems that teachers face in their classrooms each day.

GLOSSARY OF TERMS

Academic learning time. That portion of the classroom time where students are actively and successfully involved in the lesson's activities.

Academic organization. The teacher's means of ordering and arranging information for instruction so that students will be able to understand the information communicated, e.g., diagrams, outlines, hierarchies, etc.

Active listening. Specific approach to listening where the teacher gives full attention to both the emotional as well as intellectual meaning of what the student is saying; often involves mirroring back what a student has said confirming that the listener is attentive, interested, and nonjudgmental.

Advance organizer. Described by David Ausubel as the teacher's use of introductory statements or activities that frame the new content to be taught as a part of the lesson focus.

Advancework. The process of preventing problems before they begin rather than reacting to problems after they have already occurred.

Aggression. A serious behavior problem in that the possibility exists that one or more students may be injured; fighting is the ultimate form of aggression though aggression may also include pushing and shoving, overly physical play, name-calling, or other verbal attacks.

Allocated time. The amount of time a particular teacher or school designates to an identified course topic or activity.

Anticipatory set. The mental or attitudinal foundation established by the teacher for the students at the beginning of the instructional experience that helps students understand what they may anticipate in the instruction which will follow.

Antisocial behavior. A behavior directed toward bringing about a negative consequence for someone or something.

Applied Behavior Analysis. An approach to behavior management based on the work of B. F. Skinner's operant conditioning theory that focuses on the positive, rewarding appropriate behaviors, as opposed to the negative, punishing unwanted or inappropriate behaviors.

Anxiety. Feeling of apprehension, worry, tension, or nervousness.

Assertive Discipline. Management theory established by Lee Canter based on the position that teachers have the right to teach while students have the right to learn, and no one has the right to disrupt the learning environment; clear rules are established along with identified consequences for students who choose to break the rules.

Attainment value. Value determined by how a task or domain fulfills a person's needs; it concerns the relevance of an activity to a person's actual or ideal self-concept.

Attention-seeking. Student behavior problem often exhibited by tattling and showing off, class clowning, or in some other way drawing focus to one's self.

Avoidance strategies. To reduce stress, strategies such as simply ignoring an upcoming situation and/or engaging in something totally unrelated to the stressful situation.

Attribution. Cognitive theory that represents a student's view of the causes of outcomes or of an event and how this view influences his or her future expectations and behavior.

Autonomy. In self-determination theory, independence and the ability to alter the environment when necessary.

Behavior modification. Associated with the work of B.F. Skinner, now more popularly called Applied Behavior Analysis; management approach that utilizes rewards for modifying student behavior.

Behaviorism. Theory of motivation that focuses on the use of reinforcements or rewards to modify student behavior.

Bullying. A negative behavior which is intentionally designed to cause real, or threatening injury or discomfort to another individual that may reflect physical harm, psychological harm, or both.

Chronic avoidance of work. Potentially a serious student behavior problem where a student consistently fails to complete his or her assigned work following repeated teacher effort to get the work completed.

Clarity. Important teacher characteristic in being able to be understood in communications with students so that they understand the different teacher messages used during instruction, how the instruction will be conducted, and what is expected of them.

Class meeting. Management strategy recommended by William Glasser where the teacher meets regularly with students as a process to involve students in establishing guidelines for acceptable behavior and as a forum for collaborative problem solving.

Closure. Type of review that occurs at the end of the instructional period that enables the student to end the lesson with a better understanding of the topic and a place to build on in the future.

Coercive strategies. Behavior strategies used by the teacher in maintaining a well-managed classroom that are based on the power of punishment.

Cognitive memory level question. Question at the lowest level of cognition that asks students to recall previously learned and memorized information; behaviors such as recalling, recognizing, and reporting are typically included at this level.

Cognitive theories. Theories of motivation that stress the student's need for order, predictability, and the understanding of events around him.

Competence. In self-determination theory, the ability to function effectively in the environment.

Conflict Resolution. Management strategy developed by David and Roger Johnson that relies on training students to deal with their own problems and those of their fellow students; peer mediation is an important part of this strategy.

Connected discourse. Communication where the teacher's presentation is thematically well connected and leads to a goal, going point by point.

Convergent level question. Question at the second lowest level of cognition that asks students to put facts or concepts together to obtain the single correct answer; questions may require students to make comparisons, explain facts or concepts, state or describe relationships, or solve problems using learned procedures.

Criterion material. Information that students will be held accountable for which has been communicated to them prior to instruction; the criteria or standard upon which the teacher will base student success.

Debilitating anxiety. Anxiety so extreme that it gets in the way of successful performance.

Defiance. A serious form of student misbehavior where the student refuses to do what the teacher asks or boldly talks back to the teacher in a hostile or threatening way.

Deficiency needs. Needs at the lower levels of Abraham Maslow's Hierarchy of Needs including survival, safety, belonging, and self-esteem.

Desists. The use of verbal or nonverbal communications by teachers for the purpose of stopping student misconduct or misbehavior.

Discipline. Action taken on the part of the teacher to enforce rules and respond to student misbehavior.

Disequilibrium. A state of being out-of-balance.

Dishonesty. Considered by some to be the most serious form of student misconduct often exhibited through cheating and/or stealing and telling untruths and lying.

Disruptive talking. Student behavior problem through talking that interferes with the learning process by interrupting the teacher while teaching, students as they are listening to the teacher, or as they are involved in completing activities that the teacher has assigned.

Divergent level question. Question that asks students to engage in divergence of thought and produce a response that is original for that student; questions may require students to predict, hypothesize, or infer.

Diversity. In the school or classroom, pertains to the variety of backgrounds or circumstances from which students come as they enter the schooling environment.

Emotion-focused strategies. To reduce stress, efforts to deal with anxious feelings that could include relaxation exercises or describing one's feelings to a friend.

Emphasis. An element of communication where the teacher specifically identifies for students important points to be remembered, e.g., through the use of such statements as "this is important" or "be sure to remember this."

Engaged time. The portion of instructional time that students actually spend directly involved in learning activities; often referred to as time-on-task.

Enthusiasm. The amount of energy and vigor shown by the teacher; felt to communicate to students the degree to which the teacher enjoys teaching and the degree to which the teacher believes that the students will be successful in their learning.

Equilibration. The process of searching for order or balance, i.e., equilibrium, and, in so doing, testing one's understanding against the real world.

Equilibrium. A state of balance.

Equitable distribution. A recommended approach to asking questions where all students are called on equitably or as equally as possible.

Expectancy X value theory. Theory that students are motivated to engage in learning tasks to the extent that they expect to succeed on the tasks and the degree to which they value achievement on the tasks or other potential outcomes that may come as a result of task achievement.

Expulsion. Process exercised by a school district's governing authority, generally the school board, of banning a student from attending school for the remainder of the school year or the remainder of the school year plus an additional period of time carried over into the next school year.

External locus of control. When students feel that forces external to or outside themselves control their lives.

Extrinsic motivation. Motivation to become involved in an activity as a means to an end, e.g., to receive a reward, praise, or some other recognition.

Evaluation level question. Question at the highest level of cognition that asks students to make judgments based on logically derived evidence; students must defend or explain their judgments based on criteria that they designate or which have been established by others.

Facilitating anxiety. Anxiety in such a small amount that it actually helps to improve performance.

Feedback. Information provided students by teachers, generally in oral or written form, that lets them know the status of their learning progress; the more specific, regular, and in-depth the feedback the better.

Focus. Attention given to and maintained on the most important points to be made during instruction; when teachers have good focus, students understand what will take place during instruction and what will be expected of them.

Frequency. Important aspect of question-asking that deals with the number of questions that the teacher asks; generally the more questions the better.

Goal. That which an individual is striving to achieve or accomplish; in teaching, goals are generally broad as opposed to narrow and more long-term as opposed to short-term in nature.

Group focus. On-task behavior where all students in the classroom attend to the teacher or activities that the teacher has assigned at the same time.

Growth needs. Needs at the higher levels of Abraham Maslow's Hierarchy of Needs including intellectual achievement, aesthetic appreciation, and self-actualization.

Hierarchy of Needs. Humanistic theory of motivation developed by Abraham Maslow that identifies a hierarchy of needs associated with underlying reasons for human behavior; needs are identified as deficiency or growth needs.

Humanism. Theory of motivation that views behavior as an individual's effort to satisfy or fulfill his ultimate potential as a human being.

I message. Three-part communication from the teacher that: (1) delineates the student's undesired behavior, (2) describes the effect the behavior has on the teacher, and (3) lets the student know how the teacher feels when the behavior occurs.

Inattention. Student behavior seen as the least severe management problem; students may engage in daydreaming, staring into space, doing unrelated work, etc., as examples of not being involved in the learning process.

Indirect teaching. Approach to teaching that focuses heavily on the use of student ideas and student active participation in the learning process.

Instructional time. The portion of allocated time that is actually devoted to learning activities.

Instructional variety. The use of a number of different instructional techniques or strategies by the teacher rather than relying on only a very few; see also variability.

Inquiry. Logical approach to problem solving that includes the statement of the problem, development of a hypothesis, collection and analysis of data, and the drawing of conclusions.

Internal locus of control. When students feel that they are responsible for what happens to them.

Intrinsic motivation. Motivation to become involved in an activity for its own sake.

Intrinsic value. Value reflected by the immediate enjoyment one gets from doing a task.

Learned helplessness. The belief held by students that no amount of effort on their part will produce success and that events and outcomes in their lives are beyond their control.

Learner-focused classroom. Classroom where emphasis is given to a focus on student learning as opposed to student performance with special attention given to student self-regulation, climate, teacher characteristics, and instruction.

Learning goal. Goal that emphasizes the challenge of learning and the mastery of a task as opposed to performance; also referred to as a mastery goal.

Locus of control. The degree to which students perceive that both positive and negative events in their lives are under their control.

Logical consequences. Recommended by both Rudolph Dreikurs and William Glasser as representing understandings on the part of students that when certain behaviors are exhibited certain responses or consequences will follow.

Management. A system of organization that addresses all elements of the classroom (i.e., students, space, time, materials, and behavioral rules and procedures) that enables the teacher to reach optimum levels of instruction and learning.

Management organization. The general organizational structure used by the teacher to coordinate the classroom, e.g., starting on time, having specific learning routines, etc.

Mastery-focused classroom. Learning environment (classroom) where the focus is on student effort, continuous improvement, and understanding.

Mastery goal. Also referred to as learning goal; goal that emphasizes the challenge of learning and the mastery of a task as opposed to performance.

Misbehavior. Student behavior seen as being unacceptable or inappropriate for the setting or situation in which it occurs.

Model for Reflection and Inquiry. Five-step model for logical problem solving recommended for teachers to use as they analyze problems with student management and motivation; the model includes the statement of the problem, development of a hypothesis, collection of relevant data, analysis of data, and the interpretation and reporting of results, drawing conclusions, and making generalizations.

Modeling. Being able to see someone else perform a particular task successfully influences the observer to do the same; use of demonstration to assist students in the learning process.

Motivation. An internal state that arouses students to action, directs them to certain behaviors, and assists them in maintaining their arousal and action with regard to behaviors important and appropriate to the learning environment.

Motivation to learn. Motivation represented by the quality of a student's cognitive engagement in a learning task or activity.

No-lose approach. Approach to help students resolve their own conflicts or problems in such a way that all students involved feel positive about the resolution and no one is considered a loser.

Normative strategies. Behavior strategies used by the teacher in maintaining a well-managed classroom based on all involved doing what is traditionally expected of them, e.g., teachers are expected to ask certain things of students, and students are expected to do what they are asked by their teachers.

Operant conditioning. A form of learning where an observable response changes in frequency or duration as a result of a consequence; the response increases in frequency as a result of its being followed by reinforcement.

Pedagogical content knowledge. Knowledge of teaching methods and approaches that are specific to the particular subject, or the application of certain strategies in a special way, that the teacher teaches; this includes an understanding of the content in order to teach it in a variety of ways, drawing on the cultural backgrounds and prior knowledge and experiences of the students.

Pedagogical knowledge. Knowledge that includes the general concepts, theories, methods, and research about effective teaching, no matter the content area.

Peer mediation. Important aspect of the Conflict Resolution approach to behavior management where students, after formal training, lead the problem-solving process by helping each other (i.e., peers) reach acceptable solutions to problems that they have experienced.

Performance-focused classroom. Learning environment (classroom) that emphasizes high grades, public displays of ability, and performance and achievement compared to others.

Performance goal. Goal that emphasizes the demonstration of high ability and the avoidance of failure.

Potency. The strength or power of a reinforcer, reward, praise or criticism, to change behavior.

Power-seeking. Student behavior problem where the student seeks to control the teacher instead of being directed by the teacher.

Precise terminology. Teacher communication that eliminates or restricts the use of vague and ambiguous words and phrases from presentations and interactions with students.

Premack principle. The principle that a high-probability or desired activity or behavior can serve as a reinforcer for a low-probability or perhaps less desired activity or behavior; the principle can be a helpful guide for choosing the most effective reinforcers.

Primary reinforcer. A reinforcer that meets a basic physiological need such as food, water, and safety.

Principle of least intervention. Principle that, when dealing with routine classroom behavior, misbehaviors should be corrected with the simplest, least intrusive intervention that will work.

Proactive teacher. A teacher who, through prior planning and knowledge gained, has the ability to "head off" most management problems before they occur and respond to management problems when they occur in such a way that sets the stage for learning to continue in the future.

Probing behaviors. Verbal techniques used by teachers, typically through question-asking, that request in a nonthreatening way that a student go deeper into an answer given or comment made and reflect on his or her ideas.

Problem-focused, self-regulating strategies. To reduce stress, strategies could include planning a formal study schedule, getting notes from a friend, or finding a quiet place to study.

Professional knowledge. Knowledge about teaching in general; this includes knowledge about learning, diversity, technology, schooling and education, and the profession of teaching as a whole.

Prompting. Question-asking strategy that helps students respond to questions by providing cues after an incorrect or incomplete answer or silence.

Prosocial behavior. A behavior directed toward promoting the well-being of someone else.

Prosocial literature. Stories that teachers use in their classrooms that emphasize desired values such as fairness, kindness, tolerance, and honesty.

Proximity control. Control exercised by the teacher based on the teacher's nearness to or distance from the student; generally, the nearer the teacher is to a student, the less likelihood there will be for the student to display inappropriate behaviors.

Psychological membership. The feeling of membership in a group that is determined by the degree to which students feel personally accepted, respected, included, and supported.

Psychological state. Emotional or attitudinal state of a student with respect to performing a task, e.g., tired, anxious, or fearful students will experience a lowered level of self-efficacy.

Punishers. Consequences used by a teacher to weaken an undesired student behavior or decrease the likelihood of it recurring in the future.

Punishment. The process of using punishers to decrease behavior.

Reactive teacher. Teacher whose behavior is characterized by reacting or responding to classroom management and motivation problems after they have occurred rather than ascertaining the causes of such problems and, through prior planning and the use of relevant information, reduce the likelihood that they will ever take place.

Reality Therapy. Management approach recommended by William Glasser, now more popularly referred to as Choice Theory, where students play an active role in the decision-making processes in the classroom.

Reflection. A way of thinking that involves the ability to use information to make rational choices and to assume responsibility for those choices; it requires that the teacher be introspective, open-minded, and willing to accept responsibility for decisions and actions.

Reflective practitioner. Educator who regularly utilizes formal problem solving strategies to develop solutions to problems related to motivation, management, and instruction.

Reinforcer. Something given or a consequence that, depending on whether it is positive or negative, either adds to or reduces the frequency or length of a behavior.

Relatedness. In self-determination theory, the feeling of being connected to others in one's social environment and feeling worthy of love and respect.

Remunerative strategies. Behavior strategies used by the teacher in maintaining a well-managed classroom that are based on the power of rewards.

Resilience. The ability to recover quickly from some type of misfortune or adversity; resilience results in a heightened likelihood of success in school and in other aspects of life, despite environmental adversities.

Resilient self-efficacy. The belief that one can perform a task successfully even after experiencing setbacks with the recognition that effort and perseverance are essential for success.

Retreating. When a teacher is aware that a student is violating a rule governing student conduct yet does not react to correct and extinguish the behavior.

Revenge-seeking. Student behavior problem where a student may do something to cause other students to be punished to "get back at them."

Review. When the teacher summarizes important points from previous work in helping students link what has been learned to what will be taught in the future; review can occur at different points of the lesson, either close to the beginning, midpoint during the body of the lesson, or at the end.

Ripple effect. The effect on other students in the classroom when the teacher reinforces or corrects particular students for their behavior.

Sane messages. Recommended by Haim Ginott; a way for teachers to communicate to students so that they focus on the students' undesired behaviors and not on them as individuals on a personal level.

Secondary reinforcer. A reinforcer that may address a particular psychological need such as praise, grades, and money.

Self-actualization. The full development or use of one's potential.

Self-determination. The process of deciding how to act on one's environment.

Self-efficacy. One's beliefs about his or her capability of succeeding on specific tasks.

Self-fulfilling prophecy. Phenomenon that a student's performance is greatly influenced when a teacher holds certain beliefs about the student's ability to perform.

Self-regulation. The process of using one's own thoughts and actions to reach academic learning goals and to govern one's own behaviors; includes taking responsibility for learning to identify goals, develop strategies for reaching them, and monitoring progress toward their attainment.

Shaping. The practice of gradually changing a student's unwanted actions to more acceptable behavior over time through the use of reinforcements.

State anxiety. Temporary feeling of anxiety brought about through the presence of certain situations that typically result in a sense of fear, concern, or threat.

Structuring comments. Verbal statements used by the teacher, normally at the beginning of the lesson, that alerts students to the events which are to follow and the important points that they should focus on during the instruction.

Student success rate. The rate at which students gain an understanding of and correctly complete their work.

Suspension. Removal of a student from the regular school environment for a stated period of time for the breaking of identified school rules; most schools have both in-school as well as out-of-school suspension programs.

Task orientation or business-like behavior. Manner of conducting instruction where the teacher is focused on the desired learning outcome and in so doing communicates to students that there is a clear and important goal to be achieved and that they will stay on task during the period of time needed to reach the desired goal.

Teacher burnout. Point of teacher extreme stress where a teacher has lost his or her enthusiasm for teaching and has little energy to focus on helping students learn.

Teacher Effectiveness Training (**TET**). Developed by Thomas Gordon as a model for classroom management focusing on problem solving, active listening, and assisting students to resolve their own conflicts through no-lose processes.

Teacher efficacy. The teacher's belief in his or her ability to be successful in getting students to learn.

Teacher expectation. What a teacher expects or thinks a particular student will be able to accomplish.

Time-on-task. See engaged time.

Trait anxiety. When students are anxious in circumstances that should not be seen as threatening.

Transition signals. The use of specific communication signals to blend one topic with the next that follows so that the flow of instruction will be smooth and not abrupt.

Unity-building activities. Activities designed to build a feeling of community and belonging to the group or team; such activities help students communicate better and develop understanding and empathy for one another.

Unruliness. Serious behavior problem where the student exhibits a lack of self-control; unruliness may be exhibited by talking loudly, running in hallways, using unacceptable language, etc.

Utility value. Value that focuses on the usefulness of a task as a means to achieve goals that might not be related to the task itself.

Variability. The teacher's diversity of teaching strategies used during the presentation of lessons; see also instructional variety.

Wait-time. The amount of time the teacher allows after asking a question before speaking again; average wait time is about one second; a minimum of three seconds is recommended to increase student achievement.

Withitness. When a teacher displays the ability to have an ongoing awareness of events throughout the entire classroom and not just one area of the setting.

You message. A statement used by a teacher to a student that may be interpreted as a personal attack or put-down of the student.

Zero tolerance. Policy for managing student behavior, usually adopted on a school district-wide basis, represented by the use of certain pre-determined consequences when particular rules are broken; the consequences are applied automatically regardless of the circumstances surrounding the rule being broken.

Zone of proximal development. A range of tasks that a student cannot yet do alone but can accomplish when assisted by a more skilled partner.

REFERENCES

Adair, J. (2000). Tackling teens' no. 1 problem. *Educational Leadership, 57*, 44–47.

Adams. R., & Biddle, B. (1970). *Realities of teaching: Explorations with video tape*. New York: Holt.

Albert, L. (1996). *Cooperative discipline*. Circle Pines, MN: American Guidance Service, Inc.

Alberto, P., & Troutman, A. (2012). *Applied behavior analysis for teachers: Influencing student performance* (9th ed.). Upper Saddle River, NJ: Pearson.

Alderman, M. (2008). *Motivation for achievement: Possibilities for teaching and learning* (3rd ed.). New York: Routledge.

Ames, R., & Lau, S. (1982). An attributional analysis of student help-seeking in academic settings. *Journal of Educational Psychology, 84*, 261–271.

Anderman, E., & Anderman, L. (2010). *Motivating children and adolescents in schools*. Columbus, OH: Merrill/Prentice-Hall.

Anderson, L., & Krathwohl, D. (Eds.). (2001). *A taxonomy for learning, teaching, and assessing: A revision of Bloom's taxonomy of educational objectives*. New York: Addison Wesley Longman.

Angel Green: Teen's suicide moves Indiana Anti-bullying initiative forward. (2013). Retrieved April, 26, 2013, from http://www.policymic.com/articles/33439/angel-green-teen-s-suicide-moves-indiana-anti-bullying-initiative-forward.

Armstrong, D., Henson, K., & Savage, T. (1997). *Teaching today: An introduction to education* (5th ed.). New York: Macmillan.

Ashton, P., & Webb, R. (1986). *Making a difference: Teachers' sense of efficacy and student achievement*. White Plains, NY: Longman.

Aspy, C., Oman, R., Vesely, S., McLeroy, K., Rodine, S., & Marshall, L. (2004). Adolescent violence: The protective effects of youth assets. *Journal of Counseling and Development, 82*, 268–276.

Association for Supervision and Curriculum Development (ASCD). (2006).The definition of classroom management. Retrieved August 3, 2007, from www.ascd.org.

Association for Supervision and Curriculum Development (ASCD). (2007). Poll. Retrieved May 31, 2007, from www.ascd.org.

Atkinson, J. (1964). *An introduction to motivation*. Princeton, NJ: Van Nostrand.

Audrie Pott, Rehtaeh Parsons suicides show sexual cyber-bullying is "pervasive" and "getting worse," expert says. (2013). Retrieved April 26, 2013, from http://www.cbsnews.com/8301-504083_162-57579366-504083/audrie-pott-rehtaeh-parsons-suicides-show-sexual-cyber-bulling-is-pervasive-and-getting-worse-expert-says/.

Auguste, B., Kihn, P., & Miller, M. (2010). Closing the talent gap: Attracting and retaining top-third graduates to careers in teaching. Retrieved February 23, 2013, from http://mckinseyonsociety.com/closing-the-talent-gap/.

Ausubel, D. (1978). In defense of advance organizers: A reply to the critics. *Review of Educational Research, 48*, 251–259.

Bandura, A. (1986). *Social foundations of thought and action: A social cognitive theory.* Upper Saddle River, NJ: Prentice-Hall.

Bandura, A. (1989). Human agency in social cognitive theory. *American Psychologist, 44*, 1175–1184.

Bandura, A. (1993). Perceived self-efficacy in cognitive development and functioning. *Educational Psychologist, 28*(2), 117–148.

Bandura, A. (1997). *Self-efficacy: The exercise of control.* New York: Freeman.

Banks, J. (1994). *An introduction to multicultural education.* Needham Heights, MA: Allyn & Bacon.

Battistich, V., Solomon, D., Kim, D., Watson, M., & Schaps, E. (1995). Schools as communities, poverty levels of student populations, and student attitudes, motives, and performances: A multilevel analysis. *American Educational Research Journal, 32*(2), 627–658.

Baugous, K., & Bendery, S. (2000). Decreasing the amount of classroom disruptions in order to increase the amount of time on task in elementary students. Retrieved from ERIC database (ED443554).

Bennett, B. (1997). Middle level discipline and young adolescents: Making the connection. In J. L. Irvin (Ed.), *What current research says to the middle level practitioner.* Columbus, OH: National Middle School Association.

Benton, J., & Hacker, H. (2007). Analysis shows TAKS cheating rampant. Retrieved June 8, 2007, from www.dalasnews.com/sharedcontent.

Berk, L. (2010). *Development through the lifespan* (5th ed.). Boston: Allyn & Bacon/Pearson.

Bernhard, J., & Siegel, L. (1994). Increasing internal locus of controls for a disadvantaged group: A computer intervention. *Computers in the Schools, 11*(1), 59–77.

Bindel, J. (2006). Absent enemies. Retrieved November 21, 2006, from http://education.guardian.co.uk/schools/story.

Black, S. (1998). Forever plaid? *American School Board Journal, 185*, 42–45.

Black, S. (2004). Beyond zero tolerance. *American School Board Journal, 9*(191). Retrieved May 21, 2007, from asbj.com journal.

Blair, F. (1999). Does zero tolerance work? *Principal, 79*, 36–37.

Bloom, B., Englehart, M., Furst, E., Hill, W., & Krathwohl, D. (1956). *Taxonomy of educational objectives. Handbook I: Cognitive domain.* New York: David McKay.

Borich, G. (2011). *Effective teaching methods: Research-based practice* (7th ed.). Boston: Pearson.

Borich, G., & Tombari, M. (1997). *Educational psychology: A contemporary approach* (2nd ed.). New York: Longman.

Borman, S., & Levine, J. (1997). *A practical guide to elementary instruction: From plan to delivery.* Boston: Allyn & Bacon.

Borum, R., Cornell, D., Modzeleski, W., & Jimerson, S. (2010). What can be done about school shootings? A review of the evidence. *Educational researcher, 39*(1), 27–37.

Bottoms, G. (2007). Treat all students like the "best" students. *Educational Leadership, 64,* 30–37.

Bracey, G. (2009a). Identify and observe effective teacher behaviors. *Phi Delta Kappan, 90*(10), 772–773.

Bracey, G. (2009b). Some thoughts as "Research" turns 25. *Phi Delta Kappan, 90*(6), 530–531.

Brock, B., & Grady, M. (1998). Beginning teacher induction programs: The role of the principal. *The Clearing House, 71,* 179–183.

Brophy, J. (1983). Conceptualizing student motivation. *Educational Psychologist, 18,* 200–215.

Brophy, J. (1998). *Motivating students to learn.* New York: McGraw-Hill.

Brophy, J. (2004). *Motivating students to learn* (2nd ed.). Boston: McGraw-Hill.

Brophy, J. (2010). *Motivating students to learn* (3rd ed.). New York: Routledge.

Brophy, J., & Evertson, C. (1976). *Learning from teaching: A developmental perspective.* Boston: Allyn & Bacon.

Brophy, J., & McCaslin, M. (1992). Teachers report of how they perceive and cope with problem students. *Elementary School Journal, 93*(1), 3–68.

Brown, J. (1997). Curriculum: Listen to the kids. *American School Board Journal, 184,* 38, 40–47.

Brubaker, J., Case, C., & Reagan, T. (1994). *Becoming a reflective educator: How to build a culture of inquiry in the schools.* Thousand Oaks, CA: Corwin Press.

Bruner, J. (1971). *Toward a theory of instruction.* Cambridge, MA: Belknap Press of Harvard University Press.

Bruning, R., Schraw, G., & Ronning, R. (1995). *Cognitive psychology and instruction* (2nd ed.). Upper Saddle River, NJ: Prentice-Hall.

Bryner, J. (2007). Study: School culture affects student violence. *LiveScience,* 1–4. Retrieved May 21, 2007, from LiveScience database.

Buhs, E., Ladd, G., & Herald, S. (2006). Peer exclusion and victimization: Processes that mediate the relation between peer group rejection and children's classroom engagement and achievement. *Journal of Educational Psychology, 98,* 1–13.

Bullying is behind teen suicide wave in Japan. (2006). Retrieved February 15, 2013, from http://news.monstersandcritics.com/asiapacific/article.

Bullying and suicide – Bullying statistics. (2013). Retrieved April 26, 2013, from http://www.bullyingstatistics.org/content/bullying-statistics.html.

Burden, P. (2006). *Classroom management: Creating a successful K-12 learning community* (3rd ed.). New York: John Wiley & Sons.

Burden, P. (2010). *Classroom management: Creating a successful K-12 learning community* (4th ed.). Hoboken, NJ: John Wiley & Sons.

Burden, P., & Byrd, D. (2013). *Methods for effective teaching: Meeting the needs of all students* (6th ed.). Boston: Pearson.

Burden, P., & Cooper, J. (2004). *An educator's guide to classroom management.* New York: Houghton-Mifflin.

Bushaw, W., & Lopez, S. (2012). The 44th annual Phi Delta Kappa/Gallup Poll of the public's attitudes toward the public schools. *Phi Delta Kappan, 94*(1), 8–25.

Butler, A. (2006). Uniforms take pressure off. Retrieved February 16, 2013, from www.baltimoresun.com/news/education.

Cameron, J., Pierce, W., & Banko, K. (2005). Achievement-based rewards and intrinsic motivation: A test of cognitive mediators. *Journal of Educational Psychology, 97,* 641–655.

Cangelosi, J. (2000). *Classroom management strategies: Gaining and maintaining students' cooperation.* New York: John Wiley & Sons.

Canter, L. (2010). *Lee Canter's assertive discipline: Positive behavior management for today's classroom* (4th ed.). Bloomington, IN: Solution Tree Press.

Canter, L., & Canter, M. (1976). *Assertive discipline: A take-charge approach for today's educator.* Seal Beach, CA: Canter and Associates.

Canter, L. (1988). Let the educator beware: A response to Curwin and Mendler. *Educational Leadership, 46*(2), 71–73.

Caruso, P. (1996). Individuality vs. conformity: The issue behind school uniforms. *NASSP Bulletin, 80,* 83–88.

Cassady, J., & Johnson, R. (2002). Cognitive anxiety and academic performance. *Contemporary Educational Psychology, 27,* 270–295.

Charles, C. M. (2011). *Building classroom discipline* (10th ed.). Boston: Pearson.

Charles, C. (1976). *Educational psychology: The instructional endeavor* (2nd ed.). St. Louis, MO: C. V. Mosby.

Children's Defense Fund. (1994). *The state of America's children 1994.* Washington, DC: Children's Defense Fund.

Clark, D., Martin, C., & Cornelius, J. (2008). Adolescent-onset substance use disorders predict young adult mortality. *Journal of Adolescent Health, 42,* 637–639.

Clement, M. (1998, April 8). *Beginning teachers' perceptions of their stress, problems, and planned retention in teaching.* Paper presented at the annual meeting of the Midwest Association for Teacher Educators, Urbana, IL.

Clough, D., Smasal, R., & Clough, M. (1994). Managing each minute. *The Science Teacher, 61*(6), 30–34.

CNN Staff. (2013). Former Atlanta schools superintendent reports to jail in cheating scandal. *CNN Justice.* Retrieved April 5, 2013, from http://cnn.com/2013/04/02/justice/georgia-cheating-scandal/index.html.

Cole, A., & Knowles, J. (2000). *Researching teaching: Exploring teacher development through reflective inquiry.* Boston: Allyn & Bacon.

Coloroso, B. (1994). *Kids are worth it: Giving your child the gift of inner discipline.* New York: Morrow.

Coloroso, B. (2000). *Parenting with wit and wisdom in times of chaos and loss.* Toronto: Penguin.

Conway, P., & Clark G. (2003). The journey inward and outward: A re-examination of Fuller's concerns-based model of teacher development. *Teaching and Teacher Education, 19,* 465–482.

Cooper, D., & Snell, J. (2003). Bullying – Not just a kid thing. *Educational Leadership, 60*(6) 22–25.

Corpus, J., McClintic-Gilbert, M., & Hayenga, A. (2009). Within-year changes in children's intrinsic and extrinsic motivational orientations: Contextual predictors and academic outcomes. *Contemporary Educational Psychology, 34*, 154–166.

Cotton, K. (1999). *Research you can use to improve results.* Alexandria, VA: Association for Supervision and Curriculum Development.

Corzine: Train teachers to help children avoid Web predators. (2007). *South Jersey News Online.* Retrieved February 15, 2013, from http://blog.nj.com/gloucester/2007/08/corzine_train_teachers_to_help.html.

Covaleski, J. (1992). Discipline and morality: Beyond rules and consequences. *The Educational Forum, 56*(2), 56–60.

Covington, M., & Omelich, C. (1987). "I knew it cold before the exam": A test of the anxiety-blockage hypothesis. *Journal of Educational Psychology, 79*, 393–400.

Croft, G. (2006). Back-to-school: Books and bullies. Retrieved February 17, 2013, from http://abcnews.go.com/Primetime/story.

Cruickshank, D. (1985). Applying research on teacher clarity. *Journal of Teacher Education, 35*(2), 44–48.

Crute, S. (2004). Teacher stress: Stressed out. *NEA Today.* Retrieved May 10, 2007, from www.nea.org/neatoday.

Cummings, C., & Haggerty, K. (1997). Raising healthy children. *Educational Leadership, 54*, 28–30.

Curtner-Smith, M., Smith, P., & Porter, M. (2011). Family-level interventions with bullies and victims. In E. Vernberg & B. Biggs (Eds.). *Preventing and treating bullying and Victimization* (pp.75–106). New York: Oxford University Press.

Curwin, R., & Mendler, A. (2004). *Discipline with dignity* (2nd ed.). Alexandria, VA: Association for Supervision and Curriculum Development.

Curwin, R., Mendler, A., & Mendler, B. (2008). *Discipline with dignity: New challenges, new solutions* (3rd ed.). Alexandria, VA: Association for Supervision and Curriculum Development.

Curwin, R., & Mendler, A. (1988). Packaged discipline programs: Let the buyer beware. *Educational Leadership, 46*(2), 68–71.

Curwin, R., & Mendler, A. (1999). Zero tolerance for zero tolerance. *Phi Delta Kappan, 81*, 119–120.

Dacey, J. (1989). *Fundamentals of creativity.* Lexington, MA: D. C. Heath/Lexington Books.

Dale, E. (1972). *Building a learning environment.* Bloomington, IN: Phi Delta Kappa, Inc.

Danforth, S., & Boyle, J. (2000). *Cases in behavior management.* Columbus, OH: Merrill.

Darling-Hammond, L., & Goodwin, A. (1993). Progress toward professionalism in teaching. In G. Cawelti (Ed.), *Challenges and achievements in American education.* Alexandria, VA: Association for Supervision and Curriculum Development.

Dayton, J. (2000). Discipline procedures for students with disabilities. *The Clearing House, 73*, 151–156.

Dealing with school violence. (2006, October). Retrieved October 17, 2006, from www.startribune.com.

Deci, E., & Ryan, R. (1992). The initiation and regulation of intrinsically motivated learning and achievement. In A. K. Boggiano & T. S. Pittman (Eds.), *Achievement and motivation: A social-developmental perspective.* Cambridge, England: Cambridge University Press.

Dempster, F. (1991). Synthesis of research on reviews and tests. *Educational Leadership, 48*(7), 71–76.

DiGiulio, R. (2000). *Positive classroom management* (2nd ed.). Thousand Oaks, CA: Corwin Press.

Dillon, J. (2012). *No place for bullying: Leadership for schools that care for every student.* Thousand Oaks, CA: Corwin Press.

Dinkes, R., Cataldi, E., & Lin-Kelly, W. (2007). Indicators of school crime and safety: 2007 (NCES 2008-021/NCJ 219553). Washington, DC: National Center for Education Statistics, Institute of Education Sciences, U. S. Department of Education, and Bureau of Justice Statistics, Office of Justice Programs, U.S. Department of Justice.

Doi, E. (2006). Schoolyard bullying in Japan leads to rash of student suicides. Retrieved December 7, 2006, from www.mercurynews.com/mld/mercurynews/news/world.

Doll, B., Zucker, S., & Brehm, K. (2004). *Resilient classrooms: Creating healthy environments for learning.* New York: Guilford Press.

Dowling-Sendor, B. (1998a). Watching what students wear. *American School Board Journal, 185,* 12–13.

Dowling-Sendor, B. (1998b). Gangs and rosaries. *American School Board Journal, 185,* 22, 24.

Dreikurs, R. (1968). P*sychology in the classroom* (2nd ed.). New York: Harper & Row.

Dreikurs, R., & Cassell, P. (1972). *Discipline without tears.* New York: Hawthorn Books.

Dunlosky, J., Rawson, K., Marsh, E., Nathan, M., & Willingham, D. (2013). Improving students' learning with effective teaching techniques: Promising directions from cognitive and educational psychology. *Psychological Science in the Public Interest, 14*(1), 4–58.

Dweck, C. (2007). *Mind set: The new psychology of success.* New York: Ballantine Books.

Dwyer, K., Osher, D., & Hoffman, C. (2000). Creating responsive schools: Contextualizing, early warning, timely response. *Exceptional Children, 66,* 347–365.

Eccles, J., Adler, T., Futterman, R., Goff, S., Kaczala, C., Meece, J., & Midgley, C. (1983). Expectancies, values, and academic behavior. In J. T. Spence (Ed.), *Achievement and achievement motives: Psychological and sociological approaches* (pp. 75–146). San Francisco: Freeman.

Educational Testing Service. (1998). Beyond assumptions. *American Educator, 22,* 32–35.

Eggen, P., & Kauchak, D. (2007). *Educational psychology: Windows on classrooms* (7th ed.). Upper Saddle River, NJ: Pearson.

Eggen, P., & Kauchak, D. (2013). *Educational psychology: Windows on classrooms* (9th ed.). Boston: Pearson.

Eggen, P., & Kauchak, D. (2012). *Strategies and models for teachers: Teaching content and thinking skills* (6th ed.). Boston: Pearson.

Eisner, E. (1998). *The kind of schools we need: Personal essays.* Portsmouth, NH: Heinemann.

Elam, S., & Rose, L. (1995). The 27th annual Phi Delta Kappa/Gallup poll of the public's attitudes toward the public schools. *Phi Delta Kappan, 77*(1), 41–56.

Elam, S., Rose, L., & Gallup, A. (1996). The 28th annual Phi Delta Kappa/Gallup poll of the public's attitudes toward the public schools. *Phi Delta Kappan, 78*(1), 41–59.

Elawar, M., & Corno, L. (1985). A factorial experiment in teachers' written feedback on student homework. *Journal of Educational Psychology, 77*(2), 162–173.

Elias, M., Gager, P., & Leon, S. (1997). Selecting a substance abuse prevention program. *Principal, 76,* 23–24, 27.

Elliott, S., Kratochwill, T., Cook, J., & Travers, J. (2000). *Educational psychology: Effective teaching, effective learning* (3rd ed.). New York: McGraw-Hill.

Emery, M. (2010). UH study suggests school uniforms reduce student absences, disciplinary problems. Retrieved February 25, 2013, from http://www.uh.edu/news-events/stories/2010articles/April2010/0405SchoolUniforms.php.

Emmer, E., Evertson, C., & Worsham, M. (2006). *Classroom management for middle and high school teachers* (7th ed.). New York: Pearson.

Essex, N. (2000). Classroom harassment: The principal's liability. *Principal, 79,* 52–55.

Evans, D. (1996). School uniforms: An `unfashionable' dissent. *Phi Delta Kappan, 78,* 139.

Evertson, C. (1980, May). Effective classroom management at the beginning of the school year. *Elementary School Journal,* 219–231.

Evertson, C., Emmer, E., & Worsham, M. (2005). *Classroom management for elementary teachers* (7th ed.). Boston: Allyn & Bacon.

Evertson, C., & Weinstein, C. (2006). Classroom management as a field of inquiry. In C. Evertson & C. Weinstein (Eds.), *Handbook of classroom management: Research, practice, and contemporary issues* (pp. 3–15). Mahwah, NJ: Erlbaum.

Feather, N. (Ed.). (1982). *Expectations and actions.* Hillsdale, NJ: Erlbaum.

Feitler, F., & Tokar, E. (1992). Getting a handle on teacher stress: How bad is the problem? *Educational Leadership, 49,* 456–458.

Flannery, D., Webster, K., & Singer, M. (2004). Impact of violence exposure at school on child mental health and violent behavior. *Journal of Community Psychology, 32,* 559–574.

Fletcher, A., Bonell, C., & Hargeaves, J. (2008). School effects on young people's drug use: A systematic review of intervention and observational studies. *Journal of Adolescent Health, 42,* 209–220.

Freiberg, H., & Driscoll, A. (2004). *Universal teaching strategies* (4th ed.). Boston: Allyn & Bacon.

French, J., & Raven, B. (1959). The bases of social power. In D. Cartwright (Ed.), *Studies in social power* (pp. 150–168). Ann Arbor, MI: University of Michigan Press.

Froyen, L., & Iverson, A. (1999). *Schoolwide and classroom management.* Upper Saddle River, NJ: Prentice-Hall.

Gagne, R., Wagner, W., Golas, K., & Keller, J. (2005). *Principles of instructional design* (5th ed.). Independence, KY: Cengage Learning.

Gallagher, J., & Aschner, M. (1963). A preliminary report of the analysis of classroom interaction. *Merrill-Palmer Quarterly, 9,* 183–194.

Garcia, E. (1994). *Understanding and meeting the challenge of student cultural diversity.* Boston: Houghton-Mifflin.

Gathercoal, F. (1993). *Judicious discipline* (3rd ed.). San Francisco: Caddo Gap.

Ghezzi, P. (2006, March 20). Zero tolerance for zero tolerance. *Atlanta Constitution.*

Giammona, C. (2013). California case another three-part tragedy of rape, cyber bullying and suicide, NBC News. Retrieved May 25, 2013, from http://usnews.nbc-news.com/_news/2013/04/14/17747411-california-case-another-three-part-tragedy-of-rape-cyber-bullying-and-suicide?lite.

Ginott, H. (1965). *Between parent and child.* New York: Avon.

Ginott, H. (1969). *Between parent and teenager.* New York: Macmillan.

Ginott, H. (1972). *Teacher and child.* New York: Macmillan.

Glasser, W. (1997, April). A new look at school failure and school success. *Phi Delta Kappan,* 596–602.

Glasser, W. (1986). *Control theory in the classroom.* New York: Harper & Row.

Glasser, W. (2001). *Counseling with choice theory: The new reality theory.* New York: Harper-Perennial.

Glasser, W. (2000). *Every student can succeed.* Chatsworth, CA: Black Forest Press.

Glasser, W. (1965). *Reality therapy: A new approach to psychiatry.* New York: Harper & Row.

Glasser, W. (1969). *Schools without failure.* New York: Harper & Row.

Glasser, W. (1990). *The quality school: Managing students without coercion.* New York: Harper & Row.

Glasser, W. (1992). *The quality school: Managing students without coercion* (2nd ed.). New York: Harper-Perennial.

Glasser, W. (1998). *The quality school teacher.* New York: Harper-Perennial.

Good, T., & Brophy, J. (1986). *Educational psychology: A realistic approach* (3rd ed.). New York: Holt, Rhinehart & Winston.

Good, T., & Brophy, J. (2000). *Looking in classrooms* (8th ed.). New York: Addison Wesley Longman.

Good, T., & Brophy, J. (2003). *Looking in classrooms* (9th ed.). New York: Pearson.

Good, T., & Brophy, J. (2007). *Looking in classrooms* (10th ed.). New York: Allyn & Bacon.

Goodenow, C. (1993). The psychological sense of school membership among adolescents: Scale development and educational correlates. *Psychology in the Schools, 30,* 79–90.

Goodlad, J. (1984). *A place called school.* New York: McGraw-Hill.

Gootman, M. (2008). *The caring teacher's guide to discipline: Helping young students learn self-control, responsibility, and respect* (3rd ed.). Thousand Oaks, CA: Corwin Press.

Gordon, T. (1974). *Teacher effectiveness training.* New York: Wyden.

Gottlieb, J., & Weinberg, S. (1999). Comparison of students referred and not referred for special education. *Elementary School Journal,* 187–199.

Grant, T. (2006, August). Back to school: Zero tolerance makes discipline more severe, involves the courts. Retrieved February 14, 2013, from www.post-gazette.con/pg/062431717806-298.stm.

Greeno, J., Collins, A., & Resnick, L. (1996). Cognition and learning. In D. Berliner & R. Calfee (Eds.), *Handbook of educational psychology* (pp. 15–46). New York: Macmillan.

Gregory, A., Skiba, R., & Noguera, P. (2010). The achievement gap and the discipline gap: Two sides to the same coin. *Educational Researcher, 39*(1), 59–68.

Gschwend, L., & Dembo, M. (2001, April). *How do high-efficacy teachers persist in low-achieving, culturally diverse schools?* Paper presented at the annual meeting of the American Educational Research Association, Seattle, WA.

Hahn, E., Hall, L., Rayens, M., Burt, A., Corley, D., & Sheffel, K. (2000). Kindergarten children's knowledge and perceptions of alcohol, tobacco, and other drugs. *Journal of School Health, 70,* 51–55.

Hamachek, D. (1987). Humanistic psychology: Theory, postulates, and implications for educational processes. In J. Glover & R. Ronning (Eds.). *Historical foundations of educational psychology* (pp. 159–182). New York: Plenum Press.

Hamilton, K. (1999). Implementing a school uniform policy. *Principal, 79,* 46–47.

Hanish, L., & Guerra, N. (2002). A longitudinal analysis of patterns of adjustment following peer victimization. *Development and Psychopathology, 14,* 69–89.

Hansen, R. (1977). Anxiety. In S. Ball (Ed.), *Motivation in education.* New York: Academic Press.

Harter, S., & Jackson, B. (1992). Trait versus nontrait conceptualizations of intrinsic/extrinsic motivational orientation. Special issues: Perspectives on intrinsic motivation. *Motivation and Emotion, 16,* 209–230.

Hattie, J., & Temperley, H. (2007). The power of feedback. *Review of Educational Research, 77*(1), 81–112.

Heider, F. (1958). *The psychology of interpersonal relationships.* New York: Wiley.

Helfrich, S., & Bean, R. (2011). Beginning teachers reflect on their experiences being prepared to teach literacy. *Teacher Education and Practice, 24*(2), 201–222.

Hendrickson, B. (1979). Teacher burnout: How to recognize it, what to do about it. *Learning, 7,* 36–38.

Henson, T., & Eller, B. (1999). *Educational psychology for effective teaching.* New York: Wadsworth.

Hunt, G., & Bedwell, L. (1982). An axiom for classroom management. *The High School Journal, 66*(1), 10–13.

Hunt, G., Wiseman, D., & Touzel, T., (2009). *Effective teaching: Preparation and implementation* (4th ed.). Springfield, IL: Charles C Thomas.

Hunter, M. (1984). Knowing, teaching and supervising. In P. Hosford (Ed.), *Using what we know about teaching.* Alexandria, VA: Association for Supervision and Curriculum Development.

Hyman, I., & Snook, P. (2000). Dangerous schools and what you can do about them. *Phi Delta Kappan, 81,* 488–498; 500–501.

Jain, S., & Dowson, M. (2009). Mathematics anxiety as a function of multidimensional self-regulation and self-efficacy. *Contemporary Educational Psychology, 34,* 240–249.

Johnson, D., & Johnson, R. (2009). *Joining together: Group theory and group skills* (10th ed.). Boston: Allyn & Bacon.

Johnson, D., & Johnson, R. (2005). *Teaching students to be peacemakers* (4th ed.). Minneapolis, MN: Burgess.

Johnson, D., & Johnson, R. (2004). The three Cs of promoting social and emotional learning. In J. Zins, R. Weissberg, M. Wang, & H. Walberg (Eds.), *Building academic success on social and emotional learning* (pp. 40–58). New York: Teachers College Press.

Johnston, L., O'Malley, P., Bachman, J., & Schulenberg, J. (2011). *Monitoring the Future national results on adolescent drug use: Overview of key findings, 2010.* Ann Arbor, MI: Institute for Social Research, the University of Michigan.

Jones, F. (1980). *Adolescents with behavior problems.* Boston: Allyn and Bacon.

Jones, F. (1987). *Positive classroom discipline.* New York: McGraw-Hill.

Jones, F. (2000). *Positive classroom discipline* (3rd ed.). New York: McGraw-Hill.

Jones, R. (1997). More than just no. *American School Board Journal, 184,* 30–32.

Jones, V., & Jones, L. (2013). *Comprehensive classroom management: Creating communities of support and solving problems* (10th ed.). Boston: Pearson.

Josh Pacheco, gay Michigan teen, committed suicide after intense bullying, say parents. (2012). Retrieved April 26, 2013, from http://www.huffingtonpost.com/2012/12/05/josh-pacheco-gay-michigan-teen-suicide-bullying-_n_2246767.html.

Joyce, E. (2007). I'm, like, so being harassed online. Retrieved June 29, 2007, from www.internetnews.com/stats/article.php/3685726.

Kagan, D. (1992). Implications of research on teacher belief. *Educational Psychologist, 27,* 65–90.

Kansas schools take drug testing to extreme. (2006, September 14). *Chicago Tribune.*

Karweit, N. (1989). Time and learning: A review. In R. E. Slavin (Ed.), *School and classroom organization.* Hillsdale, NJ: Erlbaum.

Kastens, K., & Liben, L. (2007). Eliciting self-explanations improves children's performance on a field-based map skills task. *Cognition and Instruction, 25*(1), 45–74.

Kauchak, D., & Eggen, P. (2012). *Learning and teaching: Research-based methods* (6th ed.). Boston: Pearson.

Kauffman, J. (1989). *Characteristics of behavior disorders of children and youth* (4th ed.). Upper Saddle River, NJ: Merrill/Prentice-Hall.

Kazdin, A., & Rotella, C. (2013). *The everyday parenting toolkit: The Kazdin method for easy, step-by-step lasting change for you and your child.* New York: Houghton-Mifflin, Harcourt.

Kher-Durlabhji, N., Lacina-Gifford, L., Jackson, L., Guillory, R., & Yandell, S. (1997, March). *Preservice teachers' knowledge of effective classroom management strategies.* Paper presented at the annual meeting of the American Educational Research Association, Chicago.

Kidron, Y., & Fleischman, S. (2007). Research matters: Promoting adolescents' prosocial behavior. *Educational Leadership, 63*(7), 90–91.

Kids and laughing teachers bullied suicide teen. (2012). Retrieved April 26, 2013, from http://abcnews.go.com/blogs/headlines/2012/07/kids-and-laughing-teachers-bullied-suicide-teen/.

King, A. (1996). Exclusionary discipline and the forfeiture of special education rights: A survey. *NASSP Bulletin, 80,* 49–64.

Knapp, M., & Woolverton, S. (1995). Social class and schooling. In J. A. Banks & C. A. M. Banks (Eds.), *Handbook of research on multicultural education.* New York: Macmillan.

Koch, K. (2000, March 10). Zero tolerance. *Congressional Quarterly Researcher.* Washington, DC: Congressional Quarterly, Inc., 187–204.

Koenig, L. (2000). *Smart discipline for the classroom: Respect and cooperation restored* (3rd ed.). Thousand Oaks, CA: Corwin Press.

Kohn, A. (2011). *Feel-bad education . . . and other contrarian essays on children and schooling.* Boston: Beacon Press.

Kohn, A. (1992). *No contest: The case against competition.* Boston: Houghton-Mifflin.

Kohn, A. (1993). *Punished by rewards: The trouble with gold stars, incentive plans, A's, praise, and other bribes.* New York: Houghton-Mifflin.

Kohn, A. (2000). *The case against standardized testing: Raising the scores, ruining the schools.* Portsmouth, NH: Heinemann.

Kommer, D. (1999). Beyond fashion patrol: School uniforms for middle grades. *Middle School Journal, 30,* 23–26.

Kounin, J. 1983). *Classrooms: Individual or behavior settings? Micrographs in teaching and learning* (General Series No. 1). Bloomington, IN: Indiana University School of Education. (ERIC Document Reproduction Service No. 240 070).

Kounin, J. (1970). *Discipline and group management in classrooms.* New York: Holt, Rinehart & Winston.

Kranz, C. (2007). Program urges students to put a stop to bullying. Retrieved January 16, 2007, from http://news.enquirer.com.

Kummer, F. (2006). Leaders aim to curb cheating on tests. Retrieved October 26, 2006, from www.philly.com/mld/philly/living/education.

Lalwani, P. (2011). Facts about school uniforms. Retrieved February 25, 2013, from www.buzzle.com/articles/school-uniforms-facts-on-school-uniforms.html.

Langdon, C. (1996). The 3rd Phi Delta Kappa poll of teachers' attitudes toward the public schools. *Phi Delta Kappan, 78,* 244–250.

Larrivee, B. (2009). *Authentic classroom management: Creating a learning community and building reflective practice* (3rd ed.). Upper Saddle River, NJ: Pearson.

Lefrancois, G. (2000). *Psychology for teaching* (10th ed.). Belmont, CA: Wadsworth/ Thompson Learning.

Lemov, D. (2010). *Teach like a champion: 49 techniques that put students on the path to college.* San Francisco: Josey-Bass.

Levin, J., & Nolan, J. (2010). *Principles of classroom management: A professional decision-making model* (6th ed.). Boston: Pearson.

Lieberman, B. (2007). Educator to apply lessons learned to improve low-performing schools. Retrieved June 29, 2007, from www.signonsandiego.com/news/education.

Locke, E., & Latham, G. (1990). *A theory of goal setting and task performance.* Englewood Cliffs, NJ: Prentice-Hall.

Locke, E., & Latham, G. (2002). Building a practically useful theory of goal setting and task motivation: A 35-year odyssey. *American Psychologist, 57,* 705–717.

Lowry, R., Cohen, L., Modzeleski, W., Kann, L., Collins, J., & Kolbe, L. (1999). School violence, substance use, and availability of illegal drugs on school property among U.S. high school students. *Journal of School Health, 69,* 347–355.

Manning, L. & Bucher, K. (2013). *Classroom management: Models, applications, and cases* (3rd ed.). Upper Saddle River, NJ: Pearson.

Margolis, H., & McCabe, P. (2004). Self-efficacy: A key to improving the motivation of struggling learners. *The Clearing House,* July/August, 241–249.

Marshall, H. (2001). Cultural influences on the self-concept: Updating our thinking. *Young Children,* November, 12–22.

Martin, N., & Baldwin, B. (1996). Helping beginning teachers foster healthy classroom management: Implications for elementary school counselors. *Elementary School Guidance & Counseling, 31,* 106–113.

Martinez, S. (2009). A system gone berserk: How are zero-tolerance policies really affecting schools? *Preventing School Failure, 53*(3), 153–157.

Marzano, R. (2007). *The art and science of teaching: A comprehensive framework for effective instruction.* Alexandria, VA: Association for Supervision and Curriculum Development.

Marzano, R. (2003). *What works in schools: Translating research into action.* Alexandria, VA: Association for Supervision and Curriculum Development.

Marzano, R., & Marzano, J. (2003). The key to classroom management. *Educational Leadership, 61*(1), 6–18.

Marzano, R., Gaddy, B., Foseid, M., & Marzano, J. (2009). *A handbook for classroom management that works.* Upper Saddle River, NJ: Pearson.

Marzano, R., Pickering, J., & Pollock, J. (2004). *Classroom instruction that works: Research-based strategies for increasing student achievement.* Boston: Pearson.

Maslow, A. (1970). *Motivation and personality* (2nd ed.). New York: Harper & Row.

Matthews, J., Ponitz, C., & Morrison, F. (2009). Early gender differences in self-regulation and academic achievement. *Journal of Educational Psychology, 101,* 689–704.

Matus, D. (1999). Humanism and effective urban secondary classroom management. *The Clearing House, 72,* 305–307.

Mayer, M., & Furlong, M. (2010). How safe are our schools? *Educational Researcher, 39*(1), 16–26.

McCaslin, M., & Good, T. (1992). Compliant cognition: The misalliance of management and instructional goals in current school reform. *Educational Research, 21*(3), 4–17.

McCaslin, M., & Good, T. (1998, Summer). Moving beyond management as sheer compliance: Helping students to develop goal coordination strategies. *Educational Horizons,* 169–176.

McCormack, S. (1989). Response to Render, Padilla and Krank: But practitioners say it works! *Educational Leadership, 46*(6), 77–79.

McCormick, C., & Pressley, M. (1997). *Educational psychology: Learning, instruction, assessment.* New York: Longman.

McEwan, B. (2003). *The art of classroom management: Effective practices for building equitable learning communities* (2nd ed.). Upper Saddle River, NJ: Merrill.

McEwan, B. (2000). *The art of classroom management: Effective practices for building equitable learning communities.* Upper Saddle River, NJ: Prentice-Hall.

Melnick, S., & Meister, D. (2008). A comparison of beginning and experienced teacher concerns. *Education Research Quarterly, 31*(3), 39–56.

Merrell, K., Gueldner, B., Ross, S., & Isava, D. (2008). How effective are school bullying intervention programs? A meta-analysis of intervention research. *School Psychology Quarterly, 23,* 26–42.

Morgon, M. (1997). Dear colleague: A letter from a new teacher to experienced teachers. *The Clearing House, 70,* 250–252.

Moir, E. (2011, August). Phases of First-Year Teaching. Santa Cruz, CA: New Teacher Center. Retrieved February 24, 2013, from http://www.newteachercenter.org/blog/phases-first-year-teaching.

Morral, D., McCaffrey, D., Ridgeway, G., Mukherji, A., & Beighley, C. (2006). The relative effectiveness of 10 adolescent substance abuse treatment programs in the United States. *Rand Technical Reports TR-346.* Retrieved May 14, 2007, from www.rand.org/pubs/technical_reports.

Morris, R. (1998). Conflict: Theory must inform reality. *The Kappa Delta Pi Record,* Fall, 14–17.

Morrison, G., & D'Incau, B. (2000). Developmental and services trajectories of students with disabilities recommended for expulsion from school. *Exceptional Children, 66,* 257–272.

National Center for Education Statistics. (2012). Fast facts – School uniforms. Retrieved February 25, 2013, http://nces.ed.gov/fastfacts/display.asp?id=50.

National Institute of Education. (1980). *Teachers opinion poll.* Washington, DC: U.S. Department of Health, Education, and Welfare.

New York police probe possible cyberbullying after girl found hanged, CNN (2013). Retrieved May 25, 2013, from http://www.cnn.com/2013/05/23/us/new-york-girl-death/index.html.

Newman-Carlson, D., & Horne, A. (2004). Bully Busters: A psychoeducational intervention for reducing bullying behavior. *Journal of Counseling and Development, 82*(3), 259–267.

Nishina, A., Juvonen, J., & Witkow, M. (2005). Sticks and stones may break my bones, but names will make me feel sick: The psychosocial, somatic, and scholastic consequences of peer harassment. *Journal of Clinical Child and Adolescent Psychology, 34,* 37–48.

Nissman, B. (2009). *Teacher-tested classroom management strategies* (3rd ed.). Boston: Pearson.

Noguchi, S. (2006). Schools fight cheaters who use tech tools. Retrieved September 26, 2006, from www.mercurynews.com.

O'Flahavan, J., Hartman, D., & Pearson, D. (1988). Teacher questioning and feedback practices: A twenty-year retrospective. In J. Readence, R. Baldwin, J. Konopak, & P. O'Keefe (Eds.), *Dialogues in literacy research* (pp. 183–208). Chicago: National Reading Conference.

Ofer, U. (2011/2012). Criminalizing the classroom: The rise of aggressive policing and zero tolerance discipline in New York City Public Schools. *New York Law School Law Review, 56,* 1373–1411.

Olweus, D. (2003). A profile of bullying at school. *Educational Leadership, 60*(6), 12–17.

Olweus, D. (1993). *Bullying at school: What we know and what we can do.* Cambridge, MA: Blackwell.

Olweus, D. (2013). Olweus bullying prevention program. Retrieved February 25, 2013, from http://www.violencepreventionworks.org/public/olweus_scope.page.

Ormrod, J. (2011). *Educational psychology: Developing learners* (7th ed.). Boston: Pearson.

Osborne, A. (1998). The principal and discipline with special education students. *NASSP Bulletin, 82*, 1–8.

Pawlas, G. (1997). Seven tips to reduce teacher stress. *High School Magazine, 4*, 42–43.

Peterson, R., & Skiba, R. (2001). Creating school climates that prevent school violence. *The Clearing House, 74*, 155–163.

Pfiffner, L., Rosen, L., & O'Leary, S. (1985). The efficacy of an all-positive approach to classroom management. *Journal of Applied Behavior Analysis, 18*, 257–261.

Piaget, J. (1952). *Origins of intelligence.* New York: International Universities Press.

Pianta, R. (2006). Classroom management and relationships between children and teachers: Implications for research and practice. In C. M. Evertson & C. S. Weinstein (Eds.), *Handbook of classroom management: Research, practice and contemporary issues* (pp. 685–710). Mahwah, NJ: Lawrence Erlbaum.

Pintrich, P., & Schunk, D. (2002). *Motivation in education: Theory, research, and application* (2nd ed.). Upper Saddle River, NJ: Merrill/Prentice-Hall.

Poole, M., Okeafor, K., & Sloan, E. (1989, April). *Teachers' interactions, personal efficacy, and change implementation.* Paper presented at the annual meeting of the American Educational Research Association, San Francisco.

Poplin, M., Rivera, J., Durish, D., Hoff, L., Kawell, S., Pawlak, P., Hinman, I., Straus, L., & Veney, C., (2011). Highly effective teachers in low-performing urban schools. *Phi Delta Kappan, 92*, 39–43.

Powell, R., McLaughlin, H., Savage, T., & Zehm, S. (2001). *Classroom management: Perspectives on the social curriculum.* Upper Saddle River, NJ: Merrill/Prentice-Hall.

Ratcliff, N., Jones, C., Costner, R., Knight, C., Disney, G., Savage-Davis, E., Sheehan, H., & Hunt, G. (2012). No need to wait for Superman: A case study of one unique high school. *Journal for the Education of the Gifted, 35*(4), 391–411.

Ratcliff, N., Jones, C., Costner, R., Savage-Davis, E., Sheehan, E., & Hunt, G. (2010). Teacher classroom management behaviors and student time-on-task: Implications for teacher education. *Action in Teacher Education, 32*, 38–51.

Ratcliff, N., Jones, C., Costner, R., Savage-Davis, E., & Hunt, G. (2010). The elephant in the classroom: The impact of misbehavior on classroom climate. *Education, 132*(2), 306–314.

Ratcliff, N., Pritchard, N., Costner, R., Knight, C., Jones, C., & Hunt, G. (2013). *Traditional versus 4X4 block scheduling: The impact on learning environments and student academic performance.* Manuscript submitted for publication.

Reis, J., Trockel, M., & Mulhall, P. (2007). Individual and school predictors of middle school aggression. *Youth and Society, 38*(3), 322–347.

Render, G., Padilla, J., & Krank, H. (1989). What research really shows about assertive discipline. *Educational Leadership, 46*(6), 72–75.

Richards, J. (2004). Zero room for zero tolerance policies: Rethinking federal funding for zero tolerance policies. *University of Dayton Law Review, 30*, 91–117.

Rigby, K. (2007). What is bullying? Bullying in schools. Retrieved April 19, 2007, www.education.unisa.edu.au/bullying.

Rimm-Kaufman, S., La Paro, K., Downer, J., & Pianta, R. (2005). The contribution of classroom setting and quality of instruction to children's behavior in kindergarten classrooms. *Elementary School Journal, 105*(4), 377–394.

Rizzo, J., & Zabel, R. (1988). *Educating children and adolescents with behavioral disorders: An integrative approach.* Boston: Allyn & Bacon.

Rogers, C., & Freiberg, H. (1994). *Freedom to learn* (3rd ed.). Columbus, OH: Charles E. Merrill.

Rose, C. (2010). Bullying among students with disabilities: Impact and implications. In D. L. Espelage & S. M. Swearer (Eds.), *Bullying in North American schools: A socio-ecological perspective on prevention and intervention* (2nd ed.), pp. 34–44, Mahwah, NJ: Lawrence Erlbaum.

Rose, C., & Monda-Amaya, L. (2012). Bullying and victimization among students with disabilities: Effective strategies for classroom teachers. *Intervention in School and Clinic, 48*(2) 99–107.

Rose, C., Monda-Amaya, L., & Espelage, D. (2011). Bullying perpetration and victimization in special education: A review of the literature. *Remedial and Special Education, 32,* 114–130.

Rose, L., & Gallup, A. (1998). The 30th annual Phi Delta Kappa/Gallup poll of the public's attitudes toward the public schools. *Phi Delta Kappan, 80*(1), 41–56.

Rose, L., & Gallup, A. (1999). The 31st annual Phi Delta Kappa/Gallup poll of the public's attitudes toward the public schools. *Phi Delta Kappan, 81*(1), 41–56.

Rose, L., & Gallup, A. (2000). The 32nd annual Phi Delta Kappa/Gallup poll of the public's attitudes toward the public schools. *Phi Delta Kappan, 82*(1), 41–58.

Rose, L., & Gallup, A. (2003). The 35th annual Phi Delta Kappa/Gallup poll of the public's attitudes toward the public schools. *Phi Delta Kappan, 85*(1), 41–52.

Rose L., & Gallup, A. (2004). The 36th annual Phi Delta Kappa/Gallup poll of the public's attitudes toward the public schools. *Phi Delta Kappan, 86*(1), 41–52.

Rose L., & Gallup, A. (2005). The 37th annual Phi Delta Kappa/Gallup poll of the public's attitudes toward the public schools. *Phi Delta Kappan, 87*(1), 41–54.

Rose L., & Gallup, A. (2006). The 38th annual Phi Delta Kappa/Gallup poll of the public's attitudes toward the public schools. *Phi Delta Kappan, 88*(1), 41–53.

Rose L., & Gallup, A. (2007). The 39th annual Phi Delta Kappa/Gallup poll of the public's attitudes toward the public schools. *Phi Delta Kappan, 89*(1), 33–45.

Rose, L., Gallup, A., & Elam, S. (1997). The 29th annual Phi Delta Kappa/Gallup poll of the public's attitudes toward the public schools. *Phi Delta Kappan, 79*(1), 41–56.

Rosenshine, B. (1988). Explicit teaching. In D. Berliner & B. Rosenshine (Eds.), *Talks to teachers* (pp. 75–92). New York: Random House.

Rosenshine, B., & Furst, N. (1971). Research in teacher performance criteria. In B. O. Smith (Ed.), *Research in teacher education.* Englewood Cliffs, NJ: Prentice-Hall.

Rosenshine, B., & Stevens, R. (1986). Teaching functions. In M. Wittrock (Ed.), *Handbook of research on teaching* (3rd ed.), pp. 376–391. New York: Macmillan.

Rosenthal, R., & Jacobson, L. (1968). *Pygmalion in the classroom: Teacher expectation and pupils' intellectual development.* New York: Holt, Rinehart & Winston.

Ross, T. (2007). 150,000 pupils targeted by homophobic bullies. Retrieved June 28, 2007, from http://education.independnet.co.uk/news/article2710599.ece.

Rossman, S., & Morley, E. (1996). Introduction. *Education and Urban Society, 28,* 395–411.

Rowe, M. (1986). Wait-time: Slowing down may be a way of speeding up. *Journal of Teacher Education, 37*(1), 43–50.

Safe Schools Climate Act. (2006). Retrieved June 7, 2007, from http://ed.sc.gov.

Santrock, J. (2008). *Educational psychology* (3rd ed.). New York: McGraw-Hill.

Savage-Davis, E., Costner, R., Ratcliff, N., Jones, C., Sheehan, H., Scott, M., & Hunt, G. (2011). Comparing elementary and middle school classrooms: Teachers make the difference. *Teacher Education Journal of South Carolina, 11*(1), 36–46.

Schlechty, P. (1976). *Teaching and social behavior: Toward an organizational theory of instruction.* Boston: Allyn & Bacon.

Schreier, L. (2006). Crime prevention group tracks cyberbullying. Retrieved August 18, 2006, from www.contracostatimes.com/mld/cctimes/news/nation.

Schunk, D. (1994, April). *Goal and self-evaluative influences during children's mathematical skill acquisition.* Paper presented at the annual meeting of the American Educational Research Association, New Orleans, LA.

Schunk, D., Pintrich, P., & Meece, J. (2008). *Motivation in education: Theory, research, and applications* (3rd ed.). Columbus, OH: Merrill.

Schwartz, D., Gorman, A., Nakamoto, J., & Tobin, R. (2005). Victimization in the peer group and children's academic functioning. *Journal of Educational Psychology, 97*, 425–435.

Seligman, M. (1975). *Helplessness.* San Francisco: Freeman.

Shavelson, R. (1973). What is the basic teaching skill? *Journal of Teacher Education, 24*, 144–151.

Shukla-Mehta, S., & Albin, R. (2003). Twelve practical strategies to prevent behavioral escalation in classroom settings. *The Clearing House, 77*(2), 50–56.

Sixty percent of U.S. high school students cheat, 28% steal, study finds. Retrieved October 17, 2006, from www.financialexpress.com.

Skiba, R. (2001). *Zero tolerance, zero evidence: An analysis of school disciplinary practice.* Bloomington, IN: Indiana Educational Policy Center, Indiana University.

Skiba, R., & Peterson, R. (2000). School discipline at a crossroads: From zero tolerance to early response. *Exceptional Children, 66*, 335–346.

Skiba, R., & Peterson, R. (1999). The dark side of zero tolerance: Can punishment lead to safe schools? *Phi Delta Kappan, 80*, 372–376; 381–382.

Slavin, R. (2000). *Educational psychology: Theory and practice* (6th ed.). Boston: Allyn & Bacon.

Smith, C. (2000). Behavioral and discipline provisions of IDEA '97: Implicit competencies yet to be confirmed. *Exceptional Children, 66*, 403–412.

Smith, J., & Colon. R. (1998). Legal responsibilities toward students with disabilities: What every administrator should know. *NASSP Bulletin, 82*, 40–53.

Smith, J., Schneider, B., Smith, P., & Ananiadou, K. (2004). The effectiveness of whole-school antibullying programs: A synthesis of evaluation research. *School Psychology Review, 33*(4), 547–560.

Snowman, J., McCown, R., & Biehler, R. (2012). *Psychology applied to teaching* (13th ed.). Belmont, CA: Wadsworth.

Snyder, S., Bushur, L., Hoeksema, P., Olson, M., Clark, S., & Snyder, J. (1991, April). *The effect of instructional clarity and concept structure on students' achievement and perception.* Paper presented at the annual meeting of the American Educational Research Association, Chicago.

Sokolove, S., Garrett, S., Sadker, M., & Sadker, D. (1990). Interpersonal communication skills. In J. Cooper (Ed.), *Classroom teaching skills*. Lexington, MA: D.C. Heath.

Sprague, J., & Walker, H. (2000). Early identification and intervention for youth with antisocial and violent behavior. *Exceptional Children, 66*, 367–379.

Stanley, M. (1996). School uniforms and safety. *Education and Urban Society, 28*, 424–435.

Sternberg, R. (1985). *Beyond IQ: A triarchic theory of human intelligence*. New York: Cambridge University Press.

Sternberg, R. (1999, Spring). Ability and expertise: It's time to replace the current model of intelligence. *American Educator, 10:13*, 50–51.

Sternberg, R. (2006). Recognizing neglected strengths. *Educational Leadership, 64*, 30–35.

Stevahn, L., Johnson, D., Johnson, R., Green, K., & Laginski, M. (1997). Effects on high school students of conflict resolution training integrated into English literature. *The Journal of Social Psychology, 137*(3), 302–313.

Stipek, D. (2002). *Motivation to learn: Integrating theory and practice* (4th ed.). Boston: Allyn & Bacon.

Stollsteimer, J. (2010). Give us the truth about school violence. *Education Week, 29*(35), 34.

Strong, M. (2006, January). Mentoring new teachers to increase retention: A look at the research. *Research Abstracts*. Santa Cruz: CA: New Teacher Center.

Strother, D. (Ed.). (1991). *Learning to fail: Case studies of students at risk*. Bloomington, IN: Phi Delta Kappa.

Swearer, S., Espelage, D., & Napolitano, S. (2009). *Bullying prevention and intervention: Realistic strategies for schools*. New York: Guilford.

Swearer, S., Espelage, D., Vaillancourt, T., & Hymel, S. (2010). What can be done about school bullying? Linking research to educational practice. *Educational Researcher, 39*(1), 38–47.

Tauber, R. (1999). *Classroom management: Sound theory and effective practice* (3rd ed.). Westport, CT: Bergin & Garvey.

Taylor, H. (2000). Meeting the needs of lesbian and gay young adolescents. *The Clearing House, 73*, 221–224.

Taylor, J., & Baker, R. (2002). Discipline and the special education student. *Educational Leadership, 59*(4), 28–30.

Teicher, S. (2006). Social norms strategy aims to tame bullying. Retrieved August 17, 2006, from www.csmonitor.com/2006/0817/p15s02-legn.html.

The MetLife Survey of the American Teacher: Challenges for School Leadership. (2013). www.metlife.com/teachersurvey. New York: Metropolitan life Insurance Company.

Thorndike, E. L. (1905). *The elements of psychology*. New York: Seiler.

Thorndike, E. L. (1911). *Animal intelligence: Experimental studies*. New York: Macmillan.

Tiletson, D. (2005). *10 best teaching practices: How brain research, learning styles, and standards define teaching competencies* (2nd ed.). Thousand Oaks, CA: Corwin Press.

Tobin, K. (1987). Role of wait-time in higher cognitive level learning. *Review of Educational Research, 57*(1), 69–95.

Tollefson, N. (2000). Classroom applications of cognitive theories of motivation. *Education Psychology Review, 12*, 63–83.

Tolson, E., McDonald, S., & Moriarty, A. (1992). Peer mediation among high school students: A test of effectiveness. *Social Work in Education, 14*, 86–93.

Townsend, B. (2000). The disproportionate discipline of African American learners: Reducing suspensions and expulsions. *Exceptional Children, 66*, 381–391.

Tracy, J. (2006, December 29). School crime rises, reflects Hub violence. Retrieved January 2, 2007, *Boston Globe.*

Travers, R. (1977). *Essentials of learning.* New York: Macmillan.

Tschannen-Moran, M., & Woolfolk Hoy, A. (2001). Teacher efficacy: Capturing an elusive construct. *Teaching and Teacher Education, 17*, 783–805.

Tschannen-Moran, M., Woolfolk Hoy, A., & Hoy, W. (1998). Teacher efficacy: Its meaning and measure. *Review of Educational Research, 68*, 202–248.

Tseng, N. (2006, August 9). Districts grapple with web bullying. *Orlando Sentinel.*

Ttofi, M., Farrington, D., & Baldry, A. (2008). *Effectiveness of programs to reduce school bullying.* Stockholm, Sweden: Swedish Council for Crime Prevention, Information and Publications.

Tucker, J., Ellickson, P., Collins, R., & Klein, D. (2006). Does solitary substance use increase adolescents' risk for poor psychosocial and behavioral outcomes? A 9-year longitudinal study comparing solitary and social users. *Psychology of Addictive Behaviors.* Retrieved from www.ncbi.nlm.nih.gov/pubmed/17176171

Van Cleave, J., & Davis, M. (2006). Bullying and peer victimization among children with special care needs. *Pediatrics, 118*, 1212–1219.

Veenman, S. (1984). Perceived problems of beginning teachers. *Review of Educational Research, 54*, 143–178.

Villegas, A., & Lucas, T. (2007). The culturally responsive teacher. *Educational Leadership, 64*, 28–33.

Vreeman, R., & Carroll, A. (2007). A systematic review of school-based interventions to prevent bullying. *Archives of Pediatric and Adolescent Medicine, 161*, 78–88.

Wagner, M., Knudsen, C., & Harper, V. (1999/2000). The evil joker. *Educational Leadership, 57*, 47–50.

Wagstaff, L. (2004). Zero-tolerance discipline: The effect of teacher discretionary removal on urban minority students. Unpublished dissertation, University of Texas, Austin.

Walker, H., Ramsey, E., & Gresham, F. (2004). Heading off disruptive behavior: How early intervention can reduce defiant behavior – and win back teaching time. *American Educator,* Winter, 6, 8–21.

Wallace, M. (2000). Nurturing nonconformists. *Educational Leadership, 57*, 44–46.

Wang, M., Haertel, G., & Walberg, H. (1995, April). *Educational resilience: An emerging construct.* Paper presented at the annual meeting of the American Educational Research Association, San Francisco.

Waxman, H., & Huang, S. (1997). Classroom instruction and learning environment differences between effective and ineffective urban elementary schools for African American students. *Urban Education, 32*(1), 7–44.

Weatherly, J. (2000). Special rules for special ed. *American School Board Journal, 187*, 26–27.

323

Webster, D. (1993). The unconvincing case for school-based conflict resolution programs for adolescents. *Health Affairs*, Winter, 127–141.

...iner, B. (1985). An attributional theory of achievement motivation and emotion.
Psychological Review, 92(4), 548–573.

... (1990). History of motivational research in education. *Journal of Education-*
al ...logy, 82, 612–622.

... *Human motivation: Metaphors, theories, and research.* Newbury Park,

...ity versus effort revisited: The moral determinants of achieve-
...chievement as a moral system. *Educational Psychologist, 29,*
...557–573.

...cial and personal theories of achievement striving:

..., A., Jr. (2011). *Elementary classroom manage-*
...th ed.). New York: McGraw-Hill.

... Checklist of Tips. (1998). Retrieved
...ar/checklist.html.

... Retrieved February 25, 2013,
...ning-your-ideal/121-school-

... *The Clearing House,*

...on. A develop-

...f effective

Zero tolerance (schools). (2007). Retrieved February 17, 2013, from http://en. wikipedia.org/wiki/zero-tolerance- (schools).

Zirkel, P. (1997). The Midol case. *Phi Delta Kappan, 78*, 803–804.

Zirkel, P., & Gluckman, I. (1997). Due process in student suspensions and expulsions. *Principal, 76*, 62–63.

Zirpoli, T. (2007). *Behavior management: Applications for teachers and parents* (5th ed.). Upper Saddle River, NJ: Prentice-Hall.

INDEX